FOOTBALL LEAKS

UNCOVERING THE DIRTY DEALS BEHIND THE BEAUTIFUL GAME

Rafael Buschmann and Michael Wulzinger

Translated from the German by Jefferson Chase

First published by Guardian Faber in 2018

Guardian Faber is an imprint of Faber & Faber Ltd,
Bloomsbury House, 74–77 Great Russell Street,
London WC1B 3DA

Guardian is a registered trade mark of
Guardian News & Media Ltd,
Kings Place, 90 York Way, London N1 9GU

This paperback edition published in 2019

Typeset by Ian Bahrami
Printed and bound by CPI Group (UK) Ltd, Croydon CR0 4YY

A CIP record for this book
is available from the British Library

ISBN 978–1–78335–141–1

10 9 8 7 6 5 4 3 2 1

FOOTBALL LEAKS

Rafael Buschmann, born in Zabrze, Poland, in 1982, studied German, psychology, sport and education. He joined the sports desk of Spiegel Online as a reporter in 2010 and then moved to the *Spiegel* in 2013. For his report on the disclosure of the irregularities behind the 2006 World Cup he and his co-authors were awarded the 2016 Henri Nannen Prize.

Michael Wulzinger, born in 1965, studied history, political science and German, joined the *Spiegel* sports desk in 1997 and was its head until September 2016.

Rafael Buschmann and Michael Wulzinger were named Business Journalists of the Year 2018 by *Wirtschaftsjournalist* magazine.

Contents

Prologue — 1

The Whistle-Blowers — 5
Inshallah Kings — 16
The Search — 36
Tax Tourists — 43
The Breakthrough — 55
Indentured Servants — 75
The Crisis — 85
Other People's Success — 112
The Sugar Daddies — 120
A Mountain of Data — 130
Flogged-Off Favourites — 135
Rebellion — 143
The Golden Goal — 160
The Final Place of Refuge — 165
The Big Payday — 178
The Captive — 182
The Partners — 187
On the Silk Road — 191
Swiss Swamps — 201
Tax Haven Heaven — 208
The Visit — 214
Documents of Greed — 219

Hero or Blackmailer?   234
Burning Issues   247
The Earthquake   256
Euphoria   297

Acknowledgements   305
Index   309

Prologue

On 2 December 2016, Germany's leading news weekly, *Der Spiegel*, published an issue that had two alternative covers. One featured the face of Cristiano Ronaldo, the other that of Mesut Özil, two of the biggest football stars in the world. Their eyes were aglow with € signs. The headline read 'The Money Champions'. The issue contained major investigations into both players' questionable sense of ethics when it came to paying taxes.

The next issue of the magazine featured a cover story examining the highly confidential contracts of professional football players in the German Bundesliga. And in dozens of follow-up stories in the magazine, on *Spiegel Online* and on *Spiegel* TV, readers and viewers learned about the dirty, criminal side of the billion-euro business that is football.

One story was about a sports marketing agency that did business with the biggest clubs in Europe and had close ties to the Balkan underworld. Another was about how agents representing world-class players from South America at clubs like Real Madrid, Juventus and Manchester United earned millions in fees for transfers and contract extensions, which were then transferred to bank accounts of a company located in the tax haven of the British Virgin Islands. Another concerned the reprehensible trade in talented children from developing countries who dreamed of having great careers but fell into the hands of the wrong people. Many of the articles were about what seemed to be everyday business practices in football, one of the most glamorous branches of the global entertainment industry. They concerned secret side deals, million-euro favours, unfair contracts and suspicions of embezzlement and fraud. But all of these stories had one thing in common: they were about money – and greed.

This look at professional football's dark underbelly was made possible by the whistle-blowing platform Football Leaks, which began posting internal industry documents on the Internet in September 2015. Original contracts, top-secret clauses and labyrinthine flows of money were now available for public scrutiny. But activities on the website then suddenly ceased. One of the creators had decided to work together with *Der Spiegel* and had given the magazine 1.9 terabytes' worth of data – the largest leak in the history of professional sport. It was impossible to determine exactly where this material had come from, but it clearly originated from football associations, clubs, agencies and companies in several different countries. One thing was for sure: there was no one single source for the documents. From Football Leaks' point of view, a good reason for passing on the data was to tell the overall story and reveal the larger context surrounding dubious business practices instead of just leaking individual facts and figures.

Confronted with some 18.6 million documents, *Der Spiegel* decided to share this treasure trove with its partners at the research network European Investigative Collaborations (EIC). Members of this association include *Mediapart* in France, *NRC Handelsblad* in the Netherlands, *Politiken* in Denmark, *Le Soir* in Belgium, *L'Espresso* in

Italy, *El Mundo* in Spain, *Newsweek* in Serbia, *Falter* in Austria and RCIJ/The Black Sea in Romania. Investigations were also supported by the *Sunday Times* in Britain and *Expresso* in Portugal.

For seven months, sixty reporters and film journalists worked together with IT experts and lawyers to give the world an unprecedented look into the inner workings of the football industry. This book describes how that work was done and the extent of the dirty dealings that were uncovered. It also tells the story of the whistle-blower who took on the representatives of a rapacious and increasingly powerful industry. He's a young man from Portugal who lives without a fixed address in Eastern Europe. He's intelligent, reckless, obsessed and restless, a football romantic and a passionate fan torn between his bravery in challenging authority and despair about whether anything will change.

He is someone who, as he himself has said, can't bear to see unscrupulous businessmen infiltrating football. He says that one of his main motivations in publishing this colossal cache of data via Football Leaks was anger: anger at those who profited from the dirty money that football attracts and that underpins the sport. He calls them 'the enemies of the game', and aims to unmask them using the hard data of contracts, side agreements, account balances and bills to reveal what's truly behind their facades. But in the process, he himself has gone from the hunter to the hunted, as the enemies of the game have become his own personal enemies.

Professional football has always been comparatively non-transparent. The general public is scandalised when politicians or business leaders evade their taxes, but the same does not apply to football heroes, whom people seem quicker to forgive. The passion at play in football – the hopes and fears, the power of the mob mentality, the longing for salvation and the constant swirl of emotions – exerts a seductive power that trumps human reason. Fans may suspect that club presidents and players' agents are lining their own pockets, that transfer fees often end up in tax havens and that pro footballers frequently build up networks of companies to conceal their advertising revenues, but as long as nothing is proven, supporters aren't particularly bothered.

The Football Leaks revelations are threatening to the sporting industry because they turn those suspicions into certainties, using facts obtained from original trade documents. The clearer it becomes how rotten the system of professional football is, how grotesquely overpaid the players and agents are, how corruptly club officials behave and how far removed the theatre of dreams is from the everyday lives of supporters, the greater the chance that those supporters will turn their backs on the sport.

Football is a wonderful, beautiful game. But the patience of the people who love and pay for it is not boundless.

Rafael Buschmann and Michael Wulzinger
Hamburg, April 2018

The Whistle-Blowers

There he is. The invisible man. The phantom. The one who never leaves a trace behind. Finally. For months we've only been allowed to communicate in writing. At first he wouldn't answer at all. Then just irregularly and with obvious hesitation. His emails usually contain only the most necessary information. Short sentences, with hardly any details.

This is not someone who trusts others easily, that much is clear. It's hard to blame him. After all, he's on the run, hiding from the criminal underworld and from private detectives and police. One mistake could reveal his identity. So it's understandable that someone like that would need some time to emerge from hiding. Now, in February 2016, he has written that he needs to discuss something personally. It's urgent.

The first meeting takes place in a city in Eastern Europe. There's snow on the ground, but inside the small hotel room it's unbearably hot and sticky. There's no way to turn the heat down. It's not a feel-good atmosphere.

How does he want to be addressed? He's never even revealed his name.

'Call me John,' he says.

This is the beginning of an adventure that will take us on a months-long journey into the murkiest depths of the football industry. John is Football Leaks. The tiny website that has been creating so much uproar of late is his mouthpiece.

Its data is his voice, and it has carried weight, right from day one.

Football Leaks appeared out of nowhere on the Internet in late September 2015, without any reference to John or anyone else behind it and without any explanation or manifesto. It was just an Internet page with documents. The first leaks documented outlandish transfer deals involving young players and contained evidence of dubious agreements between club presidents and players' agents, some of whom split the fees between themselves. These were essentially kickbacks, dirty deals that critics had long suspected were standard in the industry. Now those secrets were published for all to read on the Internet.

Portugal was the first country to be affected. The documents on the Football Leaks home page initially came from Benfica, Sporting Lisbon and, later, Porto – the country's three top clubs. They looked authentic. They had two sets of signatures, initials and stamps, and their content was strictly confidential. These were company secrets, the sort of stuff that is kept under lock and key. Where was it coming from?

Football Leaks didn't answer this question. Instead it kept posting more and more documents for people to read and, if they wished, download. The leaks were not just a one-off prank; they were an ongoing campaign and a growing threat to the football industry.

One European club official, speaking on condition of anonymity because he did not want to provoke the group, told the *New York Times*, 'No one knows exactly what is happening, but everyone knows that they don't want to be next.'

When that was printed, John, this mystery man from the depths of the Internet, was sitting somewhere in the world in front of his computer having a good laugh. He combed fan forums and the media for speculation about who or what could be behind Football Leaks. Was the site the work of an individual or a group? An employee of the Portuguese football league or a former member of FIFA? Or perhaps an ex-agent who wanted to get revenge on his competitors, perhaps the entire industry? What were the motivations of the person or persons responsible? Revenge? Greed? Insanity? The desire to stir up trouble? There were lots of questions and wild speculation. The only thing that was certain was that the material on the Football Leaks site was explosive. Publishing it was a full-frontal attack on the unfathomably wealthy business of football.

Major leaks, involving huge caches of data, had been made public in the worlds of business, politics and even religion. But sports? Football? The Football Leaks revelations were a first, and the whistle-blowers' attacks caught the industry completely off guard. Reading the Football Leaks documents, you could only conclude that professional football had never imagined its dirty laundry could ever be aired in public.

Over the years, the industry had increasingly become something of a parallel universe – with its own concepts of right and wrong, integrity and ethics. Perhaps it was inevitable that the billions pumped into the industry by fans, sponsors and broadcasters had led to arrogance, vanity and even megalomania.

As an entertainment industry, football had achieved a social significance that went way beyond sport itself. On matters concerning the interests of this industry, be it tax laws, government charges on corporations or public subsidies for stadiums, no politician could avoid being lobbied by football's representatives.

Professional football and political power are closely connected, and the boundaries between the two are fluid. Just look at Germany. Chancellor Angela Merkel has visited the dressing room of the German national team after big wins. German national coach Joachim Löw and German Football League head Reinhard Rauball were delegates to the convention that elected the German president. The boss of the German Football Association, the DFB, Reinhard Grindel, is a former deputy in the German Bundestag, and the chairmen of the boards of Deutsche Telekom and Audi also sit on the supervisory board of Bayern Munich. Such connections are also global. When FIFA awards the World Cup, the emir of Qatar flies in to Zurich.

If political and business leaders all over the world want to bask in the reflected glamour of professional football, who's supposed to ensure that everything in the industry is on the straight and narrow? The media? Football marginalises and excludes critical journalists. Reporters enjoy very little direct, unmediated access to players and coaches, and media consultants and agents also try to control their clients' public image.

Reporters who refuse to play ball, who sniff around too much or try to write about reality rather than the carefully constructed images, are pressured and not infrequently pushed aside. Critical journalists often find they can't get any more interviews and are cut off from background information sessions.

It's a simple fact: football has become so huge and so powerful that it no longer needs the media. Everything clubs, associations, functionaries and players have to say they can say via YouTube, Twitter and Facebook – unedited and unverified by journalists. Weekend after weekend, millions of fans sit in stadiums and in front of television screens and are served up reality as the industry would like it to be. European football's governing body, UEFA, no longer thinks twice about censoring scenes of hooligans from live broadcasts of the European Championship. Hooligans, after all, damage the brand.

So can anyone regulate an industry so drunk on success and so convinced of its own perfection? The judicial system? The police? Sometimes, yes. Mostly, no. The football industry is rich enough to afford the finest attorneys, tax experts and business consultants, whose task is clear: to find ways of making dirty deals look clean.

The Football Leaks data reveal that almost every professional footballer on an above-average wage is behind one or more companies. In Spain and England in particular, these are formed specifically for channelling players' advertising and endorsement income. Clubs are also involved in these labyrinthine business structures, which quite often end in tax havens in the South Seas or Caribbean. All this diversification, obfuscation and concealment has only one goal: minimising the taxes owed. The basic motivation of everyone concerned seems to be to extract as much net from the gross as possible. That's why in football larger sums of money rarely flow along direct routes.

Investigators chasing down promising leads are quickly limited by national borders. Players frequently change countries and even continents. Agents' fees can be paid to anywhere in the world, even to the smallest banks on the most remote islands, where dirty money can be swiftly washed clean. Police and prosecutors often can only stand by and watch helplessly, since judicial systems are still, in the main, national: UK revenue agents act according to UK laws, and German ones act according to German laws. Even in today's globalised world, national authorities have astonishing difficulties exchanging information. Requests for legal assistance from countries in Africa, South America and the Caribbean are often not worth the effort they require to file. Police in Europe know only too well how frequently such requests don't even receive an answer.

The highly paid financial and tax experts in the world of football are well acquainted with these weak spots in the system and are masters at exploiting loopholes. A nebulous transfer of money from a Premier League football club to a company in the British Virgin Islands may be a regular payment to the account of a player's agent. As long as football can do its business in such clandestine fashion, it's nearly untouchable.

In keeping with these possibilities, football has long been run according to its own set of rules, a parallel universe that purports to be about order and monitoring, but that prevents outside authorities from intruding upon the industry's business. Football associations have whole departments and staff that issue licences to professional clubs. They are supposed to check if clubs are maintaining financial responsibility, whether their books are balanced and who is investing in them. More and more ethics commissions and compliance teams also monitor deals and sound the alarm when possible conflicts of interest arise. But the Football Leaks documents reveal that much of this is simply a facade.

Revelations about the orgies of corruption within FIFA and allegations that Germany paid bribes to secure the right to host the 2006 World Cup have badly damaged the credibility of the football industry. The associations reacted by suddenly hiring anti-corruption officials, and the teams promised to follow good business practices. This was supposed to be a sign of their determination to fight corruption and win back public trust. The message was: 'Look here, we're changing the way we do business. We're ensuring greater transparency.' But who believes that such a corrupt environment can clean up itself?

The people behind Football Leaks don't believe that, at any rate. Back in the autumn of 2015, while the world was still wondering who ran the platform, the whistle-blowers launched their next attack. It was intended to show that, beyond the national borders of Portugal, anyone could be hit by revelations, that no internal document was safe, that Football Leaks was not going to let the matter go. And that the anonymous operators of the site were not afraid of taking on the dark side of big money.

Twente Enschede – A Marionette

In the autumn of 2015, Football Leaks published two contracts within a few days of one another. Each of them would have caused a scandal on its own, but together they almost spelled the end of a top Dutch club. With these revelations, the platform achieved European-wide notoriety for the first time. The agreements published contained almost everything that is slowly but surely destroying professional football.

The first contract, which was concluded on 25 February 2014 between Twente Enschede and a company named Doyen Sports, concerned an investment model that FIFA would ban fifteen months later. Third-party ownership (TPO) is a kind of wager on human beings. An investor buys shares in the transfer rights of players, usually young ones, and bets that they will perform well so that their market value will rise. If the club sells the player, the investor gets paid. That's the simplest variant of a TPO.

However, TPOs can also be set up to ensnare clubs that are highly in debt. That was the case with Twente. The Dutch club had been in the middle of the pack for most of its fifty-year history but had notched up some triumphs thanks to the millions of euros injected by wealthy fan and functionary Joop Munsterman. Twente invested a lot of money in its squad, and in 2010 it won the Dutch championship and qualified for the Champions League. The celebrations could begin.

But the party was soon over. The club had overextended itself. The squad was too expensive, and salaries were proving a burden. Twente had to play in the Champions League year in, year out to have a chance of paying its wage bill. Unfortunately for the club, it didn't manage to qualify for club football's premier competition again and, by early 2014, it was up to its neck in debt. But instead of coming to its senses, selling its expensive players and rebuilding with youth prospects, Twente chose a path that is emblematic of all the false promises of modern professional football: club bosses decided to do a deal with a shady investor.

Doyen – a sports rights company with headquarters in London and Malta – acquired shares in the transfer rights of five Twente players, who were almost all at the start of their careers. Twente are known across Europe for their excellent youth academy, and in the past the club had sold players for tens of millions of euros, so the investors smelled an opportunity. In return for signing the deal, Twente received a one-off payment of €5 million. Peanuts. The club must have been desperate to raise money quickly. That's the only explanation for why clear-headed people would have signed such a deal.

Doyen didn't just profit when Twente sold a player. The fine print of the contract virtually guaranteed the company a return, while Twente, alone, bore any real risk. Even when the transfer value of a player plummeted, Doyen got back a part of its investment. In the case of striker Luc Castaignos, the club had to pay the company €1.5 million in the first year of the deal, and that sum increased every season by 10 per cent. Twente had to cough up the money even if the player could no longer play due to injuries. Doyen also profited when the player was loaned out to another club. In addition, there was even a clause requiring Twente to immediately inform the company about all offers, negotiations and expressions of interest from another club in a given player.

As if that weren't enough, on 27 December 2013, around two months before the conclusion of the €5 million contract, Twente and Doyen had signed another agreement – the second document published by Football Leaks. This arrangement contained a clause requiring the club to pay Doyen if it decided against a transfer over the investor's wishes. It was a terrible deal for the team. It was de facto no longer the club and its sporting management that ultimately decided the make-up of the squad, but the investor, who was supposed to have no say in internal decisions of this sort.

Such agreements compromise the whole spirit of sporting competition. The clause put Twente in a lose–lose situation. In order not to have to pay off Doyen, it was almost forced to sell its best players.

Notwithstanding the devastating consequences of such a deal from a sporting perspective, the agreement between Twente and Doyen raises questions of ethics in the game and how professional clubs treat their fans. How can a club justify making profits from the sale of kits with players' names on them while hoping that those same players will bring in transfer fees? How are fans supposed to feel when clubs suggest that every time a player signs a contract extension he will definitely be wearing the team's shirt in the coming season, while simultaneously promising investors that he will be sold as soon as his performances improve and the first big offer rolls in? It's pure cynicism to exploit the loyalty of supporters and believe that they won't notice what's really going on.

Before Football Leaks published these two contracts, fans weren't the only ones who had no clue about quite how deep this cynicism went, however. The Royal Netherlands Football Association, the KNVB, also didn't know that such nebulous investment deals were being concluded. Twente only submitted the second, later contract to the association for review. The club and the investor kept the first one top secret. Once Football Leaks made that document public, the KNVB didn't waste any time in declaring the arrangement unethical and banning it.

Twente supporters protested against the immoral business practices of their club, and Doyen and the team set about immediately dissolving the contract. But this was an evasive manoeuvre, and it attracted the attention of Football Leaks. Once again documents were leaked to the website, including some controversial emails sent by Doyen's sports director Nélio Lucas, of whom we shall hear again. 'Let's not loose [*sic*] time,' Lucas writes. 'Very important they pay us something this year and as soon as possible.' Doyen would end up receiving €3.3 million when the contract was dissolved.

Things continued to decline for Twente. First, the KNVB revoked the club's licence for the first division. That punishment was struck down on appeal, but Twente were still subject to strict financial oversight and banned for three years from European competitions. They also had to pay a €180,000 fine. Instead of climbing out of their financial hole, as the club had hoped, the deal with Doyen meant that Twente Enschede were in even worse shape than before.

Was the small Dutch club just an unhappy exception? Easy prey for a predatory investor? Unfortunately not. The case was only the tip of the iceberg. The involvement of Doyen – an investor unknown even to some football insiders – would prove to be typical of the cut-throat exploitation of the beautiful game.

The Football Leaks revelations prompted further research into the nature of these investors' businesses. It would lead – of course – to tax havens, but also to clans who had accumulated huge wealth in the disintegrating Soviet Union and who were now, one generation further on, using their political contacts to co-opt the glamour of sports for their businesses. Welcome to the world of Doyen Sports.

Inshallah Kings

There you are, a newcomer to the business. And there he is, the president of Real Madrid. You want to sell him a player. He probably gets offers like this every day; you're one in a crowd. So what's your plan? You try to use the oldest incentive in the world: sex.

On 7 August 2013, Real Madrid played a friendly against Chelsea in Miami. It was the finale of the International Champions Cup, the real prize of which was not some brewery-sponsored silverware but a couple of million dollars in appearance fees. But for Doyen Sports, the ambitious newcomer in the trading of football players, this was the game of the season. A game, indeed, that wasn't decided on the pitch but in a luxury hotel suite the night before.

One year previously, Doyen had spent a modest sum acquiring transfer rights to a player under contract to Spanish side Sevilla: Geoffrey Kondogbia. If another club offered €20 million for him, Sevilla would have practically no choice but to sell – such were the terms of the contract – and Doyen, too, would cash in. It was a great piece of business for the company, so Doyen was desperately looking for a club prepared to pay €20 million for Kondogbia. And what better opportunity to kick-start such a deal than a summer exhibition match in Florida watched by a bored Real Madrid president Florentino Pérez? As chance would have it, the

Arif clan behind Doyen happened to own a 650-square-metre villa on nearby Fisher Island, a private playground for the super-rich.

On 6 August, Doyen Sports boss Arif Arif received several WhatsApp messages from Nélio Lucas describing how he had showed club presidents, including Pérez, a good evening: 'I'm in Miami . . . Yesterday was amazing . . . I took few presidents out and even Florentino came with us . . . Very funny. He removed his tie and danced.' They had gone to a Miami Beach nightclub called the Mokai Lounge, which is known for dancers and female bartenders whose work outfits leave little to the imagination.

The party was to continue the next day in the apartment on Fisher Island. 'I want to bring some girls to be with us,' Lucas wrote, asking if he could trust a woman named Violet to 'organise' the girls in question. 'Never met her bro,' responded Arif. 'Do what u have to.' He asked that Lucas take down the photos on the walls and lock his father's room. Lucas said that he was thinking of giving that room to Pérez. Arif wrote back: 'For 20 million :) For Kondogbia.' Lucas responded, 'That's why we need to look after him.' There's little doubt about what was going on in the house, regardless of who exactly was involved. At one point Arif brags about his own room in the house, 'A lot of girls have been fucked in that room.'

The next evening Lucas wrote, 'Took real madrid directors and Florentino to the house last night . . . Probably also today.' But he also had disappointing news: Real was only willing to pay €15 million, not €20 million – a sum insufficient to force Sevilla to sell. 'I'm killing my balls to find someone to pay the clause of Kondogbia,' Lucas promised.

Three weeks later, it was French side Monaco, and not Real Madrid, that would pay the requisite €20 million. Doyen turned the kind of profit on the Kondogbia transaction that is more commonly seen in a drug deal, earning a 524 per cent return in thirteen months. And getting to know Pérez apparently also benefited the company, if in a different sense. A short time later, Lucas would boast that his connections to Real Madrid were 'more solid than titanium'.

Pérez himself said with reference to the alleged 'sex party' that he didn't meet anyone on the night in question. He said that he had gone to a nightclub – presumably the Mokai Lounge – and that any one of the hundreds of patrons there might have taken pictures of him. But Pérez denied anything further, saying that there was no meeting with anyone else and no party. He also denied that Real Madrid had ever been interested in Kondogbia or that anyone had offered him the player, adding that to the best of his knowledge, Real Madrid had never worked with Doyen Sports.

It is noteworthy, however, that in a page since deleted from Doyen's website, Pérez was quoted as saying that 'Real Madrid . . . recognizes that Doyen was and is important for Spanish football and must highlight their professionalism. Our experience with them in other subjects is immaculate.' When asked about this quote, he replied, 'I can't say why in its webpage is quoted a phrase like the one you mentioned, that I don't remember to have ever said.'

The exact details of that evening's events will never be known to anyone other than those present. There is no evidence in the WhatsApp conversation about whether Pérez accepted any offer made by Lucas or participated in any sexual adventures. It's possible that the sports director was merely trying to impress his boss back home; although despite Lucas's bragging, there is no indication that Pérez was influenced in any way.

What is not in doubt, however, is how the case of Doyen illustrates the ways in which money from nebulous sources can force its way into a legitimate industry. Although hardly anyone in the public at large knows about Doyen, it earns its money through some of the biggest names in sports. The company markets Neymar, the most expensive player in football history, as well as the highest-paid ex-player, advertising icon David Beckham. Its clients also include the world's fastest man, Usain Bolt, and German tennis legend Boris Becker. Doyen not only owned a piece of the €20 million Kondogbia, now at Inter Milan, but also of the €30 million Eliaquim Mangala (Manchester City) and the €40 million Radamel Falcao (Monaco).

Football Leaks possesses numerous documents that illustrate Doyen's business practices and help explain the company's meteoric rise. These documents reveal what lies behind the carefully polished corporate facade: lies, a secret fund, one-sided contracts that force clubs to sell players, and shell firms behind which Doyen continues to conceal itself. The London-based company has become a symbol within the world of football. On the surface, everything is gleaming and nice, while the dirty reality is located below, in figures, contract clauses and agreements. Doyen is football today, and football today is Doyen.

Predators

Wembley Stadium, 25 May 2013, was a showcase for the excellence of German football. Borussia Dortmund were playing Bayern Munich in the all-German final of the Champions League. The fans were feverish with anticipation, as were the people in an office building in the exclusive central London neighbourhood of St James's. There, on the seventh floor of 12 Charles II Street, was Doyen Sports Investments. Twenty-seven-year-old Arif Arif, who had spent the past two years building up the company using his family's money, was going through everyone who needed to be accommodated in his VIP box one last time. He needed a seat for himself and his sports director, Nélio Lucas, for a couple of Doyen managers and for a player's agent. But the real VIPs on the guest list were other people crucial to Doyen Sports' survival: Arif's father, Tevfik Arif, and Tevfik's old friends Sasha and Alik. Sasha's full name is Alexander Mashkevich, while Alik is better known as Alijan Ibragimov.

Mashkevich and Ibragimov represent two-thirds of the legendary 'Kazakh trio' of oligarchs, whose company ENRC pursues a particularly lucrative form of refining raw materials. For decades they have been turning the seemingly endless natural resources in Kazakhstan into billions for their private accounts. The money is used to buy everything that a self-respecting oligarch needs. Mashkevich, for instance, owns a Rolls-Royce Phantom V, two Bentleys, a Ferrari, a Lamborghini and six Mercedes. He once spent €2.1 million buying jewellery, watches and haute couture during a two-day shopping spree in Paris.

In a tightly run kleptocracy like Kazakhstan, where dictator Nursultan Nazarbayev and his family have accumulated billions in ways that aren't public knowledge, an oligarch cannot go without political protection. US diplomats consider Mashkevich a close friend of the Kazakh potentate, who has ruled since 1990, and among those also favoured by the dictator is the Arif clan. Arif Arif's sister Ayla wrote in an Internet chat that Mashkevich 'is helping dad keep hold of his primary business'. Arif responded, 'And he's a great friend for that.' Everything to do with the clan, including the new sports marketing company in London, is related to the family's core business dealing in natural resources in Kazakhstan. And Arif Arif's guest list for the Champions League final in London sheds light on the dark origins of a family empire that is now trying to control football.

In the late 1980s, as the Warsaw Pact collapsed, Tevfik Arif and his younger brother Refik were perfectly poised to make the leap from communism to capitalism. They landed on the side of those who seized hold of assets the disintegrating Soviet government could no longer protect in the name of the people. The Arifs lived in Kazakhstan, and Tevfik worked in the Ministry of Trade as the director of its hotels department. A short time after the collapse of the Soviet Union, he quit his job and struck out on his own. As of 1991, his brother Refik occupied a key post in the Kazakh Ministry of Industry and Trade, which wanted to get involved in dealing phosphorus and iron alloys.

It is not clear how the Arifs subsequently earned their fortune. What is certain is that Tevfik worked for the Reuben brothers, David and Simon. Born in India, these two men gained control of the Russian aluminium industry in the mid-1990s. Tevfik Arif was in the middle of it all, serving as 'an agent of the ground', as his son Arif would later put it. What followed was an 'aluminium war', at the end of which a number of managers lost their lives. They were discovered with their throats cut or their bodies riddled with bullets. It's possible that this is why Tevfik disappeared from Kazakhstan. 'Once the business began intertwining with organised crime (inevetible [*sic*] in those days), he dropped everything and moved to the USA via Turkey,' Arif Arif would write in 2014.

Refik Arif stayed behind in Kazakhstan, where he had obviously picked the winning side: the trio of Mashkevich, Ibragimov and a third oligarch named Patokh Chodiev. The Arif family emerged from all the turmoil with a tidy little fortune, and since the mid-1990s they've controlled ACCP, one of the world's biggest chromium-based chemical plants. Who gave the Arifs the money for this, for the core business in which Sasha Mashkevich has been described as such a 'great friend?' It may well have been this trio of oligarchs. Their corporation just happens to own one of Kazakhstan's largest chromium ore mines. Without that ore, the Arifs' chemical plant would grind to a halt.

Scandals, Scandals

Owning ACCP is like having a licence to print money. Between 2004 and 2014, according to internal records, the Arifs made almost €400 million selling chromium-based chemicals. That's Refik Arif's war chest. His brother Tevfik also earned millions for the family. After fleeing to Turkey in 1993, he built the Rixos chain of five-star hotels. He also acquired a stake in one of Turkey's largest construction companies, Sembol. It received a conspicuous amount of work from the Kazakh government: for instance, for the university in Astana, which is, of course, named after Nazarbayev. Sembol was also hired to construct the 'Pyramid', an events centre built on the express command of the Kazakh dictator.

Around the turn of the millennium, Tevfik emigrated to the US and founded the real-estate company Bayrock. In New York City, he built a hotel and apartment complex with one of the most famous and controversial real-estate tycoons in the world, US President Donald Trump.

Over the course of his career, Tevfik Arif himself has had several brushes with controversy. Sometimes there have been full-blown scandals. Investors say they have been deceived, and connections have been made to a man who sold fraudulent investments. Arif and his friends have been known to enjoy the company of young 'models' from Russia and Ukraine – always a crucial ingredient for a shady reputation. Arif has always denied all accusations of wrongdoing, and he's never been convicted of a crime. But in 2010 he made the headlines in Turkey for weeks, after police detained him and all three of the Kazakh trio of oligarchs on board a luxury yacht with the aforementioned models.

This is the clan that decided in 2011 to get into a new lucrative industry: professional football. Such a decision is hardly surprising: the turnover from football in Europe alone is estimated at €20 billion annually, and prices have been shooting skywards like oil from a freshly drilled well. It's an ideal market for predators.

From 2011 to 2015, Refik provided some €75 million in start-up capital, and together with Tevfik he had the final say in how that money was used. The man they trusted to run the new business was Tevfik's son, Arif Arif. Apparently, the idea was for him to prove his mettle in the sports sector and show that he had what it takes to take over the family's chemical plant, real-estate business and construction company someday. Arif will no doubt pass this test. The methods he uses are the same ones that have been tried and tested in the family. They are both shady and successful.

Becoming Billionaires

When Arif Arif got involved in football in 2011, he didn't know much about the sport. What's more, his sports director, Nélio Lucas, was almost a *persona non grata* in the industry. Lucas had fallen out with his mentor, the legendary players' agent Pini Zahavi, who accused Lucas of doing deals behind his back. 'U did the mistake of ur life,' Zahavi wrote to Lucas. 'I don't want 2 do any thing with u in the world, and trust me that u won't b able 2 do any thing.' But in only four years, Lucas would become one of the stars of the industry, taking Doyen Sports, the Arifs' newly founded investment company, with him.

Arif Arif is thirty-two, Lucas thirty-nine. They're like two overgrown boys who oscillate between visions for the future and full-blown megalomania. 'What Business we create!!!' Lucas wrote to Arif. 'Money money!!!' Arif responded, 'Imagine us in 10 years inshallah kings chico.' Lucas answered, 'Together forever on good and bad. We will succeed and we will become billionaires!!!!' Their aim was to have Doyen Sports turning a profit in three years, not a decade.

The two men speak the language of gangsta rap, maintain the lifestyles of playboys and have the self-confidence of champion boxers. Once, when they were looking at a new apartment, Arif boasted that it was 'tailor made for orgies'. 'Oh yes!!!' Lucas wrote back. For Halloween, Lucas had trouble deciding whether to dress up as Napoleon, the Pope or Louis XIV. 'For me the dictator,' Arif advised him. When he's not in London, Arif likes to party in Ibiza and in southern France.

The Doyen Group is like a gigantic general store. Along with the sports division, there is Doyen Capital, which deals in raw materials and is also headed by Arif Arif. Then there is Doyen Natural Resources, which has a stake in an iron ore mine in Brazil. Through this company Arif does deals with Jamie Reuben, a son of David Reuben, and Vladimir Semzov, a real-estate mogul with a Belgian passport. Perhaps these are old friends and connections of Arif's father.

Two parallel companies take care of sport. For a commission, Doyen Marketing helps stars like Neymar, David Beckham and Boris Becker get advertising deals. But the main business is done by Doyen Sports, which is de facto run by Arif Arif, even though he has nothing to do with it on paper. This is the division of the corporation that speculates on the future transfer values of football players. It buys stakes in the transfer rights of young athletes in hopes of a quick rise in value, cashing in when those players are sold to new clubs, as was the case with Kondogbia and Twente. Doyen is a 'third party' in such transactions, along with the teams and the players. The company styles itself as a knight in shining armour that helps small clubs who would otherwise be unable to afford top talent. In particular, Doyen claims

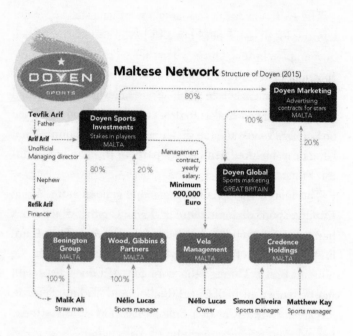

Maltese Network Structure of Doyen (2015)

to assist clubs with long traditions but limited amounts of money in closing the gap to the richest teams.

In fact, the divide between the top ten clubs in Europe and the rest gets bigger and bigger every year. Money scores goals, as the saying goes, and that certainly applies to Bayern Munich, Real Madrid, Barcelona and Paris Saint-Germain. These teams are all but unbeatable in their respective domestic leagues. The 'chance' that Doyen offers clubs unable to keep up with these giants is the same one a loan shark offers the poor debtor who can no longer get credit from a bank. Doyen's money is lent in return for signatures on unfair contracts. Interest rates are high, and stranglehold clauses in the contracts ensure that Doyen almost never loses on any of its investments.

'A Pure Financial Play'

In August 2011, the first player in whom Doyen acquired a stake was Abdelaziz Barrada, a Moroccan who played for the suburban Madrid club Getafe. Doyen paid €1.5 million for 60 per cent of Barrada's transfer rights. Less than two years later, he transferred to Al-Jazira in the United Arab Emirates for €8.5 million. After incidental costs, Doyen earned €3.35 million, a return of 223 per cent – that's according to Doyen company records. Lucas described this result as not bad, but he wasn't completely satisfied: 'We couldn't control him [any] more. His salary was 450.000€ net and they paying him now 3M usd net . . . But if the player had listen to me I will get more but fucking Muslim.'

Doyen wants its players and clubs to do as the company orders. The players are puppets, mere chips in a grand casino game of football. The ultimate aim is not what's best for them but what makes Doyen the most money. Geoffrey Kondogbia is one example. The French midfielder ended up not at Real Madrid, the biggest club in the world, but at Monaco. Lucas wrote to Arif, 'Great deal for us.'

'Congrats bro!!!!!!!' Arif replied, but added, 'I hope we didnt ruin his career . . . My heart Is broken.'

'Look to the bank account in few days and u will feel different,' Lucas told him.

'I know bro but I always envisioned this kid being a superstar at a big club,' Arif replied.

'I wanted the kid to move to a solid team . . . But this ended up being a pure financial play,' Arif wrote to a friend that same day.

Arif may have had a broken heart over this particular deal, but he clearly considers other players mere business opportunities. Emotions play no part, and the language these predatory capitalists use reflects that. After one of Doyen's stars did well for his national team, Arif wrote, 'Nigga making us money.'

In Lucas's and Arif's messages to one another, they write as if they owned the world, so the comedown is all the harder whenever they're reminded that their world actually belongs to Papa Tevfik and Uncle Refik. 'I've been getting my head fucked every day,' whined Arif Jr in July 2013. His uncle controlled the money, Arif wrote, while he took care of management. That was okay, but Arif would only amount to anything in the eyes of the older generation when he paid back the capital his father and uncle had invested. 'All our jobs depend upon me managing this relationship w my father and uncle,' he told Lucas. Once, Lucas was so fed up that he advised his buddy Arif to renounce it all. 'I can't bro I'm stuck why [sic] crazy glue,' Arif answered, adding somewhat cryptically, 'The only way is to cut myself out, but that the knife was a million miles away I can't reach it.'

So the two young men have no choice but to expand the older Arifs' business empire and make it more profitable. 'These cocksuckers want to bash third party ownership continually,' Arif cursed when FIFA began to consider banning TPO deals of the sort Doyen had with Twente. In public relations brochures, Doyen depicts itself as a business partner. Never would Doyen interfere in clubs' dealings or force them to sell players, the firm promises. But the case of Twente proved the opposite. A typical Doyen contract contains clauses that border on extortion.

There were similar provisions in the contract of Dutch winger Ola John, who transferred from Twente to Benfica in 2012. Doyen bought half of his transfer rights for €4,575,000, but the deal called for Doyen to get at least €6 million back, regardless of how John's market value developed. If Benfica sold the player for less than €12 million, the company still got its €6 million. If John brought in more than €12 million, Doyen got €6 million plus half of everything over the €12 million. If the player didn't get sold in three years, no matter: Doyen was owed €6 million. Had he been so seriously injured as to never be able to play again, €6 million for Doyen. If another club was willing to pay €20 million and Benfica refused to sell, Benfica would have to pay half that sum – €10 million – to Doyen. Doyen was also allowed to look for a club that would pay €20 million. And so on and so on.

Doyen made a 25 per cent return on its investment in three years, regardless of what happened. When the company wants to cash in, partner clubs mostly have no choice but to sell the player in question, if they still can. Benfica sent Ola John out on loan four times in two years – most likely in an attempt to get rid of him. By the end of 2016, his transfer value was only estimated at around €5 million. Assuming that Doyen activated the €6 million clause, the club would have ended up footing the difference.

This was by no means the only example of such a contract at Doyen. There were similar provisions in a contract concerning Josuha Guilavogui, who has played for Bundesliga side Wolfsburg since 2014. The year before he played for Atlético Madrid, a club that has repeatedly done business with Doyen. In this case, Doyen was guaranteed a 30 per cent profit in three years.

The idea that Doyen is a fair TPO partner is a myth, one among many. Another, even larger one is that Doyen is financially transparent. A presentation intended to differentiate Doyen from other, shady TPO investors claimed that the firm was fully registered and monitored by economic evaluators. In reality, Doyen Sports is a complexly intertwined construct of international enterprises, some based in Malta, some in the British Virgin Islands, some in the United Arab Emirates. Shell firms are founded and then dissolved in regular cycles. With his usual bluntness, Lucas explained the logic behind all these subsidiaries in a message to Arif: 'We need to put in place a structure to protect us and the company in order for nobody to disclose nothing about us.' By 'nobody' he may well have meant the tax authorities.

But nothing causes Arif Jr to break out in a cold sweat more than the prospect that the family's old friends could find out that his father Tevfik, nicknamed 'Skip', is ultimately behind Doyen Sports. In July 2013, the Bloomberg financial news service reported exactly that, and the Arifs readied themselves to shut the young business down from one day to the next. Luckily for them, no one demanded that. 'The kazakhs don't give a Fuck about u me or skip,' wrote Arif Jr. 'If they find out he is behind it they will go after our family business in kazakhstan and then it's all over . . . Get it through your head it's not funny, they will ruin us. They will expose us, our businesses and our high level relationships then it's all over.'

After the scandal on the Turkish yacht, Tevfik Arif seems to have been given a clear message to stay out of the spotlight. Did it come from his friends, the trio of Kazakh oligarchs? The young Arif's chat messages suggest that the three men disassociated themselves from Tevfik. Mashkevich seems to have wanted nothing more to do with him for a time. Arif Jr wrote that the oligarch had blamed his father to save his own skin. But soon everything was forgiven and forgotten. The two were spotted together at a football stadium in London and in a restaurant in Sardinia. But Arif Jr still feared the consequences if his father got himself back in the public eye.

Lucas thought Arif was being paranoid, but the latter countered that Lucas had only ever worked in the civilised world and explained how things worked where his family was from. 'They', wrote Arif, would ruin 'us' by exposing the family's business and high-level contacts. The Doyen brand name would be finished, and the family's other businesses would have to distance themselves from it. Things never got that far, but from that point on the older Arifs disappeared completely behind a protective wall of shell companies run by front men. Doyen became utterly non-transparent.

That was probably all for the better. In 2013, Doyen's dealings became even shadier with the establishment of a secret fund maintained in Ras al-Khaimah, one of the seven emirates that make up the UAE. Ras al-Khaimah doesn't attract much publicity. An offshore advisor of Lucas runs a letterbox company there called Denos that regularly takes in money stemming from sports deals. As a rule, 10 per cent of any given deal will be sent to the emirate, with the total sums amounting to several million euros. But the money doesn't stay there very long. Doyen Sport uses it for payments that apparently stay secret.

What is the money used for? Ahead of a construction project Lucas was negotiating, he asked Arif Jr whether he should pay off the other side. Arif answered, 'Yes bro.'

In addition, Lucas once explained to the Arif clan that the money going to Denos wasn't actually Doyen's but instead was 'for transactions we need to do' with 'no paperwork'. In a chat, Arif Jr also wrote that Lucas had to pay the people he did business with, if Doyen wanted to buy and sell. His father, the young man wrote, had made that clear from the very beginning: 'He said that he needs to compensate people that he does business with whenever we buy and sell.' But Doyen also needed to steer clear of involving itself in what was potentially dirty business. 'It's not that clear cut so that's why we stay out of it,' Arif added.

For example, in 2014, the Doyen Group bought half of the image rights for top young Belgian talent Adnan Januzaj, then with Manchester United. Officially, Doyen paid €1.5 million, but an additional €500,000 allegedly went via Denos to Januzaj's agent and then, as leaked emails suggest, most likely into the pockets of the player's father. Could this have been a covert payment made by Doyen to establish a relationship with a bright young talent? On one occasion, Denos money even seems to have ended up with agents who worked simultaneously both for a player and for a club.

By contrast, Lucas uses money from a Maltese letterbox company he personally owns to fly in women from Eastern Europe. The Twitter account of one of the ladies in question, a Kateryna S., promises that a beautiful woman is 'paradise for the eyes, hell for the mind and purgatory for the pockets'. Conspicuously often, these Eastern European women are sent to cities in which a Champions League game is being played. The reason for these trips is unclear. Do the women escort Nélio Lucas himself, or does he use them on behalf of Doyen to grease the wheels of business on the margins of football matches, as he apparently intended to do in the Arif family's luxury apartment in Florida?

Lucas has refused to answer these and other questions. All he will say is that he denies all the allegations. Doyen Sports boss Arif Arif, his father Tevfik and his uncle Refik also don't want to answer any questions. They and Lucas said via attorneys that the questions themselves were defamatory and based on false assumptions. The trio of Kazakh oligarchs, Adnan Januzaj, his father and his advisor didn't respond at all to requests for statements.

'This Football Leaks Shit'

Money, as the saying goes, doesn't stink. Some clubs have no problem working with Doyen, a company that promises them big money, even if those teams would rather not know where precisely that money comes from and it should be clear to everyone in the football industry that Doyen is a company better avoided.

Thus, Doyen's business continues to boom. Third-party ownership may have been prohibited, and the lawsuits and complaints to the EU Commission that the company launched in protest may have proven unsuccessful, but Doyen wouldn't be Doyen if it didn't try to get around the prohibition. Moreover, football wouldn't be the grubby business it is if FIFA hadn't been quick to loosen regulations. Investing in individual players is still forbidden, and looks set to remain so. But investing in a club in return for a portion of all the revenues from its sales of players is still permitted, as FIFA recently made clear in response to a query from the Danish Football Association. For example, a draft Doyen contract from November 2015 had the company buying 20 per cent of Spanish third-division team Cádiz for €1.5 million and also receiving half of the transfer rights to all of its players.

In March 2015, Bundesliga club Hamburg SV, reeling from a series of poor squads and always looking to build a new one, also entered into discussions with Doyen. Having just stepped down as chairman of the club's advisory board a few days earlier, functionary Thomas von Heesen met with Doyen representatives in Munich. The TPO ban had already been decided upon and would come into force two months later. Von Heesen explored the possibility of selling shares in six Hamburg players, including Pierre-Michel Lasogga, Cléber, Jonathan Tah and Maximilian Beister, for €12.2 million. However, a contract was necessary for Doyen to take over the shares. Apparently the idea was to negotiate at a future date how the investor would be remunerated after the sale of a player – precisely the sort of deal that would have amounted to skirting the FIFA prohibition taking force on 1 May 2015. On 10 June, a Doyen negotiating partner sent then-Hamburg chairman Dietmar Beiersdorfer a list of possible new players for HSV. With regard to a player from Sampdoria, it was noted: 'purchase shared between Doyen and Hamburg'. That would have been an instance of the now banned TPO.

In the end there was no deal. Why not? In March 2018, von Heesen confirmed that he had been in contact with Doyen but said that he had not been acting on behalf of Hamburg or been authorised to negotiate on the club's behalf. HSV and the investor confirmed that there had been an 'exchange of information with the Doyen Group'. That exchange had been about possible 'refinancing', but in the end, the parties involved had backed off, in part because of FIFA's bans on TPO.

But Doyen's sports director Nélio Lucas may also have been forced to change his strategy. Football Leaks published the first Doyen documents in September 2015, and roughly two-months later, Lucas wrote to his attorney that he might not be able to pay a bill because after 'this Football Leaks shit' all the structures were being changed. That sounded as if Lucas himself had to build up new structures, and perhaps establish a few additional letterbox companies, before business could proceed.

The Search

Why would someone voluntarily take on people like the Arif brothers or Nélio Lucas? Because they personally wanted to unmask them or because they had been hired to do so? Or was this a case of revenge? With every new document it published, Football Leaks raised new questions and became an ever-greater mystery. The people who ran the platform worked anonymously. Even their Internet presence wasn't simple to follow: over the course of the Twente Enschede affair, Football Leaks changed its web address twice. Why? What was the point of this game of hide and seek?

At the bottom of the website was a contact address, and in early December 2015, in the middle of the maelstrom surrounding the dubious contracts signed by Twente, we sent an email, asking the people behind Football Leaks who they were, where they came from and what they were trying to achieve. A week went by without us getting an answer. We sent a second mail with additional questions. Is this material genuine? Why did they choose to publish precisely this material? Are there more leaks on the way? Was Football Leaks the work of an individual or a group? We attached a document with the questions we had sent the week before, adding that it would be nice if we could get an answer.

It's not easy to write to people who want to remain anonymous. What tone should you use? What questions would be of interest to the person hiding behind anonymity? What sort of answers can you hope for? If you know nothing about the person you'd like to converse with, you're flying blind.

We took another look at the contracts and the other documents published on the Football Leaks website. Maybe we had overlooked some clues about who could be behind it? Perhaps the way the page was set up contained information about the whereabouts of those behind it? We made notes about the tiniest details, hoping that they might shed light on the identity of the authors. Because a lot of the documents are in Portuguese, we surmised that the people behind Football Leaks might also be connected with Portugal.

The material seemed genuine. All the contracts were signed by multiple parties, and the dates, addresses and mode of speech of the emails looked authentic. Conspicuously, a lot of what was published had to do with Doyen Sports. Had the sports marketer been hacked? Was Football Leaks in reality a hacker collective? Or was this the work of a former employee who had stolen the data?

The major leaks of the past, as we'd learned, were usually the work of a former member of a company or organisation who wanted to do something about abuses at his or her previous employer. Take, for example, Edward Snowden, probably the world's most famous whistle-blower, whose theft of data from the NSA raised fundamental questions about individual freedom versus the state's need for security. The former soldier Bradley (now Chelsea) Manning gave WikiLeaks material about the US military that revealed the brutal behaviour of American soldiers in war zones. Hervé Falciani and Bradley Birkenfeld, two former bankers, helped bring down

Switzerland's principle of banking secrecy; their leaks represented a major step in combating tax fraud. We added former employees and possible hackers to our list of potential explanations for Football Leaks. We had no idea how we could test our theories, but at least it felt good to have a few.

Days went by, and we still hadn't received any answer from Football Leaks. We refused to give up and sent a third email. 'Are you Portuguese?' we asked. 'Are you hackers? Have you hacked into Doyen Sports and stolen the material? Did you use to work for Doyen? Can we talk – anonymously, if you wish?' Perhaps, we thought, such direct, targeted questions would help provoke a response. We sent our email. And lo and behold, we got some answers to our questions.

Unfortunately for us, they were printed in the *New York Times*.

On 15 December, the newspaper ran a long article with the headline: 'Mysterious Website Aims to Shed Light on Soccer Dealings'. It contained a summary of the Twente affair, but the scoop in the story, the one we had been after, came right at the beginning of the report: 'Football Leaks is shrouded in mystery, and no one involved with it has offered any significant details about the identities of the organizers. Over the course of a lengthy email exchange with *The New York Times*, however, someone who identified himself as a leader of Football Leaks discussed the site's background, its motivations and its intentions.'

Damn, damn, damn. Our colleagues from the *Times* had an exclusive.

The person providing the information about Football Leaks in the article identified himself only as John – a common nom de plume among anonymous whistle-blowers.

John said that he lived in Portugal, and that he and his partners established the platform to draw attention to TPO investment deals in the Portuguese football league. 'This kind of secrecy about contracts and secret clauses is killing this sport,' John was quoted as saying.

So John and his partners were football fans trying to do something to clean up the sport. They saw themselves as somewhat like international watchdogs. By now the Football Leaks page was only accessible via a Yandex address hosted on a Russian server. John told the *Times* that the hosts of the two previous Football Leaks pages had been put under so much pressure that they closed down the whistle-blowing platform. Yandex, too, John said, had closed the site's cloud account after a complaint from Doyen. 'The fight has been hard,' he told the *Times*. 'But we won't stop.' When asked why he had used a Russian server, John answered, 'Because it's publicly known Russian authorities rarely cooperate with Western authorities.'

That raised further questions. Were the people behind Football Leaks criminals? Hackers? Thieves? John's response was that while 'people may think we are hackers, we are only regular computer users'. A rather thin explanation. And where did the documents come from? John said nothing on this issue, but he did let it drop that Football Leaks was in possession of more than 300 gigabytes of data from within the football industry – a huge amount. John didn't reveal whom the material concerned or who would be affected by the next revelations, saying only that Football Leaks needed time to examine the data.

This was John's first major media appearance, but he didn't reveal much. Most of his answers remained vague, and it was difficult to draw conclusions about his personality and character from what he was quoted as saying. But he did at least seem to be someone with a fighting spirit who wasn't easily deterred and enjoyed rebelling against authority.

Doyen spokesman Francisco Empis was far clearer in his statements, describing Football Leaks as a 'scam' and saying, 'It's now a police matter.' The Spanish sports newspaper *As* cited an anonymous source in the Portuguese police who claimed that Football Leaks was an 'international criminal organisation'. Tough talk. One thing was clear: Football Leaks had made some serious enemies.

First Signs of Life

We wrote some more emails. It was our only chance of contacting John and his associates. We asked for interviews, phone calls, a meeting. But neither John nor anyone else reacted to our messages. Shortly before the end of 2015, we sent email number sixteen. This time we listed all the articles about football and corruption we had been involved in over the past few years: they covered allegations that Germany paid bribes to win the rights to the 2006 World Cup, Lionel Messi's tax evasion, scandals at FIFA, betting frauds, match fixing and the influence of agents over clubs and players. We wanted John to see that for years we'd been doing what he was doing, that we had tried to look behind the facade of the sport, not just report about exciting matches and brilliant stars.

Our email sounded pompous and boastful, and we weren't happy with it. But it was our last straw, a kind of cry for help.

And it did the trick. On 3 January 2016, the first email from Football Leaks was waiting in our mailbox. It was written in English and sent from a Russian address. The message itself was exceedingly terse: 'What's your problem with football? Best regards, FL.' It wasn't what we had expected. 'FL' could hardly have formulated a bigger, more open question. We got to work phrasing our response, declaring that after all our past research and all our conflicts with corrupt functionaries, players, coaches, sponsors and agents, we considered the problems in the football business just as serious as those in the banking sector. Wherever so much money was allowed to flow unmonitored, it would inevitably attract shady characters. We wrote that we were interested in exposing everything that damaged the game and its credibility. We promised that we would publish articles in *Der Spiegel* that would encourage more transparency and give readers and football fans the chance to make up their own minds. Then we hit 'send'. There was nothing left to do but wait.

That evening, documents appeared on the Football Leaks page that left us speechless. They were contracts with MIM and Polaris, two companies that would keep us plenty busy in the months to come, both part of the network of firms managing Cristiano Ronaldo's marketing rights. How did these contracts get on the Football Leaks page? Normally, such documents are treated like state secrets. A careful reading of them revealed that Ronaldo's marketing rights were administered by companies in Ireland. Was a football superstar using a European tax haven to minimise his tax burden?

The documents were written in complex legal English, with lots of clauses and paragraphs. At first glance they weren't as gripping or spectacular as a contract between a team and a player. There were no astronomical transfer fees or wages leaping out at you. Among the many revelations Football Leaks had published, these documents failed to attract much notice. Hardly anyone discussed them. We, too, would need nine months of intense work to understand these contracts and appreciate what a bombshell they really were. Football Leaks would give us the key to do so.

More on that later. For now, suffice it to say that the Ronaldo documents gave us insight into the secret world at the absolute pinnacle of football where honestly paying your taxes is considered the height of stupidity, a world structured by a system that allows almost everyone in the sport to profit – players, coaches, managers and agents.

Tax Tourists

What's a day in the life of Cristiano Ronaldo worth? That's hard to say exactly, but there are indications. You can find them, for example, in Saudi Arabia or, to be more precise, at the Saudi telecommunications corporation Etihad, one of Ronaldo's countless advertising partners.

In early 2013, the corporation engaged the Portuguese superstar for a photo shoot in which Ronaldo allowed himself to be filmed and photographed for four and a half hours in Madrid and also signed five shirts and posted two messages on his Facebook and Twitter sites. For that, the Middle Eastern company paid €1.1 million. There are worse days at work.

This windfall was agreed in an eleven-page agreement to which the world now had access. Football Leaks published the contract between Ronaldo's marketer Multisports & Image Management (MIM) and the Saudis in February 2016. One clause in the contract stipulated that the mobile-phone provider from Riyadh was allowed to use the exorbitantly expensive images from the shoot for advertising purposes for a duration of one year. But only in the Middle East and northern Africa. Even for such scraps, Ronaldo receives a fortune.

Cristiano Ronaldo dos Santos Aveiro, as the Real Madrid forward's full name goes, is a global star and advertising icon. His major current and former sponsors include Unilever, Kentucky Fried Chicken, US nutrition supplement company Herbalife, Danish underwear label JBS, computer and video-game manufacturer Konami and car-maker Toyota. Clients line up to sponsor the CR7 brand. *Forbes* magazine put Ronaldo's advertising earnings alone at $32 million in 2016.

Professional football is show business – and the biggest show in the sports business. The sums of money earned are seemingly limitless. This applies not only to transfer fees, but also to endorsement deals, salaries and commissions. Money is flooding into football, and Cristiano Ronaldo has profited more than most. From Real Madrid alone, with whom in late 2016 he extended his contract to June 2021, he earns around €40 million a year. His new contract set his mandatory transfer fee at €1 billion.

Ronaldo is a football player who concentrates to the point of obsession on physical fitness and shooting technique. But reading his contracts, you could be forgiven for thinking that he was a medium-sized business instead of an athlete. Ronaldo takes in hundreds of millions every year and maintains a whole entourage of agents, tax advisors, lawyers and acrobatic accountants to maximise his net worth. The guiding principle is that every euro Ronaldo earns should end up as intact as possible in one of his many bank accounts. Indeed, if feasible, there should be no difference at all between gross and net, particularly for the millions he earns from advertising contracts.

To optimise his finances, Ronaldo has taken a page out of the book of big multinational companies like Google, Apple, Starbucks or Amazon and become a tax tourist. The big multinationals reduce the amount they owe in taxes by forming subsidiaries in places where taxes are low. The result of money being transferred back and forth is that state coffers are deprived of billions every year. Making money from money is a primordial capitalist instinct. Politicians in the West have been fighting against this form of tax evasion for years, but as soon as they shut down one tax haven, another one or two – usually on some group of islands – appear to take its place. The system is skewed towards the rich, especially super-rich companies and individuals, because only they can afford to maintain the complex set of structures needed to avoid taxes effectively. This is nothing new. What is new and disturbing is that football players now also behave like large international corporations.

Football Leaks documents from Switzerland, Morocco, Portugal and England illustrate how Ronaldo's money travels around the world. He has various companies and one foundation working for him in Panama, Hong Kong, Switzerland, Bermuda and the British Virgin Islands. This amounts to a virtual chain of tax havens and letterbox companies. In the end, his money is deposited, safe and sound, at a small private bank in Switzerland. In 2015, according to numbers published by his advisory company Gestifute and uncovered during EIC research, Ronaldo's total wealth amounted to €227 million – a proud sum accumulated over thirteen years of professional football. It makes you ask, why does someone as rich as Ronaldo find it necessary to squeeze every last cent out of football, and especially out of the country in which he plays? Why do Ronaldo and his advisors put such huge effort into juggling his millions, transferring them from one company to the next? Is it to make the tax authorities' heads spin so that (almost) nobody knows where his money is any more?

In December 2017, Spain – the country in which Ronaldo is paid so handsomely to play football – had an unemployment rate of 16.4 per cent and 36.8 per cent of young people were without a job. In Portugal – the country where Ronaldo was born and where people worship him – the figures weren't much better: 7.8 per cent unemployment and 22.1 per cent youth joblessness. But it's been a long time since football stars like Ronaldo have had anything in common with regular people and their concerns. The sums the top players earn are so astronomical that greed and megalomania become many stars' constant companions. Such players want to give back as little as possible – preferably, nothing at all – to society. After all, the faithful are supposed to make sacrifices to their gods, not the other way around. In order to be able to keep the largest possible percentage of the monstrous sums they earn, these footballers and their financial advisors push the limits of tax law.

In the business of football, there's a difference between the regular salary a club pays a player and the image rights through which that player also earns money. With salaries, it's not as easy to get around paying taxes. The laws concerning them are clear, the paper trail obvious and the tax authorities stricter. Image rights are another matter entirely. 'Image rights' is an umbrella term used by lawyers for everything professional football players earn through their names, faces, voices or autographs: from advertising to the stickers kids collect in Panini albums. Where image rights are concerned, lawyers have raised the construction of complex labyrinths for money into an art form. Tax authorities that try to follow the trail of this money usually quickly lose their way.

The basic situation is this: on his salary, a professional football player is usually subject to the top tax rate, often 50 per cent, in the country where he plays. That hurts. But a player can keep a lot more of the money he earns from advertising, if he's clever. To do that, the player transfers the rights to his advertising revenues to a company that works on his behalf. The company takes in the money he earns by smiling into the camera for a brand of chocolate or deodorant, and companies customarily only pay corporate tax. In Ireland, for instance, that amounts to a rate of 12.5 per cent.

Crisp manufacturers and shampoo-makers who feature a football star in their advertising aren't the only ones who pay money to a player's personal image-rights company. Clubs also fill its coffers. Arsenal, Chelsea, Manchester United and Barcelona all purchase partial image rights from their players for yearly payments, which are also taxed at the low corporate rate.

Various countries' tax authorities take differing attitudes towards this practice. The Germans tend to be difficult, considering payments from clubs to image-rights companies as potential covert salaries. In England, the taxman takes a considerably more relaxed approach to millionaire football stars. In 2015, Her Majesty's Revenue and Customs agreed that clubs are allowed to pay up to one-fifth of players' salaries as compensation for the use of their images. This special treatment was understandably quite popular with Premier League professionals. According to research carried out by the *Sunday Times*, in 2016 more than 180 players received payments to image-rights companies taxed at the rate of 20 per cent. That was seventy-four more players than at the beginning of 2015.

Image-rights companies often serve as deposit boxes or pension funds. As long as the professionals are still playing, they don't touch the money they earn from their images. They usually only dip into these savings when their careers are over. Then they liquidate the companies and transfer the money into their private bank accounts, paying as little additional tax as possible.

So it's no wonder many players avail themselves of this mechanism. Wayne Rooney reportedly had £9 million in his image-rights company Stoneygate 48 – a sum that increased by £2.43 million during the 2014–15 season. Goalkeeper Joe Hart is alleged to have £2.3 million in advertising earnings resting in the company JCLC Promotions. At Arsenal, eight players put around £7.3 million into various image-rights companies; the corresponding figure at Liverpool is £5.5 million. All the players and clubs concerned insist that they're not doing anything illegal.

That's the way business is done in lots of European football leagues. In 2000, in a case concerning Arsenal star Dennis Bergkamp, a British court ruled that this practice was legal. But, of course, that doesn't make it legal – or morally above board – in other countries or individual cases. Tax authorities frown upon these clever divisions of players' finances. After all, they cost the state millions in revenue. For that reason, the authorities regularly audit individual players to check whether they might be using their image-rights companies to evade taxes.

The borders here are murky. Auditors can challenge whether the image rights a club purchased from a player are

in fact worth the money paid. Can the club recoup its investment, for example, by selling shirts or autograph cards? If
not, the authorities may conclude that the deal is nothing
but a way of paying a player a portion of his salary at a dis-
counted tax rate. That's illegal in many countries.

With superstars who earn their clubs millions in kit sales
alone, tax authorities usually ask very different questions.
Is the image-rights company merely a shell firm without
an office or any personnel? In that case, depending on
national law, the money it earns could be treated as domestic income, subject to the normal tax rates. As is often the
case in money matters, the greater the profits, the greater
the risk. The advantage of taking in money for image rights
is immense. But so, too, is the danger of getting in trouble
with the tax authorities.

The most prudent thing to do would be to give such
financial constructs a wide berth. But if players have an
agent like Jorge Mendes, they rarely do. They simply live
with the risks. Mendes is currently the world's most successful agent, with the biggest names, the biggest deals and
probably the greatest sense of recklessness when it comes
to complex financial arrangements to avoid taxes. He's a
man who makes players rich. But he also turns them into
fools of fortune with clandestine letterbox companies in the
Caribbean. His clients include Spain's national goalkeeper
David de Gea, Colombian World Cup Golden Boot winner
James Rodríguez and half of the European Championship-
winning Portugal team, including Pepe, André Gomes and
Ricardo Carvalho.

He also advises star coach José Mourinho and, first and
foremost, Cristiano Ronaldo. In a feature film released in

2015 telling Ronaldo's life story, the player called Mendes a surrogate father and part of the family (Ronaldo's real father died when he was young). But, of course, 'Big Jorge' is more than a surrogate. He's also the world's best agent, a distinction that he received six years in a row at the Global Soccer Awards.

Like his protégé Ronaldo, Mendes knows what it is to be poor. And how good it feels to have more money than fits into the safe at home, as Ronaldo says at another juncture in the film. Both men come from families that couldn't afford to give them much beyond a boundless ambition to work their way up from their humble circumstances and earn money, success and fame. Mendes made his career as a salesman. He flogged videos, then opened a bar, then sold one of his customers, goalkeeper Nuno Espírito Santo, to Deportivo La Coruña. In one fell swoop, he was an agent. Soon, thanks to his ability to generate infectious enthusiasm, he was dealing with ever-bigger names. In the film there's a scene where he's eating dinner with Ronaldo, some of the forward's friends and his family. Mendes falls into raptures: 'You're a monster, the best in the world . . . I'm proud to be standing next to a man like this . . . if I didn't know you, I'd ask for your autograph.'

It's easy to understand why football players would be so taken with him, especially since Mendes has had more success than anyone else in negotiating big contracts with big clubs. From 2001 to 2010, at least as far as he claims, Mendes was involved in more than half of all the transfers involving the top Portuguese clubs Benfica, Sporting and Porto. He brought players to the true giants of football in England, Spain and Italy. 'Nothing is impossible,' Mendes preaches in the film. 'Nothing, nothing, nothing!' He can't stop intoning the word as though he were a guru motivating his disciples. And the dictum that nothing is impossible seemed for many years to apply to his players' taxes, too. One of his services is apparently to provide them with financial models with which the top earners lose as little as possible to the government.

Several of Mendes's clients have been in considerable trouble with the Spanish tax authorities. In October 2017, a Spanish court sentenced Ricardo Carvalho, formerly a hard-as-nails defender with Real Madrid, to seven months in prison and fined him €142,882 for tax evasion. In the summer of 2017, the club's former manager José Mourinho was accused of evading €3.3 million in taxes on income from his image rights. At the time of writing the case is still ongoing, but Mourinho insists he has settled his accounts with the tax authorities in Spain.

And what about Mendes's top client, Cristiano Ronaldo? The footballing gods' favourite son is apparently also the chosen one when it comes to questions about his taxes. The forward profited from the so-called 'Lex Beckham', a law passed in 2004 under Spain's conservative prime minister José María Aznar in order to lure highly gifted scientists and top managers into the country with the promise of low tax responsibilities. Foreign footballers like David Beckham and Ronaldo received the status of *'impatriado'*, given to people who hadn't lived in the country in the previous ten years. *Impatriados* were allowed to pay a tax rate of just under 25 per cent on all their Spanish income, whereas their Spanish teammates were subject to a rate of more than 50 per cent. The biggest gift, however, was that Ronaldo was only required to pay taxes on the money he earned in Spain. The Spanish tax authorities left income from elsewhere, including foreign advertising revenue, untouched. For Ronaldo, that meant that money such as his fee for his four-and-a-half-hour PR session with Etihad was net profit. Spain's new socialist government repealed the controversial law in 2010, but foreigners who had moved to the country before the end of 2009 enjoyed a period of grace until 2015. The law was a multimillion-euro loophole made for the super-rich. But just because something is legal doesn't make it morally right.

Doesn't someone who is cheered on fervently by millions of people also have some sort of social responsibility? For Ronaldo, that question would probably be absurd. The dozens of millions he earns from endorsements are diverted around the globe, and to that end financial advisors and lawyers have constructed an impenetrable network of companies, as the documents released on Football Leaks show. Some were posted in the spring of 2016, and some apparently came from the Portuguese and Swiss attorneys who advise Ronaldo. For years, this international icon's marketing deals have been administered by the same entity that concluded the deal with the Saudi mobile telecommunications giant: MIM. The company has its headquarters in Dublin and was opened on 4 February 2004 by an Irish tax consultancy that counts 'Big Jorge' Mendes among its customers. The consultancy also advises the super-agent's primary company, Gestifute. The fact that Ireland is part of the EU is important for companies like Nike, Unilever òr Toyota, which don't want to pay fees for image rights to tiny tax havens, where shady characters and tax cheats abound. Ronaldo's endorsement partners paid him via MIM in Ireland. What happened afterwards with the money was none of their concern. That was Ronaldo's business. And that of his advisors and lawyers.

By that time there already existed a channel for his advertising revenues: to Panama, one of the most secretive and well-guarded financial centres in the world. Back in February 2003, when Ronaldo was eighteen years old and about to move to the Premier League, a financial administrator in Geneva was instructed by Ronaldo's mother to set up something called the Brockton Foundation in the Latin American tax haven. The foundation was given special rights to market her son around the world, with the exception of Great Britain. It was the start of a massively complex intertwined network of financial entities. In 2004, Mama Ronaldo transferred all the Brockton Foundation's marketing rights to the company Tollin Associates in the British Virgin Islands. From there, they were passed on to the newly established marketing agency MIM. From tax haven 1 to tax haven 2 to tax haven 3. This sort of Russian Matryoshka doll-like structure allows sums in the hundreds of millions to evade notice.

Among the Football Leaks documents was a letter dated 1 March 2017 from a company in Panama that was represented by two Swiss administrators, a man and a woman, who both had power of attorney over Tollin. In that letter, they confirmed that Tollin Associates was 'the assignee of Mr. Cristiano Ronaldo dos Santos Aveiro's image rights, since 6th February, 2004'. The beneficial owner of 100 per cent of the company was Mr Cristiano Ronaldo dos Santos Aveiro. Tollin Associates, the authors of the letter continued, 'is soon to be striked off from the registrar [sic]'. Ronaldo, they wrote, had been 'the only beneficiary of all the profit generated' by the company from the marketing of his image rights, from its founding to its closure.

Ronaldo and Mendes have refused to answer any specific questions about such offshore financial transactions. Gestifute published a general statement on its website: 'As reported in recent days, the player has been aware of his tax obligations right away from the beginning of his professional career in all of the countries in which he has resided, and has not and has never had any issue with the Tax Authorities of any of those countries.'

There's nothing illegal about the advertising revenues of a professional football player flowing through the British Virgin Islands, as long as he declares such income on his annual tax return and pays the corresponding amounts due in accordance with the law. The tax authorities in Spain are now interested in whether this truly was the case. As of early 2018, Ronaldo was still in a legal battle with the Spanish authorities over whether he owed some €14.7 million in unpaid taxes.

The Breakthrough

Ronaldo, Mourinho, offshore financial transactions . . . In early 2016, we had no idea that the Football Leaks material would be so explosive. At that point, we still hadn't received a response to our email and were getting impatient. Then, finally, on 5 January, the waiting was over. 'We have a huge amount of documents that could be of help to you,' wrote 'FL'. 'Are you interested in them?'

Were we interested in them? We were over the moon. We answered that we would gladly receive any and all contracts and promised to look through and evaluate whatever material was sent.

The following days brought only silence. No answer. Nothing. Had something happened? Had we been too direct? Had we scared off John and his colleagues? Or had the police intervened? The Football Leaks page remained in operation, publishing new contracts and documents almost every day. Many of them were related to Portugal, but others concerned transfers between Argentinian, English and Chinese clubs. It was impossible to identify any sort of pattern connecting the documents leaked on the site.

On 12 January, after a week that seemed like an eternity, 'FL' got back in touch. The material was on its way, he wrote, but it needed a bit of time. At the end of his email, 'FL' advised us to refresh the Football Leaks site very regularly. Our curiosity was piqued.

The online whistle-blowers weren't kidding. Four days later, they dropped a bombshell: the contract of Anthony Martial, who had transferred from Monaco to Manchester United for a reported €50 million. The document, which contained three clauses that had previously not been reported on, made it clear that even this exorbitant fee for the nineteen-year-old was likely to increase dramatically, making Martial potentially the most expensive acquisition in the club's history at that point. If the striker scored twenty-five competitive goals for the Red Devils before the summer of 2019, played twenty-five times for the French national team or was nominated as a Ballon d'Or finalist, United would owe an additional €10 million in each case. Martial's transfer fee could thus rise to €80 million. For days, international sports newspapers dissected and analysed whether a nineteen-year-old could possibly be worth that much. Football Leaks was a force for transparency, there was no question about that.

However, we were still waiting for the material we'd been promised. We congratulated John and his associates on the Martial contract revelations. The leak had given the website's reputation a big boost. Martial, Monaco and Manchester United were in a whole different league to Doyen, Benfica and Twente Enschede. But where were these contracts coming from? And what would the material we were to receive contain? FL reassured us that Martial was only the beginning. As soon as things had calmed down somewhat, they would send us a package of data. They apologised for the delay, saying that they'd been very busy.

There was nothing for us to do but keep waiting, despite our impatience.

Still, there was no shortage of fireworks on the Football Leaks page. As their next scoop, the online whistle-blowers released a contract between the French international Eliaquim Mangala, Porto and Manchester City. City had signed the central defender in 2014 for an official transfer fee of £32 million. But that wasn't the whole story. Here, too, the documents showed that the club presidents, managers and the player had tried to pull the wool over the public's eyes. In Mangala's case, the true transfer fee was almost £42 million, making him at the time the most expensive defender ever to move to the Premier League. More interestingly, what made the transfer so expensive was that City had to pay off two companies owning around 40 per cent of Mangala's transfer rights. Once again, it was clear how the TPO model had the capacity to pull football apart. A group of investors demanding dividends seemed to be behind almost every player of note.

In general, clubs try to say as little as possible about investors. In Mangala's case, Manchester City and Porto hushed up the payment of the additional £10 million. But if no one in the public at large knows why and to whom such payments are made, if business deals remain non-transparent, it is almost inevitable that the market will be open to corruption, kickbacks and embezzlement.

Football Leaks was lifting the veil of secrecy, and its work was by no means done. Before long, it had published the contracts of Argentinian international Marcos Rojo, who had also moved to Manchester United, and Brazilian international Hulk, who had transferred from Porto to Zenit St

Petersburg. For days, the media and fans discussed the salaries, the real transfer costs and the secret clauses. Football Leaks was the talk of town.

But the platform would first become world famous with another scoop. This one was about Gareth Bale and a completely absurd contract provision. The Welsh winger had transferred in the late summer of 2013 from Tottenham Hotspur to Real Madrid. Bale was coming off a stand-out season in which he had scored thirty-one goals in all competitions. In England, he was showered with awards and named the Premier League's player of the year. Such a breakthrough year quickly attracted the attention of Europe's elite clubs. Representatives of Real contacted the Welshman, and the two sides quickly agreed terms.

For the selling club, an offer from Real usually means a windfall. Ever since the first decade of the new millennium, when the Spanish powerhouse paid horrendous sums for players like Luís Figo, David Beckham and Zinedine Zidane, Real has been known as a big spender. Until PSG's deal for Neymar in the summer of 2017, Real's purchase of Cristiano Ronaldo in summer 2009 held the official record for the world's highest transfer fee, with the club reportedly paying Manchester United €94 million. That transfer was to play a major role in the uproar surrounding Real contacting Bale.

Before the Welshman could move to the Spanish capital, Real had to win over Tottenham president Daniel Levy. The bald businessman is known for his stubbornness and his negotiating skills, and for weeks he nearly drove Madrid's representatives crazy. Levy had a history of refusing massive transfer offers if he felt the money didn't match a given player's worth. In 2007, he had bought Bale for a rumoured £10 million from Southampton, and now he wanted a hefty dividend for his gamble back then and the years of trust he had put in the Welshman. As is typical of Levy, who often opts simply to ignore the other side early on in negotiations, he reportedly never responded to Real's initial offer. Instead, he took to the media, saying that Bale was a top superstar who, for that very reason, would be very, very expensive.

A lengthy tug of war ensued before Real and Levy settled upon a deal, and all three parties agreed not to disclose the transfer fee. But in football, wherever money is concerned, rumours always seep out. In Bale's case, newspapers speculated that he had become the most expensive player in the world. Real's president Florentino Pérez felt compelled to deny the idea, telling Spanish TV that Bale had cost €91 million. A lot of money. But not quite as much as Real had paid for Cristiano Ronaldo.

Then came Football Leaks with a six-page PDF of Gareth Bale's transfer agreement. Paragraph 15 turned out to be an excellent illustration of the machinery of lies underlying professional football. It stipulated that Real Madrid were allowed to publicise a false transfer fee of €91,589,842 for the Welshman. The real fee, as the agreement also revealed, was €100,759,418. Bale was actually the first football player to break the €100 million transfer mark. He was also the most expensive player in the world, having cost around €6 million more than Ronaldo.

Why did Real lie? In order not to bruise Ronaldo's ego? Is it really so important to the Portuguese superstar to be the world's most expensive player? Or were there other reasons? Tax, perhaps?

Real never commented upon the leak, nor did Ronaldo, Bale or Tottenham. The only one who did say anything was Bale's agent Jonathan Barnett, who called the publication of the agreement 'disgraceful' and called for an 'inquiry and independent investigation' into how 'people can get hold of this sort of stuff'. He said nothing about why all the parties concerned had lied and why they had written into the contract a provision that called for the public to be deceived.

Vocal Criticism

The Bale contract was the seventy-seventh full contract that Football Leaks had published, in addition to hundreds of verbal agreements, advertising deals and confidential emails. The whistle-blowers clearly deserved to be taken seriously. People who managed to get hold of internal documents from Real Madrid, Manchester United and several of the world's most famous football players had to have very good contacts in the industry – or else be computer-hacking geniuses. Or did they have other means of access to the high-security domain of the uppermost levels of football?

Shortly before the Bale contract revelations, FIFA presented a study of the transfer market. According to its report, in 2015, $4.2 billion (approximately £3 billion) were spent on transfers around the world. That represented an increase of 2.6 per cent over the previous year. But Football Leaks questioned the basis for FIFA's figures. Almost every contract leaked on the site contained sums that were considerably higher – sometimes by tens of millions – than those publicly announced by the clubs in question. And the leaked documents showed that clubs far beyond Twente Enschede had withheld contracts from FIFA, UEFA and the national football associations.

Mark Goddard – until June 2017, the general manager of the FIFA subsidiary Transfer Matching System, which was tasked with enforcing transparency in transfers – admitted after the report's publication that the actual transfer fees could potentially be *twice* as high as the FIFA figures. There was no way to say for sure because there simply wasn't enough transparency. With reference to Football Leaks, Goddard told an AP journalist that 'All streams of information are very, very useful and that one has been as well,' adding that the site published documents 'that we could never produce or disclose based on our current waiver program we have in place'. But he also said that 'Obviously the Football Leaks guys and girls have gone rogue,' and compared the platform with the controversial WikiLeaks.

Amidst such qualified praise, criticism of the football whistle-blowers was also growing more vocal. Several Portuguese news sources reported that the people behind Football Leaks had tried to blackmail Doyen and several of the clubs concerned, offering to cancel leaks in return for cash. Was this an insidious campaign against Football Leaks, or were the whistle-blowers not as squeaky clean and idealistic as they had claimed?

A few days later, the whistle-blowers themselves directly addressed the accusations on their home page, saying that there had been 'interesting developments in Portugal' and that the site was frightening the 'right people'. The statement continued: 'Once again we have to state that Football Leaks never contacted Doyen Sports and all their allegations are a pure fantasy in another desperate attempt to discredit Football Leaks.' They vowed to continue their work: 'As a reminder, no one can silence Football Leaks and our war against TPO and football business.'

There was no denying that the Football Leaks whistle-blowers were not easily cowed. But it remained unclear who exactly was telling the truth.

Data, Data, Data

In late January 2016, an email in our inbox immediately grabbed our attention. The message from 'FL' said that they believed that players' agents had been systematically dodging taxes for years using a complex system of companies. As a small 'present', because they had not been in touch for so long, they were giving us two contracts pertaining to Germany.

The email contained four links leading to encrypted files. On initial inspection, the data that appeared before our eyes seemed very jumbled. It was a mix of contracts, account balances and emails. A lot of it was in Spanish and English; a couple of the documents were in Portuguese.

We started reading, clicking our way through the folders and paths. There were around 300 megabytes of data, some sixty contracts taking up 400 pages. We split the material up between us. The first thing was to evaluate whether it was genuine. We compared some of the agencies that appeared with entries in the commercial registers. Every one of them matched. The chronology of when a given transfer had taken place and who had profited financially in the form of fees, as well as the logic of the documents, also checked out. Later, we would write to the parties mentioned in the documents and confront them with the accusations contained therein.

As we looked through the data, we immediately noticed the transfer agreement between Bayern Munich and Real Madrid for midfielder Xabi Alonso, dated 28 August 2014, and Real Madrid's transfer deal for Bayern's Toni Kroos. The transfer fee for Kroos was listed at €25 million, payable in three instalments by 15 July 2016. The contract, which also bore Kroos's signature, was dated 10 July 2014. That was two days after the German national team had thrashed Brazil in the semi-finals of the World Cup and three days before the final. Kroos first signed his contract of employment with Real on 17 July, but the deal was actually done while Germany were still competing in the World Cup.

Kroos had aspired to be one of the top earners at Bayern, but the club's bosses had refused to grant his wish, and the squabbles surrounding Kroos's salary had preoccupied fans and the media for months. According to his new contract, the money Kroos got in Madrid would have made him one of the better-paid Bayern players at the time. The German earned €11.3 million gross in his first season, followed by €10.9 million from his second to sixth seasons. Kroos was paid every six months, rather than monthly, with payments coming on 10 January and 10 July.

One detail that says a lot about the glamour of Kroos's new employer appeared on page three of one of the supplements to the employment contract. It stated that the midfielder would receive a one-off payment of €1,818,182 gross from Real should he make the final list of candidates for the Ballon d'Or, and that this sum would automatically be added to his salary in the years that followed. Kroos would also receive the equivalent bonus and salary rise if he were actually voted the world's best player. Kroos has refused to comment on his contract.

We were mostly convinced of the authenticity of the documents, whose sources were unknown, but a few niggling doubts remained. In one of the contracts, Kroos's first name is spelled 'Tony' and not 'Toni'. Could a top club like Real make a mistake like that in a document that dealt with many millions of euros? (We later determined that it could.) To be on the safe side, we called up Kroos's agent, Volker Struth, and his company, SportsTotal in Cologne. Cologne was celebrating Carnival, and Struth didn't want to be disturbed. He didn't want to make any public statements about the contract and refused to confirm or deny anything. He did, however, threaten us with legal action.

In this case, though, we felt pretty confident. We had written documentation. The contracts looked genuine and had been signed by all parties. In addition, a long-time informant of ours who is well networked in football checked for us whether the figures and provisions were plausible. If necessary, we could have presented all this as evidence in a German court. In that case, the other side would have had to prove that the material was faked or manipulated.

At our editorial meetings, we discussed not just the legal but also the ethical ramifications of what we were doing. Publishing salary figures and the details of employment contracts is controversial. To do so, there has to be a legitimate public interest in such information and the person in question has to possess a minimum level of public importance. Our discussions were heated. In the case of Kroos, we decided to publish the figures we had because his salary demands were one of the main reasons for him leaving Bayern Munich, and his was one of the most spectacular transfer stories of the summer of 2014. The details of the contract – the fact that negotiations with Madrid were going on during the World Cup and that it was signed so soon after the final against Argentina – were interesting and meaningful to our audience. In other cases, and with other sorts of documents, we decided that individuals' right to privacy outweighed the arguments in favour of publication.

There was no doubt at all about publishing one of the other stories we found in the Football Leaks data. It concerned the questionable business deals of the Dutch agent Martijn Odems and his Amsterdam-based company Orel B.V. Odems himself is very well connected in Italy's Serie A, and in 2013, he did a deal sending Argentinian goalkeeper Juan Pablo Carrizo from Lazio to Inter Milan. As we could see from the Football Leaks documents, he transferred his fee to a company based in Panama. This arrangement was top secret. Not even Inter Milan knew about it.

After Carrizo's transfer, the club paid Orel B.V. €300,000 in three instalments. Odems's fee initially arrived in the Netherlands, but it wouldn't stay there long. The company in Panama with which Odems had his secret contract sent Orel B.V. three bills totalling €277,500 for the transfer. It isn't a huge stretch to imagine that the real purpose of this activity was tax-related. Only €22,500 from the transfer stayed with Odems's company in the Netherlands. The Dutch agent has refused to answer questions about why he sent nearly all of the fee Inter Milan paid him to a company based in Panama. He has also said nothing about whether that company paid him back a part or all of this fee.

We wrote Football Leaks another email, describing what we had been able to make of the data. We were about to write our first article about the whistle-blowers and how nervous their activities were making the world of football. We were particularly interested in agents' tax tricks. We wrote that we'd like to go into more depth on this issue and asked whether Football Leaks had further material about overseas deals.

Two hours later, the whistle-blowers answered that they had thousands of documents concerning tax evasion by players' agents. They said that they believed a system to cheat European taxpayers had been in place for years. Did we want to do some further research? Of course we did. We requested more material, particularly documents concerning German agents and naming companies and individuals. We also attached articles we had done in the past about agents. The idea was to reinforce the message that we had been investigating these issues for years and that every further piece of evidence would be of great help.

By now 'FL' was answering our emails within the space of a few hours. They would check their material, the whistle-blowers told us, and send us a selection. We were beginning to discuss with 'FL' the overarching questions in sport. What does fair competition mean? Where does all the money for top-flight sport come from? What does football give to the fans? Why are supporters sometimes so willing to go along with everything? We spent hours discussing these questions, swapping dozens of emails. The nights were getting longer and longer. Often 'FL' only became talkative after 11 p.m. That gave us time during the day to go through the data and work on our articles. Every message revealed more about the personality and character of the whistle-blowers. They had interesting ideas about how to change sport and where the world's governing bodies and, above all, investigators needed to adjust their strategies to limit criminal influence.

We asked 'FL' if he would give us an interview, either on the telephone or in person, telling him we were willing to travel anywhere in the world. 'FL' refused, saying that would be too dangerous. But he did agree to answer questions via email. The next morning, we sent a whole list of queries. Twelve hours later, we had our answers, which were published in *Spiegel Online*.

Spiegel Online: Where is Football Leaks operated?
Football Leaks: We live in Portugal. We are all Portuguese citizens.
Spiegel Online: Are you employed by anyone?
Football Leaks: We are totally independent and none of us is paid for working here. The fact that we have stirred football up so much with the publication of the documents has made us realize that we have turned a few powerful enemies against us. That's why we are unable to say anything further about our identities. We have to protect ourselves.
Spiegel Online: Why did you create Football Leaks?
Football Leaks: We had been thinking about this project for a long time. At some point, we began collecting documents from the football business and waited for the right moment to publish them. Last summer it was time. There were numerous dodgy player transfers on the Portuguese transfer market and we wanted to untangle the lies and inconsistencies.

The more documents we obtained and analysed, the clearer it became to us that this non-transparent football industry needs help.

Spiegel Online: How many contracts and documents do you possess?

Football Leaks: We have more than 500 gigabytes of documents and are constantly receiving new ones.

Spiegel Online: You publish player contracts like those of Mesut Özil, Hulk or Gareth Bale as well as legally explosive documents that shed light on illegal scheming of clubs, player agents and investment funds. What criteria and principles do you apply in your selection of documents for publication?

Football Leaks: Generally, we publish the documents at random. We try to post two documents online each day. Sometimes they spark discussions on social media channels that we seek to stimulate further with our publishing efforts.

Spiegel Online: Who is the target audience for the documents you are publishing?

Football Leaks: We are big football fans ourselves and our first priority is to help other football fans to better understand this secretive football business. Clauses, contracts, consultant fees – all of these have become taboo subjects in football. There needs to be a public debate about the sport in order to clear it of this secretiveness. A business that lacks transparency the way football does is a paradise for corruption, money laundering and tax fraud.

Spiegel Online: Some critics also accuse you of publishing the contracts of players like Gareth Bale,

Mesut Özil or Hulk merely to service the public's sense of voyeurism.

Football Leaks: Each of these contracts tells its own story. They show everything from the endless amount of clauses to astronomical fees and the possibility of hidden signing fees. These documents are very important for understanding today's football business.

Spiegel Online: Another allegation is that you have obtained the documents illegally by hacking a sporting rights agency.

Football Leaks: We haven't hacked anyone. The accusation is ridiculous. We have a variety of sources who supply us with the contracts and agreements. Our network is very stable.

Spiegel Online: You are taking on the world's largest football teams and are also getting under the skin of superstars and their influential agents. Are you not afraid at all?

Football Leaks: We are very aware of the risks involved, especially the legal ones. The football lobbyists also have a great deal of influence over the investigative authorities; we would never be given a fair trial.

Spiegel Online: How do you draw that conclusion?

Football Leaks: Our disclosures have created many problems for a sporting rights agency. The company uses a tax avoidance system and has broken several FIFA rules. Our revelations made things uncomfortable for them. We are very certain that they are also putting pressure on the investigative authorities in an effort to silence us. And that's not all: They have also hired private detectives to blow our cover.

Spiegel Online: How is this pressure manifested?

Football Leaks: Our home page has already been attacked, a sporting rights agency sent abusive DMCA takedowns and pressured the host providers. Our Russian provider closed our cloud and then showed us documents from this company, which had massively pressured them to do it. We're now victims of censorship.

Spiegel Online: What is your ultimate goal with Football Leaks?

Football Leaks: We want to make the transfer system more transparent and we want to reduce the influence of player agents and investment funds that have a growing hold on football. We would also like to see the creation of a publicly accessible database that would include all the details about transfers and breakdowns of transfer fees, signing fees, clauses and third-party ownership of players.

Spiegel Online: Those are very ambitious goals.

Football Leaks: We are driven by our desire to put a stop to those who are unfairly enriching themselves through football. We also want to ring in a new era in football: The age of transparency.

Spiegel Online: Do you consider yourselves to be in the same vein as portals like WikiLeaks?

Football Leaks: People like Julian Assange, Edward Snowden or Antoine Deltour are a big inspiration for us. They sacrificed everything for their convictions and dreams. Now we are trying to make our contribution to a more transparent world.

Spiegel Online: How long do you plan to go on publishing explosive documents on the Web?

Football Leaks: Until we no longer have any documents.

The interview was reprinted and quoted by a number of other journalistic outlets. It was a declaration of war by Football Leaks, and also a warning about what was in store for the football world in the months to come: uncontrollable leaks and 500 gigabytes of data – around double the amount John had spoken of in his interview with the *New York Times*. No one knew what it contained.

While we were working on our article and the interview, new revelations continued to appear on the Football Leaks website: transfer agreements and employment contracts for international superstars like German midfielder Mesut Özil, Colombian striker Radamel Falcao and Argentinian forward Carlos Tévez. The company secrets of top clubs like Chelsea, Arsenal, Tottenham, Real Madrid and Atlético Madrid were being posted on the Internet for anyone to see. At regular intervals mega-agent Jorge Mendes could read confidential documents connected with his agency Gestifute, while sports marketer Doyen Sports was becoming more transparent by the day. That's how much material was appearing on the platform. The football world could only stand by and watch, as if paralysed, as the Internet insurgents did their thing, the international media analysed the leaked documents and fans vacillated between outrage and resignation at what was happening in their beloved sport.

By that point, we had daily contact with 'FL'. Sometimes we spent hours exchanging emails. The whistle-blowers sent us material concerning legal cases surrounding FIFA's ban on third-party ownership and documents from the European

Parliament laying out the danger such investment models posed for football. Those behind Football Leaks were very systematic in their analysis of the data, examining companies and owners and trying to establish connections. This was the same way tax auditors, criminal investigators or investigative journalists worked.

'FL' even sent us a kind of organigram illustrating the relationship between several leading functionaries of the Portuguese football league and three players' agents and a lawyer. These people control European football and are constantly doing backroom deals with one another, 'FL' told us. Players and clubs were little more than their marionettes. Football Leaks claimed that it had the documents to prove such allegations. 'FL' promised us that when we read them, we would question how anyone could still have faith in the sport.

We suggested that we evaluate the material, but first we wanted a guarantee that it was exclusive. Otherwise, the risk was simply too great that we would spend weeks working on a mountain of data only to read about it in some other publication first. To our surprise, 'FL' got back to us within a few hours, writing simply, 'Deal!'

Online whistle-blowers are people of few words. In the attachment to this email, we found several links leading to some 700 megabytes of encrypted data, some 800 documents in all. At first, we were baffled. Many of the documents were in Chinese. They seemed to be about the takeover of a club and a partnership between a Chinese sports agency and Mendes. We weren't prepared for Chinese documents. Obviously, we were going to have to get some help on this story.

A few minutes later, the next email followed. This time the data was in Spanish and English, and it concerned the tax tricks used by South American and Dutch agents. After just a quick glance, we saw that some of the biggest names in world football were involved: the winner of the Golden Boot at the 2014 World Cup, James Rodríguez; €90 million striker Gonzalo Higuaín; and PSG superstar Ángel Di María. 'FL' also specifically highlighted individual pages, contracts and bank account statements that made it easier for us to gain an initial overview of the material. It was clear from how 'FL' sent us the documents that the people behind the website knew their way around the material and understood its contents.

We could start researching.

Depressed

In early February 2016, our first article about Football leaks appeared in *Der Spiegel*. It was about Martijn Odems. A short time later, 'FL' got in touch.

'Your story isn't bad,' he wrote, 'but you should look more closely at the offshore deals in Panama. In the documents you'll find the names of the economic beneficiaries within the companies, and they reveal how many conflicts of interest there are in the football business. The whole industry is a gigantic bubble that is prevented from bursting by the fact that everyone earns a lot of money and keeps quiet. But many of the deals are illegal.'

'FL' kept sending us further material and links, promising that in the coming days around a gigabyte of data concerning Panama would be arriving in our mailbox. All the while, we kept coming across interesting contracts and documents that we could use in our reports: for instance, about the transfer deal between Manchester United and Bayer Leverkusen for Javier Hernández, aka Chicharito, and the quantum leap in salary Nuri Şahin made when he moved from Borussia Dortmund to Real Madrid. Şahin earned around €5 million a year in the Spanish capital – more than double what he could have made in Dortmund. It was no wonder that the Turkish international midfielder became one of the first players to abandon coach Jürgen Klopp's title-winning side in 2011.

We were satisfied with the cache of material we had been given, but we had no idea how many contracts we would receive in the weeks that followed. Thanks to Football Leaks, we were given a deeper look than we had ever thought imaginable into the most confidential agreements in the top echelons of football. Document by document, we were becoming able to understand the business of football in all its shady detail, to reveal the logic behind transfer fees, and to expose why salaries and bonuses had exploded, how bets were made on increases in the market value of professional footballers and how ever more millions were being diverted through the industry. Every contract, every agreement, every supplemental clause uncovered new secrets. We gradually came to conclude that, as a whole, all the clauses, provisions and paragraphs amounted to a portrait of the ethics of the football business.

Indentured Servants

The life of a world champion football player follows a strict regimen. Free choice of doctors? Forbidden. Personal clothing at public appearances? Forbidden. Contact with the press? Only with the permission of club bosses.

The contract German international Bastian Schweinsteiger signed on 13 July 2015 with Manchester United Football Club Limited consisted of twenty-nine pages. The midfielder, who had played a big part in Germany lifting the World Cup the previous year, had seen a lot in his career. There were clear rules of conduct at his boyhood club Bayern Munich, for whom he had played for most of his career. But they were nothing compared to the rules contractually imposed by the Premier League giants.

They ran to twenty-nine pages, with dozens of paragraphs whose legalese exudes paranoia, a need for control and a mania for rules. Schweinsteiger's duties included self-evident things like participating 'in any matches in which he is selected to play for the Club' and not wearing 'anything (including jewellery) which is or could be dangerous to him or any other person' when playing or training. But most of the contract laid out the two roles Schweinsteiger had to play: make the brand name Manchester United sparkle, and work diligently. Were Schweinsteiger to violate any of these endless-seeming clauses – for example, by sharing his opinion of the manager with the media – the consequences were crystal clear, neatly listed and ordered in the section 'Disciplinary Procedure and Penalties'. They included oral and written reprimands, monetary fines (a maximum of two weeks' base salary for first offences), suspensions and termination of the contract. In return, Schweinsteiger had the right to contact the board of directors within fourteen days to tell his side of the story and ask them to review any disciplinary measures.

For his first year at United, Schweinsteiger received £7,548,357 base salary, *regardless of whether he played a single match*. It's not hard to understand why Premier League players stick strictly to the details of their contracts and refuse to do interviews or give only empty, pre-scripted answers. Money makes them toe the line, even when, as was the case with Schweinsteiger in August 2016, the manager demotes them to the reserve team.

Reading through players' contracts and learning about the salaries, bonuses, provisions and confidential agreements is to run a gamut of emotions, including astonishment, outrage, anger and envy. In any case, you understand what both the biggest stages of world football and the grittiest relegation battles are really about, the thoughts of players and agents, and the considerations of managers and club bosses. You begin to comprehend how professional football players sell a measure of their personal liberty for sometimes obscene sums of money and why they allow themselves to become temporary indentured servants, tools of agents and marketers.

At the same time, every contract is unique. There are huge differences between world-class and run-of-the-mill players, between youngsters who have a bright future ahead of them and veterans who aren't sure themselves of how long they will measure up to the demands of elite sport. Contracts vary according to league and country, the aura of the club and the reputation of the player. Some of these documents clearly reveal how bitterly the two sides fought over every tiny detail in search of the very last euro, an advantage if the player moves on or the minimisation of risk that he will blow out a knee. A contract is sometimes a tale of horse trading – told in three acts.

The Salary: The Lure of Millions

When a club and a player, represented by his agent, negotiate a contract, the starting point is relatively banal. The club only wants to fork out a large sum of money if the player plays a lot and the team wins plenty of matches. The player, on the other hand, wants to minimise the risks of suffering an injury or a dip in form or having to work with a manager who prefers other players within the squad. The player wants the biggest possible base salary, and he doesn't want the money he earns to depend on how the season goes. A rational club boss will offer a low base salary with lots of bonuses, since if a club has sporting success, it will easily earn these bonuses back in stadium, TV and sponsorship revenues.

But some players enjoy a special status – those in the category of a Toni Kroos, Zlatan Ibrahimović or Robert Lewandowski, who are capable of carrying a team and thus are in a superior bargaining position. They don't have to agree to salaries based on the number of appearances they make. They may be able to increase their astronomical base salaries by a million or two in bonuses, but that's almost peanuts when you're talking about high seven- or eight-digit figures.

In the Bundesliga, striker Chicharito enjoyed such a status at Bayer Leverkusen. Without a huge base salary, there would have been no way to entice the then twenty-seven-year-old from Manchester United to the River Rhine. According to the contract he signed on 31 August 2015, Chicharito earned €350,000 a month. In addition, he received a 'special payment' of €1.8 million every season. Together that totalled €6 million a year, guaranteed.

Add to that a couple of add-ons if he was playing regularly: €12,000 for every Bundesliga match won, and €4,000 for a draw. The goal-getter also earned €30,000 every time he played in a winning Champions League match. The bonuses agreed in Chicharito's contract show how important it is for today's clubs to take part in the Champions League. The striker would have received €100,000 if Leverkusen had won either the Bundesliga or the Champions League, but he stood to gain €150,000 just for qualifying for club football's premier competition.

The discrepancy between an international and a national star at the same club becomes apparent if we look at Chicharito's fellow Leverkusen striker Stefan Kiessling. Kiessling, who had played at the club since 2006 and signed a modified contract in 2013, had to settle for a monthly wage of €140,000 – less than half that of his teammate. His appearance bonuses, on the other hand, were huge. If he was on the pitch for forty-five minutes, he got €50,000 for a win, €25,000 for a draw and €12,500 even for a loss. He also received a special payment of €120,000 if he made twenty appearances. Whether the manager included him in the starting eleven or sat him on the substitutes' bench made a big difference to Kiessling's bank account.

It's only 190 kilometres, around a two-hour drive, from Bremen to Wolfsburg, but in terms of how much players can earn at the two cities' Bundesliga clubs, these places are worlds apart. When fans ask why Brazilian defender Naldo, who always seemed happy at Werder Bremen, would move first to Wolfsburg and then Schalke, you only have to look at the three teams' account books. A comparison of three important foreign players at Bremen, Wolfsburg and Schalke, all European and all internationals, illustrates the spectrum of how much can be earned. Werder lured Austrian midfielder Zlatko Junuzović to Bremen with the following conditions: €65,000 in monthly salary, €21,000 bonus for a win and €7,000 for a draw. After twenty appearances, he received a special payment of €120,000, provided Werder weren't relegated.

In Wolfsburg, such wages would raise a wry smile. Swiss fullback Ricardo Rodríguez signed up with the Wolves in 2012 for €110,000 a month. He got an appearance bonus of €15,000 per point earned – €45,000 for a victory. He also received an extra payment of €200,000 after only fifteen appearances and a further €200,000 after his thirtieth one. Even if the fullback only got substituted in for the final ten minutes of a match, the game counted as a 'half appearance'.

Wolfsburg can afford such wages thanks to its owner and primary sponsor Volkswagen, but the figures involved still pale in comparison to the contract that Matija Nastasić concluded with Schalke in 2015. The Serbian defender had a base salary of €250,000 a month, plus a €30,000 appearance bonus per point earned. If the team qualified for the Champions League, his base salary rose to €300,000, and if it won the German Cup, he got €200,000 extra.

Far more seductive still than the lure of Schalke is a deal in England. Buttressed by the billions handed to them by pay TV broadcasters Sky and BT, the Premier League clubs are the most highly coveted destinations for professional football players because they're the ones that pay best. Liverpool, for instance, have recruited six former Bundesliga players in recent years. Brazilian midfielder Roberto Firmino swapped Hoffenheim for Anfield in exchange for £68,085 a week in basic wage, a £10,000 bonus per victory and other generous add-ons. Firmino earned an extra £300,000 for thirty appearances in a season and a supplemental £10,000 if he played in more than thirty-five matches.

The Side Deals: The Fun Is in the Details

The German Football League (DFL), the umbrella organisation that represents Germany's first- and second-division clubs, offers its members a standard contract for professional players. Using it isn't mandatory, but the Football Leaks documents show that most contracts in Germany closely follow the DFL model.

Some of the basic details are non-negotiable. Players aren't permitted to own a stake in clubs (except for the one they play for), bet on any games they're involved in or accept any victory bonuses from third parties. Doping is, of course, also forbidden. You could find many of the other provisions in any ordinary German employment contract. Most contracts contain passages to the effect that vacation pay is included in their salaries, that every player gets twenty-four paid vacation days a year and that 'they are to be taken for the purposes of regeneration in periods with no scheduled matches'.

Such legalistic clauses sound boring, and they are. The true 'fun' is in the supplemental agreements and not in the main contracts – for example, when Schalke promise one of their players €500,000 if the team were to win the Champions League. The extra side deals are where the players bet on themselves having a dream season, agents come into their own and club bosses stray from the path of reason.

Chicharito is one exemplary case. The Mexican goal-getter had to be lured into making the move from Manchester United to Leverkusen, and he wanted a bonus for every goal he scored, an idea that is scoffed at in the Bundesliga but is part of many a contract in England. So Chicharito got a special enticement. After every fifth goal in competitive matches, he received a special payment of €100,000 gross. In his first season for Leverkusen, Chicharito scored twenty-six goals in the Bundesliga, the German Cup and the Champions League. That netted him an additional €500,000.

Chicharito's goal bonus seems a bit ham-fisted compared with the subtle gradations common at Liverpool. Roberto Firmino scored his first five goals for the bargain price of £25,000. Goals six through ten cost £45,000, eleven to fifteen £65,000, and as of goal number sixteen the Brazilian got £85,000 per five-pack. But only for goals that weren't scored from the penalty spot; in a concession, Firmino's agent had agreed that penalties wouldn't count. Assists, on the other hand, are worth good money: the midfielder earned £25,000 for the first five, and £65,000 as of his eleventh.

Liverpool's bookkeeping department has its hands full with all the bonuses it has to calculate and pay out every month. Firmino's German teammate Emre Can gets £20,000 per goal and assist. There is also a 'clean sheet bonus' of £10,000 if Liverpool don't concede.

Even loyalty is a quality that can cost a club money. Although Can and Liverpool had a contract that was valid until summer 2018, he received a 'loyalty bonus' of £2 million in 2015 and 2016 for not forcing a transfer. His debut in the German national team's starting eleven was gilded with a £250,000 bonus, and he got £10,000 every time he appeared in German national dress in a qualification or tournament match.

But contract supplements don't just define the duties attached to the job and their monetary compensation; they also regulate a player's private life. Many contracts deal with living arrangements. Professional football players are modern-day nomads, and their families often get sick of moving, if the breadwinner transfers to a variety of different clubs. By contrast, clubs don't like players to have to travel long distances to get to training, and several Bundesliga teams insist that their employees live within a certain radius of the clubs' grounds. For example, paragraph 2 of all contracts with Hoffenheim reads: 'The player shall (with his family) settle in Sinsheim or the immediate vicinity.' Hoffenheim is a district of Sinsheim, a town of 35,000 inhabitants, a football stadium, a car museum, some half-timbered houses, three autobahn exits and not much else. This clause is intended to prevent players from residing in faraway Stuttgart or Frankfurt. There is a similar clause in contracts used by Wolfsburg, where it's a running joke that the best thing about the city is its direct train connection to Berlin. No doubt for that reason, a passage in a contract signed with a national team player stipulated: 'The player commits himself to move into an apartment or house near the Volkswagen Arena (radius max. 35 kilometres).'

Players who get an offer from Berlin, Munich or Hamburg can count themselves lucky, although there's no avoiding other restrictions. Players aren't free to drive whatever cars they want, since almost all first-division clubs have a car-maker as a sponsor, which of course wants to see sporting heroes tooling around town in its own product. Thus, professional footballers have to use the vehicles placed at their disposal, 'without exception on work-related occasions and regularly during private activities'. Many stars see it as a harsh privation to only be able to take out their privately owned Ferraris when no one is looking.

Many of the provisions are primarily aimed at keeping the image and brand of the club as positive as possible. Players are employees. They're the most important representatives of the clubs, and they're supposed to follow the rules of their employers. Some players need to be reminded of this in no uncertain terms.

In pedagogical terms, probably the craziest contract was the one drawn up in 2014 between Liverpool and Italian striker Mario Balotelli, who had a reputation for being an overgrown, thick-headed child. He got into fist fights with teammates, set his bathroom on fire with fireworks and racked up a mountain of unpaid parking tickets and a large collection of red cards for dangerous conduct and insulting officials. In response, paragraph 8 of the agreement between the Premier League club and Balotelli included a 'good conduct bonus'. It stipulated that if the player was sent off fewer than three times a season for bad behaviour, he would receive an extra £1 million. Balotelli was clearly keen on the money. In his first season with Liverpool, he didn't get a single red card.

His performance was similarly bloodless. After featuring in only sixteen Premier League matches and scoring but a single goal, Liverpool shipped him off to AC Milan, who sold him to Nice on 31 August 2016. Balotelli's contract with the French side also contained a 'bonus for conscientiousness and ethical behaviour'. The passage in question is lengthy, requiring the striker to behave respectfully towards opponents and officials, approach his profession seriously and maintain polite and friendly relations with Nice's fans. The long and the short of it: if Balotelli acts like a model professional, he can add €45,000 to his monthly salary of €405,000.

The Crisis

The passages here and over the course of the rest of this book that are written in the first-person singular recount the experiences of Rafael Buschmann alone. He personally met the Football Leaks whistle-blower known as John and repeatedly got together with him over a period of several months. For the purposes of storytelling, the conversations, carried out in English, have been reconstructed from notes taken afterwards. The wording may therefore differ slightly from that originally used.

My head was spinning. All we'd seen for weeks were contracts, contracts and more contracts. I needed a break from all the gigantic sums of money, absurd provisions and endless tricks and lies. It was the middle of February, and my mother-in-law was celebrating her birthday. We got together in a small ski hut in the mountains of western Germany. Everything was very rustic, and there was a party mood. Then, at around 1.30 a.m., I glanced at my telephone and saw a message from 'FL' on the screen.

I'd stopped counting, but if I had to guess I'd say we had exchanged almost a thousand emails over the past few weeks. I grabbed my beer and retreated to a corner of the room to read the message in peace. The Internet connection was weak up there on a mountain in a provincial part of Germany, and there was no Wi-Fi. It took forever for the email to open. 'Rafael I have to be honest with you,' wrote 'FL'. 'This is all beginning to depress us.' In an instant, I was sober.

'The only reason Football Leaks attracted world-wide attention was because we published a couple of contracts involving Real Madrid and other big names,' the message continued. 'But that's not what we want. Stars, celebrities and standard employment contracts don't interest us. Maybe it's one aspect in order to understand today's football business better. But our main goal is to uncover hidden clauses, illegal payments and offshore structures in football. All the criminal things. We're tired and are seriously considering ending the project. Since September, we haven't earned a single bitcoin with Football Leaks, and it's not like we have money to spare. Every day we get tonnes of mails, and we spend lots of time reading them. What is it all good for? People simply aren't interested in the dirt about football. At the moment, it feels as if the project is suffocating us. We can hardly breathe anymore. Best regards, FL.'

What had happened? Was 'FL' having a bad day? Or were the Internet insurgents really so frustrated that they no longer wanted to continue? What was going to happen to the 500 gigabytes' worth of material? I had to collect myself and get a hold of my thoughts. The Internet here was so slow it was driving me crazy. I went outside. It was cold, and a bit of snow had fallen. I walked down the mountain, and after about an hour, I had passable mobile-phone reception. It gave me time to formulate a suitable response.

I answered 'FL' that I'd been frustrated with a lot of the research we'd done over the past few years. Far too often we'd been forced to realise that the public was only partially interested in how dirty deals were done in football. I recalled a letter I'd received from a reader after we'd written about how Germany possibly paid bribes to win the right to host the 2006 World Cup. The reader had told me we should be happy the World Cup cost only €6.7 million. I told 'FL' about my pieces on match fixing and about how the Bundesliga just continued with its normal operations, even though it was clear that top-flight German football matches were being manipulated. I wrote about my belief that football had become a substitute religion for fans who had the same sort of faith in the game that the pious used to have in the Catholic Church. Tickets were latter-day letters of indulgence. I ended my long and somewhat confused response by offering to meet with him face to face, if he wanted to talk.

I sent this email a little before 3 a.m. As I slowly dragged myself back up the mountain – inclines tend to be very steep in the middle of the night – my phone blinked again. Another message from 'FL'. I stopped in my tracks when I read his words: 'I think you're right. We should meet. I have to explain a few things to you that I've never told anyone about. Would you like to meet me for a background talk. You have to promise that you won't write anything about our identities! Best regards, FL.'

It was Sunday morning, just before dawn. I wrote back to 'FL' saying that I could meet him either that evening or on Monday. But where should I go? Portugal? A few minutes later, he sent me a password. Via another means of communication he then sent a link to an encryption programme. Previously, I only used the PGP encryption software to secure my email correspondence. I was no IT freak, and now I was sitting outside in the cold, on the side of a street where no car had driven by for more than an hour, reading an end-less series of instructions in English about how to install the extra encryption programme 'FL' wanted me to use. I had never heard of this particular email software, which changes the user name every few seconds and automatically deletes sent and received mails after several minutes.

It took more than half an hour before I was ready to go. 'FL' had already sent a message to my mailbox, saying that he would like to meet me on Monday in an Eastern European metropolis and asking me not to reveal the name of the city to anyone. He didn't know whether he would be coming alone, he wrote. He hoped it would be okay with me if he did bring someone along.

I was excited and curious. Of course, he could bring along anyone he wanted, I responded. Whatever made him feel most comfortable and relaxed. I asked 'FL' exactly when and where he wanted to meet. But I didn't get an answer that night.

The First Meeting

On Sunday afternoon, I asked my department head, Michael Wulzinger, what he thought of the invitation. We weighed up the risks. At that point, no one could say for certain whether Football Leaks was a criminal enterprise or not. But some-times, if you want to get to the bottom of crimes, you have to talk to some dangerous people. In the interests of secu-rity, we agreed that I would get in touch with the editorial department at least twice a day, in whatever way I could. I booked a flight and got ready to go.

I left the return ticket open because I had no idea how long my meeting with 'FL' would last. Just before I boarded the aeroplane, a message appeared on my phone. It was 'FL' suggesting that we hook up at 2 p.m. and telling me to check into a room at a certain hotel. 'FL' would meet me there.

In the city where we were meeting, the streets have deep potholes and the urban landscape has that typical former communist charm of prefab concrete modular buildings alternating with splendid villas. A juxtaposition of poverty and wealth. Even after only a couple of metres, Eastern Europe was displaying the contradictions that make it what it is. The route from the airport to the city centre wasn't especially long. I passed a number of stores and crossed a large bridge. My hotel, which looked like a latter-day air-raid shelter, was located at the end of a pedestrian boulevard.

I arrived two hours early. It was oppressively hot in my room, and there was no way to turn down the heat. At reception they said they would take care of the problem, but there was no other room I could have. The hotel was completely booked up. It was hardly optimal to interview a source in what amounted to a sauna.

I lay down on the bed and checked the Football Leaks page. Recently, there had been a spectacular post: a contract between David de Gea, Real Madrid and Manchester United. A deal for the Spanish national keeper had been done, and he was set to go to Real, but the paperwork arrived a few minutes after the transfer window had closed. It was an unbelievable blunder that illustrated how amateurishly even the world's top clubs sometimes work. The Football Leaks documents revealed how costly the mistake was. De

Gea lost out on a signing fee of €10.9 million and a yearly salary of €11.8 million. With a contract that would have run over six years, that amounted to around €82 million. It all went up in smoke because someone couldn't operate a fax machine properly.

It was shortly before 2 p.m., and I was beginning to get a bit nervous. I stared at the door and waited. One thing was immediately apparent: 'FL' wasn't the punctual type. A little before 4 p.m., my mobile lit up. 'FL' would be arriving shortly. At 4.50 p.m., there was a knock at my door. 'FL' had made me wait almost three hours.

I jumped up from the bed and opened the door. I would be lying if I wrote that 'FL' was what I had expected. In front of me stood a young man with alert eyes. He was thin, with dark hair and a wispy beard. Although it was bitterly cold outside, he was wearing only a thin denim jacket and a T-shirt with a half-naked woman on it. His handshake was firm.

'Is anyone else coming?' I asked.

'For today, it's just us two,' he said.

'Should I call you "FL" or John?' I asked.

'John,' he said. 'Let's go out and get some breakfast.'

Two Nights, Hundreds of Thousands of Files

John led the way. The hotel corridor was long and narrow. He moved quickly but not hectically, projecting self-confidence. In front of the elevator, he turned his back to the CCTV camera and looked down at the ground. He was being careful. What else would you expect? Wordlessly, we rode down to the lobby.

Outside in the street, John seemed more nervous than in the hotel. He said he knew a good café near by, but before we headed off he looked up and down the street. He also inspected the building across the road, in particular the windows. I stood beside him, trying to follow his gaze and get a good look at him at the same time. It felt like forever before we started walking.

We engaged in some small talk. He told me a bit about the city we were in, which he said he enjoyed visiting. 'The nightlife is unbelievable!' he gushed. At the moment he was travelling a lot. He hardly ever spent two nights in a row in the same place. 'It's too dangerous otherwise,' he said, promising to tell me more later. John was a fan of plain speaking. How did that go together with the frustrated email he had written me at the weekend, the one in which he had considered ending the project? But I kept that question to myself. John had said that he didn't want to talk about 'the project', as he called Football Leaks, or about the police or anything like that as long as we were out in the street.

'If anyone asks you what you do for a living, don't tell them the truth,' he instructed me. 'Invent some other job. Say you're a lawyer or a teacher or something.'

'Why should anyone ask about my job?' I asked.

'I know a lot of people here, and even more people know me,' John replied. 'Maybe we'll run into one of them. In that case, say that we went to university together – an exchange year, for instance.'

What had I got myself into?

We arrived at the café. John skipped through the door and said in a loud voice that we wanted a table for two. The waitress looked a bit taken aback. As I would repeatedly discover, John was able to dominate a room in seconds with his aura, wit and charm. As we walked through the tables, he told the other diners that their food looked good and that he liked the smell of their coffee. He complimented a young woman on her hairdo, making her laugh and pat her head. In the space of a few moments, John had struck up a conversation with the other customers in the café. He certainly wasn't afraid of strangers.

We sat down at one of the tables towards the back, and John ordered lemonade and a piece of chocolate cake from a young waitress. When she was gone, he whispered, 'My blood sugar level is all wrong. I didn't sleep at all last night. We received hundreds of new documents. Some are contracts concerning signing-on fees, but others are about a very dubious investment fund. Later, I'll show you everything.'

As he leaned over the table, it seemed apparent that last night wasn't the first time he hadn't got any sleep. He didn't have rings under his eyes, he had deep-grey bags. Still, his face remained very youthful. He had hardly any wrinkles, and he was always smiling mischievously.

I wanted to learn more about him. I was curious about what his life had been like and why he'd become a whistle-blower. But before I could touch on these potentially tricky subjects, John laid out a few rules. 'You're not allowed to write about what I'm doing here, what I look like or where I spend my time,' he instructed. 'You gave me your word, and I take you at it. You have to understand that I have no desire to end up like Julian Assange or Chelsea Manning, confined to some embassy or prison just because they wanted to tell the world the truth.'

'I'm happy if we establish some firm rules,' I replied. 'I'll tell you in advance precisely what details about you I intend to publish. You can decide how much I'm allowed to reveal and in what form. But I want to write about the fact that we've met, just as I want to continue writing about your aims and works.'

'Those are good rules,' was all that John said.

The hours in the café with John flew by. He was entertaining and educated as he talked about topics big and small: backpacking through Asia and America, the refugee crisis and the financial catastrophe in Greece. 'I believe that everything that happens in the world is connected,' he said. 'People who form opinions about the refugee crisis without knowing anything about arms sales by the West to the nations in the Middle East don't understand a thing.'

Our conversation quickly turned to income inequality, tax systems and resources. John's views didn't fit comfortably within the conventional political spectrum. He was against letting refugees into Europe without checking them, and he was for the nations of the Middle East taking responsibility for all the people fleeing Afghanistan, Syria and Iraq. He thought it was foolish of the European Union to offer Greece massive financial assistance while billions of euros belonging to Greek citizens lay concealed in shell companies in the Caribbean.

He was an interesting conversation partner with controversial opinions. It was clear that he had read up on a lot of different subjects and was unwilling to make his opinions compatible with the mainstream. He liked challenging others and pondering complex issues. He said that he knew five

languages and was presently learning two more, one of them
Russian. He told me that he found Russia fascinating, even
though it was riddled with corruption.

I wanted to learn more about him. John said that he was
born in Portugal and still had a place to live there, but the
country drove him crazy. 'Portuguese politics are a catastrophe,' he said. 'Businessmen and banks do whatever they
want. They're the ones who really run the country, and
young people are the ones who pay all the costs. There are
hardly any laws helping young people enter the labour market in an orderly way. That's why many university-educated
Portuguese go abroad during their studies and never come
back. The country is giving away its youth, its future.'

John had a girlfriend, but it was complicated. Because of
the secrecy surrounding the 'project', he often had to blow
her off and even lie to her. 'No woman likes that,' he told
me, 'but I have to set priorities.' The past few months for
him were like a drug rush. 'I've never experienced more
adrenaline. The project makes me feel really alive, and I
think our revelations can spark important changes.'

There were only a few crumbs left of the chocolate cake,
and John shot them around his plate with his fork like tiny
footballs. I noticed that the skin around his fingernails was
bitten down to the quick.

I asked him how much time he had for me. 'In a few minutes I'll show you a few things,' he replied. 'Then we'll go
watch a Champions League match and party a bit. If you
stay tomorrow night as well, I'll take you to one of the best
parties in the world.' This was turning out to be a pretty
fun business trip. I told him that I needed to send an email
to my bosses or they would think I'd been kidnapped. John

laughed out loud and rubbed his eyes. The sugar had put a bit of colour back in his face.

John asked for the bill. He didn't want to say anything more in the café. 'We've spent too much time in one place,' he said. He then flirted a bit with the blonde waitress and even invited her to a party in the coming week. He switched from English into the local language. I didn't understand a word of it, but the waitress laughed and he jotted down her number on his mobile phone. The two hugged, and then we were back out on the street.

There he repeated the same ritual I had seen in front of the hotel, glancing back and forth twice and constantly checking to make sure the coast was clear. 'There are lots of people who will do a lot to make Football Leaks stop existing,' he said. 'We have to be careful.' John and I walked along streets full of old buildings, next to a large river, taking side alleys wherever possible. He kept looking back over his shoulder to make sure no one was following us. Then he stopped in front of a large grey office building. The plaster was peeling from the outside walls, there were deep cracks in the front steps and several of the windowsills had broken off. But the front door had an electronic security system. You could only get in with a chip.

The front hall was narrow and dark. Gigantic spiral stair-cases led to the upper floors. The elevator was out of service – or at least it was taped off. On one of the upper floors we entered either an apartment or an office – it was hard to tell in the dark. It smelled of cooking oil, and voices from a television could be heard. In a shared kitchen, a young man was flipping sausages in a pan. He didn't say hello, nor did another person who was heading off to the toilet with his head down. Were these Football Leaks people? John smiled crookedly and said nothing.

He opened a door that had multiple layers of soundproof insulation and was covered in white leather. Inside the roughly fifteen-square-metre room there was a mattress on a fold-out couch and a laundry rack with a couple of pairs of underpants that were drying out. The only window was covered with an opaque curtain. There was no television set, no decorations, photos or plants, just a white laptop on the desk.

'Don't sit on the chair,' he told me. 'It's not for sitting on. It would collapse. Sit on the bed or the floor.' He was referring to a rickety armchair piled with old newspapers and magazines. I saw English, Italian and Portuguese headlines. It seemed as though John was collecting articles about Football Leaks. He told me he would be right back and then left the room. I took the chance to look around a bit. I saw a dozen cables next to the desk. Some were connected, while others were stuck in a box. Under the desk there were other boxes that blinked and looked like routers. But what would be the point of having so many routers right next to one another? My understanding of technology is quite limited. I couldn't begin to imagine the purpose of these devices. I'd have to ask John.

A few minutes later, the bulky door reopened and John came back with some portable hard drives. He connected them to the computer, played around with the blinking boxes, entered passwords and then returned to playing around with the boxes and the hard drives. I had no idea what was going on. Suddenly, documents appeared on the screen. Thousands of them. They were player contracts.

The names on them made up a veritable world all-star team: Neymar, Alex Teixeira, Fernando Torres, Raphaël Varane, Luka Modrić and Portuguese defender Pepe.

Another box was blinking next to the computer – probably the Internet router. More and more documents were pouring into this small room.

Who was sending him all this material?

'We have very serious secure sources,' answered John calmly, without looking up. 'However, some of our sources do not realise that they are our sources. The important thing is that all our documents are genuine.' John's answer concealed more than it revealed.

'So you're a hacker,' I prodded.

'No, I'm not a hacker – none of us are,' he replied. 'I never studied IT either. We get this material, but I'm not going to tell you where from.'

'But you do know a lot about computers,' I remarked. 'Did you teach yourself everything?'

'I'm interested in technology, that's true,' John said. 'And I do some reading about it. But now let me show you something.'

He called up the Football Leaks home page and looked over the documents scheduled to be published there in the coming days. 'If I should be arrested, measures have been taken to ensure that the publications are not stopped,' he told me. To be on the safe side, there were copies of his treasure trove of documents, hidden at various locations. He showed me a map of the world with around a dozen red dots on it. The Football Leaks page had a secret code. If it wasn't entered once every seven days, a computer would begin gradually leaking the contracts and agreements to the anonymised mailboxes of WikiLeaks, other whistle-blowing platforms and select media. It was a ticking time bomb.

John squinted into his computer, typing in more digits and codes. It was almost as if he had forgotten I was in the room. He reminded me of the con artist Leonardo DiCaprio played in the film *Catch Me If You Can*. Outwardly, he seemed calm, but you could tell he was simmering underneath.

'With my current data alone, I could prove worldwide tax fraud to the tune of three-digit millions to the authorities,' John said. 'But I hope they will give me a bit more time before they arrest me.'

He laughed. Catch me if you can.

Why was he doing this? Why take the risk? As I was about to ask him, John's computer blinked. It was a message from an address consisting only of numbers and symbols. It contained a newspaper article about the transfer of Gareth Bale. Football Leaks had published documents concerning the 100-million-euro deal a couple of days previously. Now three EU parliamentarians were calling for an independent inquiry into it. The contracts published by Football Leaks had revealed that Spanish banks had issued guarantees for the deal. These very same banks had been given 40 billion euros of public funds to save them from going under in 2012. Members of parliament were now accusing them of passing on the risks of the Bale transfer to taxpayers. It was an explosive bit of news that attracted national and international attention.

John clenched a fist and then clapped his hands. 'This is why we are doing it!' he exclaimed. 'For exactly this reason! We want to open people's eyes, show them that the entire football business has become a large criminal organisation.

No transfer takes place any more without illegality, or at least borderline trickery.'

John checked the time. 'Come on,' he said. 'Let's go party.' He closed his laptop, unplugged the hard drives, fiddled with the boxes and left the room. Where did he keep all that stuff?

'I'm hungry,' he announced on returning. 'We'll get something to eat first at a place where we can watch some football.'

The Champions League match between Real Madrid and Roma was starting in a couple of minutes. We ambled off. It was already dark out, and John almost always took streets without lights. There was no question that he knew his way around this city.

'What's your favourite club?' he asked me.

'Borussia Dortmund,' I answered. We talked about Dortmund's classic matches against Juventus in the 1990s and the club's Champions League title in 1997. John could recite the Dortmund starting line-ups from back then. He remembered Jürgen Kohler blocking Eric Cantona's shot in the semi-final against Manchester United. We talked about Lars Ricken's chipped goal in the final, Matthias Sammer getting forward as a sweeper and how rock solid Júlio César had been at the back.

'But even back then, football was broken,' John said. 'Dortmund went dozens of millions of marks in debt to be able to play this brand of the game. The bosses nearly destroyed the club. How is something like that possible? Why wasn't anyone monitoring the situation? And why didn't football learn anything from this story?'

I had no answers for him.

I wasn't allowed to reveal his favourite club, he told me. Otherwise, he'd be accused of pursuing the 'project' on behalf of that team.

'That's utter nonsense,' he assured me. 'Football Leaks isn't dependent on any team. We don't work for anyone in the football industry.'

Football Leaks had published documents about John's favourite player, his fellow countryman Cristiano Ronaldo. 'He's the best player in the world, maybe of all time,' John said. Now the world could read about just how well Ronaldo was paid for his talent. In the weeks and months to come, he would often serve as an example for how unmoored, indeed insane the entire football industry had become.

'Of course we also publish documents about our favourite players and clubs,' said John. 'No one is spared.'

Shortly before kick-off, we found seats at the foot of a large video screen in a restaurant. The air smelled of meat and frying oil. The place was packed with young people. It was unbelievably loud. The match commentator seemed to be on amphetamines. But maybe the loudspeakers were simply receiving more than they could handle – music was playing at the same time the match was on. John ordered the Serbian butcher's platter with a mountain of chips. And beer. Lots of beer. The game began. Ronaldo appeared on the screen, larger than life.

'It's a funny feeling watching Real Madrid and knowing all the secrets of the players,' John confessed. 'We have almost everything. Their wages, sponsorship contracts, signing fees and, above all, their bank account statements. We know where they're sending their money.'

Those last words were said in a whisper. He didn't talk

much as we ate, watching the game on the screen instead. Real had difficulty getting going, and Roma were defending well. It was a tug-of-war affair, with nothing for those who demand fireworks.

'I've loved playing football ever since I was a small boy,' John said. 'As a kid, I used to kick the ball around with friends for hours at a time, and I still find the time to play once or twice a week with colleagues. The sport is so wonderful. It brings so many people together in joint celebration and mourning. What else is there that connects a tradesman with a doctor? That makes complete strangers exchange intimate details of their lives? But that sort of thing happens on the pitch and in the terraces all the time. Football has to preserve that. I'm not going to let the sport be destroyed by greedy business managers.'

He ordered shots with the next round of beer. The stuff smelled like bad perfume. I began to worry what I would feel like the next day.

In the fifty-seventh minute, the first goal was scored. Roma had been dominating after the interval, then, out of the blue, Ronaldo got on the end of a long pass and, with a flick of his heel, set himself up to bend the ball into the far corner. Real were ahead.

John was over the moon. He jumped up, pumped his fists in the air and bellowed with joy. For someone who didn't want to be noticed he was attracting a lot of attention to himself. 'That's just Ronaldo!' he enthused. 'A true genius. Much better, much more complete than Messi. I love watching him. His goals are works of art.' I was surprised at how emotional he was. But once John began talking about football, you could see how much the sport meant to him.

John ordered another couple of shots. Then he pulled out his mobile phone and showed me several emails. 'Our documents appear to be in great demand,' he said. Someone purporting to be a player's agent wanted to buy the entire data set. '"I could imagine a total figure of up to €650,000,"' John read out loud. He shook his head. 'If I sell myself, I am no better than everyone else out there,' he said.

He showed me other emails from tabloids who also wanted to buy Football Leaks' documents.

'They're only interested in scandals, not in real stories,' John said. 'I don't even respond to offers like this.'

'Isn't it dangerous to use a mobile phone?' I asked. 'Can't your location be determined?'

John just laughed at me. He showed me a program on his phone while he wolfed down the rest of his meat platter. The phone gave his coordinates as somewhere near the North Pole. John suspected that people were trying to track him down, so he used software that manipulated the phone's GPS receiver. The marvels of technology.

The game was over. Real had won 2–0. We drank a couple of last shots. 'Now let's go celebrate a bit,' John said. I took stock of my internal state and determined that I was already pretty much celebrated out. By contrast, John seemed completely sober. This was going to be a hard night.

We took a taxi to a gigantic concrete complex. You could hear loud music, and hordes of young people were heading in the direction of an entrance to the basement. We walked side by side in silence. The fresh air was doing me good. We entered an underground bar. There were no windows, the ceiling was low, and sweat was dripping from it. The dance-floor was hopelessly overcrowded, and somewhere amidst all the people a live band was playing. I turned around and was immediately handed a beer. John was standing in the middle of a group of people, gesticulating with both hands. Everyone was laughing.

We shot the breeze, drank, danced and played table football. At around 5 a.m., I sat down at a corner table and tried to collect myself. John joined me, sweaty from dancing.

'We'll have to work hard to clean up all the dirt,' he said. 'It won't be easy. But if you want, I can give you 800 giga-bytes of material tomorrow.'

Eight hundred? That was 300 gigabytes more than we had recently discussed. It sounded like an unbelievable treasure, a mountain of data such as the world of sport had never seen before. I was electrified. But despite my elation, I had to ask John one more question.

'Where is all this stuff coming from?'

He looked at me with something resembling pity.

'I'm not going to tell you,' he said. 'And now let's get a couple hours' sleep.'

Thank God, I thought.

We stumbled out of the bar with a young blonde woman at our side.

'We need two taxis,' John told me. 'I'll contact you tomor-row. We can get some breakfast together.'

John waved, got into a taxi with his companion and was gone. I walked a couple of metres, set my mobile-phone alarm for 10 a.m. just in case and hailed myself another taxi. I had had enough for one night.

A Headache, Joe Cocker, Hard Drives

My head felt as though it was about to explode. I tried to get up, but the room kept spinning. Eventually, I got hold of my mobile and wrote to John that I was up. He could get in touch if he wanted. Then I messaged my bosses that everything was all right and that I'd probably be back in Hamburg by tomorrow.

Slowly, I got dressed and then went outside, but it took quite some time before I felt like myself again. By 3 p.m., I still hadn't heard from John. I texted him that I was going to get a little something to eat.

As I walked through the city a thought occurred to me: What if John didn't get back in touch? What if I had said something wrong or stupid yesterday, and he simply stayed away? I was getting nervous. I decided to go back to the hotel and wait. Lying on my bed, I kept checking our chat, but there was nothing. At some point I fell asleep.

A loud knocking on my door woke me up. I looked at my phone. It was 7 p.m. Outside it was dark again. I opened the door.

'You look like shit,' John told me.

He, too, was pale as a corpse, and the skin around his nose was grey. He was wearing the same T-shirt as yesterday and smelled that way. We laughed. He said he was hungry – it was time for breakfast. We went back to the same café. Chocolate cake and lemonade seemed to be what got him back on his feet. But this time we didn't stay long. John said that he had to prepare a couple of things. We went to the same building we'd been to yesterday and sat down in front of his laptop. Thousands of PDFs and other files appeared on the screen.

'Have a look at this stuff,' he told me. 'I'm going to take a shower.'

Where was I supposed to start? I clicked through the contracts and discovered a huge amount of material about superstars like Zlatan Ibrahimović, Mesut Özil and Paul Pogba. Lots of it concerned the Spanish powerhouses Real Madrid and Atlético Madrid, and the Bundesliga clubs Borussia Dortmund and Bayer Leverkusen. I saw a couple of Bayern Munich and Wolfsburg contracts, and lots and lots of money transfers to agents. Even though I was unable to delve deeply into this material, I knew one thing: I wanted it.

John returned, looking more alive. His cheeks even had a bit of pink to them. I told him I was very interested. He nodded.

'Can I take the data with me?' I asked.

'No, not yet,' he answered. 'It still has to be finished.'

I didn't want to ask too many questions for fear of scaring him off with my curiosity, so I concentrated on the most important one.

'When can I have the data?'

'We'll see,' he replied. 'Let's go get a beer first.' My stomach did a somersault.

As luck would have it, two matches involving Portuguese clubs were being played that evening: Porto versus Dortmund and Sporting Lisbon against Leverkusen in the Europa League. There was no chance John was going to miss them. We went to an extremely run-down pub. The floor was so dirty the soles of your shoes stuck to it, and the barkeeper looked as though he had drunk beer instead of milk as a baby. John asked him to put on the Dortmund–Porto game.

The bartender asked us what we wanted to drink. He sounded just like Joe Cocker. We ordered two dark ales. Anything else? the barkeeper asked. Peanuts, I said. Two vodkas, John added. Dortmund's players appeared on the TV screen.

We sat at the bar, away from the rest of the punters. Joe Cocker hung onto the beer tap, trying not to fall over.

'Why do you guys in the media never ask where all the money in football comes from?' John said. 'Why do journalists report on massive transfer fees without explaining how dodgy sponsors are pumping cash into the sport?' He seemed to be in a hurry today to discuss the big questions. I tried to explain how difficult it was for those of us in the media to get hold of the necessary information and that it was sometimes completely unclear whose money a club was using. Most clubs, I told him, weren't obliged to reveal detailed information about their financial backers, sponsors and sources of income to the public.

Even if journalists did succeed in finding out how a given club was financing itself, I added, we often ran up against an impenetrable wall of shell-company networks. That made researching stories nearly impossible. Normally, we have no way of squeezing the information we need out of those legally in charge of running companies. Such information could only come from inside sources and whistle-blowers.

We discussed how club owners could invest huge sums in football without anyone really knowing where it came from. Whether from long-standing owners or all the Chinese investors currently flooding the European market with money, clubs seemed to have no scruples about accepting fresh capital without checking or asking questions about it.

John told me about an African despot who, he said, wanted to invest in football no matter what the cost. The same was true of members of the Kazakh and Turkish mafias and criminal bosses from South America.

'The reason is simple,' John said. 'You can earn the greatest profits at the moment in football. The market value of almost every talented young player trained professionally goes up because there is an increasing number of clubs that need increasing numbers of good players and have the ability to pay for them. Previously, the European market was the only one in which you could earn large sums of money. Today, footballers can get rich playing in Russia, Brazil, China and India. But that also means that criminals can pump dirty money into the industry and wash it clean, usually earning a profit to top it off. It's crazy.'

John was calling not only for transfer markets to be opened up, but also for flows of money to be subject to the sort of supervision that pro baseball and American football receive in the US. There, contracts, salaries and any fees associated with signings have to be made public.

'It would be important to publish agents' fees as well,' he said. He was advocating complete transparency in an industry that was practically allergic to it.

Joe Cocker brought us two more beers and two more vodkas but no peanuts. 'Are empty,' he said. Dortmund were leading 1–0, and the match was taking its course. John was on a roll.

'Watching matches live is getting more and more expensive,' he said. 'In England, hardly anyone can afford tickets, to say nothing of exploding costs for replica shirts and sub-scriptions to cable TV channels. The sport that actually belongs to the common people is becoming further and further removed from them. And we all just sit back and watch as It girls and would-be celebrities eat popcorn in VIP seating, while players and functionaries hide the millions they earn from the fans as quickly as possible in letterbox companies as far away from European tax authorities as they can get. The system is sick. It won't be able to survive in the long term.'

John said he had uncovered so many kickbacks sur-rounding the transfers of Portuguese players and so much corruption and collusion between clubs and agents that he had been forced to act.

'It took months to set up a good structure for gaining access to internal documents,' he said.

But now the network was so stable that Football Leaks could run for years, as long as he felt that it was what the public wanted.

'We get a lot of congratulatory emails that encourage us to continue,' John told me. 'But we also encounter a lot of resistance from fans of clubs affected by our publications. And that's to say nothing about attacks from the football industry itself.'

John said that he had many indications that clubs and agents had hired private detectives to track him down.

'These aren't just any detectives,' John claimed. 'They're Russians and former elite soldiers from England.'

On his mobile phone, he called up a couple of documents containing Kazakh and Turkish names. When you googled these names, hits included words like 'mafia', 'murder' and 'organised crime'. These were the people Football Leaks were taking on.

John told me he didn't know how long he would be able to remain anonymous. He ordered another round of beers – the vodka now came on the side without anyone asking for it. John believed that Jorge Mendes had hired private detectives to find him and his colleagues. A Portuguese prosecutor was investigating, and a few days ago a request for legal assistance had been filed with an Eastern European country. Things were getting serious. John was worried that agents and sports marketing companies were trying to let some genuine thugs loose on Football Leaks, the sort of people who don't use lawyers to settle disputes.

'I have no desire', John said, 'to become part of the concrete foundations of some highway bridge.'

I wasn't sure how real the danger he described actually was. Was he truly under threat or was he just being paranoid? I didn't know enough about the structure of Football Leaks, the people behind it and their motivations.

'Are you really engaged in the project completely voluntarily?' I asked. 'Who is financing you and your colleagues?'

John put his beer down. His eyes were alert and clear, and he looked straight at me.

'There is no dark force or mastermind behind Football Leaks,' he said. 'It is what it is. We are football fans who want our sport back. We want to end the industry's exploitation and to understand where our money is going and who's getting rich off it. It may seem naïve or romantic, but for me, anyone who isn't doing something to fight the destruction of football is complicit in it.'

It's possible that Snowden, Manning or Assange would

have used similar arguments in relation to abuses in politics, the military or intelligence gathering. John was just casting himself in the role of the good guy, the man of conviction, the idealistic whistle-blower. No, more than that, he was doing all he could to live it out.

We talked for a long time. The match was almost over. On the screen we watched Dortmund make a few final passes. The German club was leading Porto 2–0, but John accepted the impending defeat of his fellow countrymen without emotion. He bent over the filthy bar and asked Joe Cocker to change the channel to the Sporting–Leverkusen match, but the barman was a Liverpool fan, and they were playing at the same time against Augsburg. So we watched Jürgen Klopp return to Germany with his English team. John argued a bit with Joe Cocker and threatened not to drink any more vodka. Not that that made any difference – the next time we ordered a round, there were shots accompanying it.

We left the bar and moved on to a nightclub. There were lots of very young people. We danced, drank and partied until three in the morning and then headed back home. I had to be at the airport at 6 a.m. and was asking myself how I could have been stupid enough to book such an early flight. John interrupted this train of thought. Out of nowhere, he told me that he wanted to leave the project. It was cost-ing him too much energy. That was the real reason he had encouraged me to visit, but we'd hardly talked about it.

'Let's go to my place,' he said. We got in a taxi, and during the drive we both had a hard time keeping our eyes open. Around half an hour later, we were sitting in his tiny room with his quietly humming laptop. He handed me two hard drives.

'This is more than 800 gigabytes,' he said. 'Start by viewing the material, and we'll see whether you get any more. The data contains a lot of information about Ronaldo's schemes for saving taxes, but there's also material about a ring of agents. They also dodge their taxes.'

'How are things going to proceed at your end?' I asked.

'I don't know,' he answered. 'We'll be discussing that.'

'Can you at least tell me how many of you there are?'

'That's enough now. Get in touch when you've landed.'

I took the hard drives, we had a farewell embrace, and he brought me to the door. Outside there was a brief 'pling'. John took his mobile from his pocket and told me he had just received a new package of data. He murmured something about Adidas and the German patron of Bundesliga club Hoffenheim, Dietmar Hopp. It was something to do with a new model for investors. John immediately began reading.

Other People's Success

Dietmar Hopp once estimated his wealth at around €7.6 billion. But what did that figure actually mean? Four weeks later, it might be €7.8 or €7.4 billion, 3 per cent more or less. Hopp's wealth is based on the 10 per cent share he owns in software giant SAP, the company he founded with four partners more than forty years ago.

Hopp, who was born in modest circumstances at the start of the Second World War, is a generous fellow. Via his personal foundation, which is fed by SAP dividends, he has given away half a billion euros over the years. The money has gone into medical research, clinics and educational and social projects, mostly in his home region in south-western Germany.

He has also funded the rise of Hoffenheim football club, today known as 1899 Hoffenheim, presumably to stress that the team has a history that pre-dates Hopp. In three decades, the billionaire has sunk around €350 million into his home-town club, which until 1989 played in the lower-division amateur leagues. Since 2008, however, it has been a constant part of top-flight German football. It's a unique success story, one which would have been inconceivable without Hopp's investments in the team, management, training facilities and, above all, the stadium. This little corner of south-western Germany truly is Dietmar-Hopp-land.

The road leading to the stadium in the town of Sinsheim is named after him, as is the old sports field in the Hoffenheim district.

The former CEO's social conscience has earned him admiration, honours and prizes, but his activities as a club patron have proven divisive in German football. Fans outside Sinsheim despise the billionaire. For them, he is the ideal figure upon whom to release their pent-up envy, hatred and scorn. Hoffenheim are not just rich; Hoffenheim are also successful.

Hopp doesn't understand their hostility. He wants to be respected as a football patron just as he's respected as someone who supports medical research. Since Hoffenheim were promoted to the first division, he has given numerous interviews about his role as the almighty club benefactor. He constantly emphasises the social importance of sport, of football as a means of building character and of team games as training for real life. Hopp has insisted his millions amounted to nothing but a bit of priming money. He claims that he has been removing himself from day-to-day business operations step by step and that the club will soon be self-supporting. 'I'm insulted, but for me it was never about earning money,' Hopp once said. 'I haven't earned anything from this, if you must know. I wanted to give something back to the people in this region, which is my home.'

Dietmar Hopp, the philanthropist. The friendly billionaire next door. It's a heart-warming story. But is it the whole story?

The Football Leaks material contained documents that cast doubt on the image Hopp tries to maintain. At issue was a company called Transfair Rechteverwertungsgesellschaft mbH.Co. KG (Transfair Rights Monetisation Society). The company, which has its headquarters in the south-western German town of Wiesloch, was founded in September 2012. The liable partner was the administrative company of St Leon-Rot Golf Club Limited, which renamed itself DH-Holding Verwaltungs GmbH (DH-Holding Administration Ltd) soon thereafter. Its sole owner, as the initials would lead you to guess, was Dietmar Hopp.

Transfair earned its money from professional football players transferring from one club to another. The name of the company might have suggested that it was an upstanding representative of ethical principles in an otherwise corrupt industry. But Transfair's business model was no different to that of other investors. The company bought shares of football players' transfer rights and profited when they were sold for the highest possible price to another club. Despite its name, the firm had nothing to do with fair trade.

In early July 2013, the *Süddeutsche Zeitung* published an article reporting that Transfair owned shares in Hoffenheim players and stood to profit if they were sold before their contracts ended. The author described possible conflicts of interest between Hopp the club patron and Hopp the investor and asked a series of questions. Was Hopp, despite what he said about not profiting, trying to make money from the club? For whom? For himself? For his partners? For Hoffenheim football club? And what happened when a player in whom Transfair had invested didn't want to leave Hoffenheim or the club didn't want to sell him before his contract expired?

The problem for the *Süddeutsche Zeitung* was hard evidence. The newspaper lacked any documents that would provide incontrovertible information about these business dealings, and Hoffenheim's patron refused to comment on the matter. The article was titled 'Hopp's Silence'. But there was no fallout from its publication. Afterwards, Hopp's investment vehicle Transfair managed to keep itself out of the headlines.

The Football Leaks documents revealed the true nature of Hopp's business deals. They left no doubt that the company did in fact own shares in the transfer rights of several Hoffenheim players and thus profited when those players were sold on or loaned out. For example, on 25 January 2013, Transfair concluded contracts with Hoffenheim's registered company – TSG 1899 Hoffenheim Fussball-Spielbetriebs GmbH – concerning the 'purchase of transfer demands'. It gave Hopp's company 100 per cent of the 'economic transfer rights', as they were called, of the Peruvian players Luis Jan Piers Advíncula Castrillón and Alexander Júnior Ponce Pardo. For Júnior Ponce Transfair paid the club €415,500, and for Luis Advíncula €730,000.

Hoffenheim had bought Júnior Ponce from Peruvian first-division outfit Alianza Lima on 22 December 2012, but he never played a minute for the German side. Hoffenheim immediately loaned out their new acquisition to Brazilian club EC Pelotas for six months. In the summer of 2013, they loaned him back to Alianza Lima, in the summer of 2014 to Portuguese first-division team Vitória Setúbal, and in summer 2015 to Peruvian first-division club Universidad San Martín de Porres, where Júnior Ponce was still playing as of 2017.

Luis Advíncula's transfer history was similar. Hoffenheim purchased the defender from Ukrainian first-division side SK Tavriya Simferopol on 8 January 2013. He stayed in south-western Germany for only half a season, before being lent out for six months to Brazilian second-division club AA Ponte Preta. He then spent half a year on loan to Peruvian champions Sporting Cristal and was loaned on to Portuguese outfit Vitória Setúbal, before Hoffenheim finally sold the footballing globetrotter to Turkish first-division club Bursaspor in summer 2015.

If you were to draw the career paths of Júnior Ponce and Luis Advíncula on a piece of paper, you'd get a graphic illustration of the ice-cold economic logic of the football market. Mediocre players like these two, of whom there are thousands, are pushed around the globe from one club to another by their advisors.

The Football Leaks documents didn't reveal how much money Hoffenheim took in from all this transfer activity or how much the club had to pay Hopp's company Transfair. Nonetheless, both contracts contain model calculations for Transfair's 'transfer demands'. If Hoffenheim were to earn €1.5 million for Luis Advíncula, Transfair would stand to get €1.26 million. If someone paid Hoffenheim €1.5 million for Júnior Ponce, Transfair would be owed €960,000.

Such sums were laughable compared to the ones Transfair agreed with Hoffenheim on 22 December 2014. The player in focus in this case was midfielder Roberto Firmino Barbosa de Oliveira. Transfair paid the club €20 million in two instalments, one immediately and one upon the acquisition of Firmino, and received in return 85 per cent of his transfer rights. The remaining 15 per cent already belonged to Transfair, which it had acquired from two Brazilian companies, including one connected to people in Firmino's agent Roger Wittmann's circle. When asked to comment on these business dealings, Wittmann refused. 'I have no intention of making any public statements about internal matters or organizational structures of Rogon Sportmanagement GmbH & Co KG or the contents of any contracts,' he wrote. 'I refuse to renege on any confidentiality responsibilities I've agreed to or to reveal any business secrets of Rogon Sportmanagement GmbH & Co KG, our partners or clients.'

The deal agreed just before Christmas 2014 came in the nick of time. On 1 May 2015, FIFA banned third-party ownership of transfer rights. The ban had been announced a year and a half previously, and all TPO agreements made before it came into effect were protected, including the Firmino deal, which turned out to be a windfall for Transfair. On 1 July 2015, Liverpool bought the Brazilian midfielder from Hoffenheim. The transfer fee was €40 million, making Firmino the most expensive player ever to transfer abroad from the Bundesliga.

But the club was only a relay station for the payment. Hoffenheim was required to transfer the money to Transfair, with the exception of €8 million. Technically, Transfair was no longer Hopp's company. Coincidentally or not, a few days after the *Süddeutsche Zeitung* article had first put Transfair in the spotlight in the summer of 2013, DH-Holding Verwaltungs GmbH had itself stricken from the commercial register as the liable partner. That role was taken over by Comaro Management GmbH in Heidelberg, which had been founded expressly for this purpose.

The sole owner and operator of Comaro was Mariano Maroto López. For as long as Dietmar Hopp had been the owner of Transfair, Maroto had possessed commercial power of attorney. In autumn 2012, Hopp had named the Spaniard as the second managing executive of DH-Holding, alongside himself. Hopp's DH-Holding was located on Heidelberger Strasse in Wiesloch, at the same address as the headquarters of Transfair, even after Hopp officially departed the company. In other words: in the heart of Dietmar-Hopp-land.

In early December 2014, two weeks after the Firmino deal, Transfair's new owner, Comaro Management and Señor Maroto, moved into this very building. Why did Hopp hand Transfair over to his long-time acquaintance Maroto, who started working for SAP as a young man in 1991 and who by 2012 had worked his way up to vice president of customer strategy and sales operations? Did the Hoffenheim patron have conflicts of interest? And were there other Hoffenheim players from whom his company Transfair profited or stood to profit?

In response to a request for information, Hopp said that he would make no statements on the internal details of confidential contract agreements or speculations. His partner Maroto answered a detailed request for clarification of his position with the words: 'You will surely understand that we refuse to comment on the assertions you mention, regardless of whether they are merely presumptions or are demonstrably untrue.' The German Football League (DFL) told us that according to the information at their disposal, Hoffenheim 'has abided by the statutes in force at the time'.

Two years previously, the DFL had allowed Hopp to take over 95 per cent of the voting shares and 99.99 per cent of the capital shares of Hoffenheim's registered company. The League's reasoning was that for twenty years the patron had selflessly pumped capital into the club. The other Bundesliga clubs, with the exceptions of Leverkusen and Wolfsburg, aren't allowed to sell a majority of their shares to a financier. The majority must remain in the hands of the club itself.

This privilege is one reason German football fans see red every time they hear the name Hopp. But until recently, Hopp's many detractors didn't know that he not only invested millions in the club but was also involved in non-transparent transfer deals.

The Sugar Daddies

For fans of Real Madrid, Cibeles fountain is a mythic place. Located in the heart of the Spanish capital, it is where the club has celebrated its greatest triumphs. As part of the festivities, an open double-decker bus brings the team down the ritzy Paseo de la Castellana boulevard, and tens of thousands of supporters take to the streets. The high point of the celebrations is when the captain of the team ties a Real scarf around the statue of Cybele, the fertility goddess, and kisses her head. That was the scene in June 2017, after Real had beaten Juventus for its second straight Champions League title.

As has now become tradition, celebrating along with the club was its equipment supplier, Adidas. Everywhere in the city that Real's crest was to be seen, the three stripes of the company's logo were visible as well. The German sportswear manufacturer had ensured that this would be the case in its contract with Real, in a clause bearing the heading 'Celebrations'. It's a document that speaks volumes about the excesses of the global football industry. Adidas pays a minimum of €1 billion for its exclusive close connection with Real Madrid. €1 billion.

The gap between the biggest earners among the world's football clubs and their challengers has been growing ever wider in recent years. One reason for this is that the

Champions League creates a non-level playing field and reinforces the hierarchical status quo. In fact, since the summer of 2010, UEFA has paid out higher Champions League premiums to a few large clubs. Real has received €318 million, Barcelona €299 million and Bayern Munich €290 million. The sporting and economic dominance of this trio is suffocating. With the lone exception of Chelsea, who upset Bayern in the 2012 Champions League final in Munich, no other team has won club football's premier competition in the stretch from 2010 to 2017.

But the truth is that Champions League revenue per se isn't primarily responsible for the financial imbalance between the elite and the rest. Sportswear giants Adidas and Nike are the ones that flood the game with money and ensure the rich get richer. Both companies have an identical marketing strategy, emphasising the most well-known names, the most famous players and the most successful clubs. In their competition to associate their brands with the most high-profile teams and stars, they mutually drive up prices and pay out absurd sums of money to their advertising partners.

Conspicuously little about their business dealings ever becomes public. Whereas UEFA publicly documents, in great detail, the millions it pays out in club competitions, the sportswear giants keep their sponsorship agreements with top clubs and top stars strictly under lock and key. And no wonder – the confidential clauses and figures have increasingly taken on surreal dimensions.

Previously, the scraps of information the public got about sponsorship contracts came from the teams. In summer 2014, when Manchester United's contract with Nike expired and the club signed a ten-year agreement with Adidas, a figure was released: the Red Devils would receive at least £750 million from the deal, a press statement said. No further details were given.

For a long time, there were only rumours about the contract between Adidas and Real Madrid. But thanks to Football Leaks, we now have a deeper understanding of the twenty-year love affair between the Spanish *Galácticos* and the German sportswear giant. The Football Leaks documents contained a draft version of a new contract that would begin on 1 July 2015 and run until 30 June 2024. It contained sums that were truly out of this world.

That draft contract envisioned Adidas paying Real a fixed sum of €70 million a year. In addition, the sportswear giant would give the club 22.5 per cent of the net profits on the sale of Real Madrid merchandise worldwide. The annual total of these earnings was guaranteed at €30 million. All revenues from the sale of licensed products in excess of that sum would be meticulously calculated. Adidas promised to draw up detailed quarterly lists of its global turnover.

Moreover, Adidas committed to supplying the club with €8 million worth of clothing, shirts, shoes and footballs every year. And if Real achieved sporting success, there was also the odd bonus: for winning the Spanish first division, the club would get a further €2.5 million, rising to €3.5 million as of 2020; every Champions League title was worth €5 million, and as of 2020, €7 million.

Two comparisons serve to illustrate how otherworldly these sums are. Borussia Dortmund – Germany's second-biggest club after Bayern – got an estimated €8 million from its equipment supplier Puma for the 2015–16 season. That year, Real earned as much from Adidas alone as

Hertha Berlin did from all its sources of income (€95 million) and more than four other German first-division teams did overall. The lawyers who drew up the almost 140-page agreement between Adidas and Real seem to have thought of every eventuality, including such absurd scenarios as the club being relegated to the Spanish second division. Should that come to pass, the team would have a relatively soft landing: Adidas still guaranteed the team around €65 million a year.

In summer 2015, when Adidas began negotiating a new contract with Real, their current deal still had five years to run. It had come into force in July 2011. The fixed yearly sum the two sides had agreed upon until the summer of 2020 was €42 million. The figure now envisioned was more than €70 million, and the annual guarantee for Real's share of club merchandise sales went from €10 to €30 million. That illustrates how the Spanish club's earnings potential exploded between 2011 and 2015. Real had the power to force Adidas to renegotiate before even half of their existing deal had expired and appears to have increased guaranteed revenues by almost 100 per cent.

The 2011 contract contained an anomaly: a one-off 'advance payment' to Real of €40 million. In the confidential draft contract, there was a strange clause decreeing that Adidas would pay the €40 million 'in cash'. While we do not know if this clause persisted in the final agreed terms of the new contract, the question remains: Why would Madrid want so much money in cash? This document revealed that Adidas had once before, in summer 1998, given Real a cash payment of $40 million upon the signing of a large-scale equipment supplier contract. Could it really be that on two separate occasions Adidas's Spanish subsidiary had showed up at Real Madrid's headquarters with suitcases full of bills?

Real Madrid reacted with irritation to our request for a statement, writing: 'Your request for information seems to be based on information that has been obtained illegally from a professional office, so if you use it knowing its unlawful provenance, as we now duly inform you for the necessary legal purposes, you would be committing an offence.' Adidas responded to our list of questions by saying: 'The content of contracts is fundamentally subject to confidentiality and will not be commented upon by our side.'

That's par for the course with Adidas. Questions about business practices such as the million-euro/dollar payments roll off the company like water off a duck's back. The company strictly wants to avoid giving the impression that it gets its hands dirty in any way, despite its close proximity for decades to the most powerful people in sport. Some of them have landed in jail, as Bayern Munich potentate Uli Hoeness did for tax evasion. Some have been forced out of their posts, as happened to former FIFA president Sepp Blatter. And some have come under clouds of suspicion regarding corruption, as was the case with golden boy Franz Beckenbauer, when evidence emerged that Germany might have paid bribes to acquire the right to host the 2006 World Cup.

There was a time when the name Adidas was synonymous with non-transparent business practices. The leading figure of this epoch was Horst Dassler, the son of the company's founder, Adi Dassler. Until his death at a relatively young age in April 1987, Horst had built up a global network of protégés and dependents who could be exploited for commercial gain in almost all areas of sport.

The mechanism by which Horst Dassler and his successors greased the wheels was the rights agency ISL, which he founded in the mid-1980s in Switzerland. In the two decades of its existence, this company set new standards in the corruption of sports functionaries, before going bankrupt in mid-2001. According to Swiss court documents, the agency is alleged to have paid out 140 million Swiss francs in bribes between 1989 and 2001 alone.

Those who run the company today in the town of Herzogenaurach say that this is all in the past. The contemporary Adidas, they contend, is completely different to the family-run business of yore. But is everything today really on the up and up?

The Adidas Group has signed big-money advertising contracts with numerous football stars. The interests of the conglomerate are represented in these deals by the subsidiary Adidas International Marketing BV, which has its headquarters in a nondescript commercial park in south-east Amsterdam. It's no accident that Adidas decided many years ago to base its global marketing division in the Netherlands. The infrastructure there is top quality, while the corporate tax rates are low.

Adidas International frequently doesn't transfer money directly to players' accounts, but rather to companies to which the players have granted their image rights. As a rule, these companies pay out their profits to the players. This business construct has one primary goal: to reduce tax liability. Adidas's endorsement money is often not taxed at the highest personal income tax rate but at far lower commercial tax rates.

For instance, between 2010 and 2014, the company paid the former Ballon d'Or winner and Brazilian international

Kaká, who at the time played for Real and AC Milan, an annual sum of at least €1.5 million. The money was transferred to the Tamid Sport Marketing company in Milan. Adidas also paid €500,000 annually to Manchester United's Spanish international goalkeeper David de Gea via a company named Bedamarse Limited in Bowden, UK. And the €635,000 received from Adidas by de Gea's teammate Juan Mata in the 2016–17 season initially went to the company Depormata 88, in Oviedo, Spain.

Such deals attract major suspicion when the owners of advertising rights are companies with their headquarters in tax havens. That was the case between 2007 and 2009 with Lionel Messi. According to prosecutors in Barcelona, Adidas International Marketing BV transferred almost €4 million to two companies, Sports Consultants and Jenbril, for the right to use the Argentinian superstar in advertisements. Sports Consultants had their headquarters in Belize, Jenbril in Uruguay – two countries hardly known for their strict tax regulations. Messi's father was the head of both companies. In summer 2016, a Catalonian court handed Messi and his father a twenty-one-month suspended prison sentence and fined them millions. They were found guilty of having concealed Adidas's payments, among other sources of income, from the Spanish tax authorities. The Messis appealed the ruling, with their attorneys characterising them as 'model citizens'. In May 2017, the Spanish Supreme Court rejected that appeal.

And what about Adidas International, the Messis' contractual partner, which sent its advertising millions to Belize and Uruguay? Did the company bosses not know that Messi's father controlled Sports Consultants and Jenbril?

Do sportswear giants not bear a responsibility to refuse to sign contracts with companies that own the image rights of professional players in Europe but which are based in tax havens outside the continent? In their investigations of the Messis, prosecutors in Barcelona assumed that Adidas knew about the business construct they were using. Adidas has refused to comment on this issue.

In late 2008, the Adidas corporation tried to transfer all advertising contracts with clubs and football players from its Dutch subsidiary to the parent company in Herzogenaurach. This was the subject of a three-page letter that two high-ranking Adidas managers sent to Real Madrid. The move would have tax consequences, they wrote. The German tax authorities would in future withhold 15.83 per cent tax at source.

That didn't go down well. Striker Gonzalo Higuaín sent the Adidas Group a letter, saying that he wouldn't sign the planned change of contract because it was not in his best interests. What Higuaín meant was that the net sum he had agreed with Adidas International in the Netherlands in late April 2007 would be reduced. At that point the Argentinian striker played for Real Madrid and had inked a long-term contract with Adidas's marketing subsidiary that earned him an average of €575,000 if he played regularly. Adidas transferred the money to a company named Supat B.V. in the Netherlands, to which Higuaín had granted his image rights. Real Madrid also protested against changing the existing contracts, and in April 2009, Adidas gave in to the pressure of its most important sponsorship partner. All deals would remain as they were, Adidas wrote to the club, adding: 'On behalf of Adidas . . . we would like to sincerely apologize for any inconvenience that we may have caused.'

Higuaín turned his back on Adidas anyway. In spring 2011, he signed an agreement with Nike worth up to €800,000 a year. The US sportswear giant also concludes almost all of its deals with clubs and players via a subsidiary located near Amsterdam: Nike European Operations Netherlands BV. Like Adidas before them, Nike transferred Higuaín's endorsement money to the Supat company located in the Dutch city of Delft.

In its capacity as the owner of Higuaín's global advertising rights, Supat had contact with another Dutch company, ITB International, that did shady-looking deals with South American football stars in Europe. From the outside, ITB International seemed like an agency that represented players in negotiations with clubs and companies and collected fees on their behalf. But ITB International employees also served as front men for a firm called Paros Consulting Limited in the tax haven of the British Virgin Islands. The deal was structured like this: ITB International retained only 10 per cent of its fees for its agency work, while the rest was passed on to Paros. Paros, as the Football Leaks documents show, was controlled by Argentinian sports agents, including some with excellent connections to Higuaín.

The Paros documents contained two strange bills connected with Higuaín's Nike deal. In total, Paros billed ITB International €199,500 on 4 November 2013. The money was payable into a Paros account in Liechtenstein. The purpose of the transfer was given as semi-annual payments for Higuaín's Nike contract. But why would ITB International, which officially had nothing to do with Higuaín's Nike contract, divert almost €200,000 to a Caribbean tax haven for that purpose? Supat has refused to comment on this topic, as has ITB International. Higuaín, whom we contacted via his current club Juventus, also refused to give us a statement. Nike responded that the company didn't comment on confidential contract information.

A Mountain of Data

As my taxi turned the corner, John was still standing in front of his building, staring at his mobile phone. Later, he would tell me that he had worked straight through the night to the following noon, examining the data. I wasn't tired either. My body felt as though it consisted of nothing but adrenaline. I couldn't believe that John had simply handed over the hard drives with the data. What a cache of exclusive material! On the way to the airport, a thousand thoughts flashed through my head. What were we going to discover on the hard drives? And how were we ever going to be able to cope with such a mass of information?

But the swirling of my thoughts was interrupted by a churning of my stomach. I was feeling queasy from all the beer and vodka. With some informants you go out for a nice meal. Others prefer to talk to you in your office. John liked to party. I reminded myself reporters have to get acquainted with their protagonists in order to understand them. I had got to know John as a man of many facets and contradictions. He didn't seem to care about a lot of things, yet at the same time he was obsessed with his 'project'. He seemed able to effortlessly push aside concerns about his future, the danger he was running and the consequences he might have to face at some point. John wasn't just clever; he was intelligent. He was capable of understanding things quickly and expressing himself with eloquence. He was able to win over people, flatter them and get his way.

I didn't know any more about the structure of Football Leaks than I did before I met him, but I didn't believe that John could manage this project on his own. The leaks that appeared on the website were too varied for that – how could one person have so much access? But if that was the case, then who was John in reality? An intermediary acting at the behest of someone else? Was I being fed data in order to cause harm to some third party?

When I arrived at the airport, I was seized with panic. Were the hard drives encrypted? What would I do if I were stopped by customs and asked what I was taking home with me? In my career as a reporter, I'd been given dozens of files that I had brought onto aeroplanes, but this situation was much trickier. There were ongoing criminal investigations into Football Leaks. Would I be open to prosecution if the authorities discovered this material on me? My head whirled, and sweat was beading on my forehead even though it was unbelievably cold.

Boarding was set to begin in a few minutes. I had no time to check the hard drives. I decided to take my chances, even if I felt a bit like a drug courier. The customs officials looked me over grumpily and made me take out my laptop. But that was just routine. No one took any interest in the hard drives I had in my luggage. A few minutes after I found my seat in the plane, I was sound asleep. I didn't wake up until Hamburg, when the fellow next to me shook my arm so that he could finally disembark. In a few minutes I would be handing my bosses a much bigger cache of data than we had ever hoped for. Now the work was truly beginning.

Swamped

The two little black hard drives lay before us in the office. We decided to store them away and only take them out when we had some spare time. In the past, we had dealt with files containing up to 100,000 pages, but we'd never encountered anything like the volume of information held in the Football Leaks data. This was uncharted territory.

Soon we were staying at the office until late at night, poking around in the documents, printing out those contracts that seemed most interesting, googling names and figures and reporting back to our colleagues the following day about what we had discovered. Ours was an exciting search, but it was completely unsystematic. We didn't have any structure. There were simply too many documents and they weren't ordered in any way. By going through them file by file, we could only grasp individual threads. We went from one to another and kept getting entangled, rather than putting them together into a cohesive whole. The data was complex, and the documents were written in various languages. Many of the names were completely unfamiliar. To understand who they were, we needed colleagues who knew their way around the countries concerned.

Where could we get help? A few months previously, *Der Spiegel* had helped found an investigative journalism network together with several other European media companies. It was called European Investigative Collaborations (EIC). Jürgen Dahlkamp, Jörg Schmitt and deputy editor-in-chief Alfred Weinzierl coordinated this collaboration for *Der Spiegel*. When we told them about what we were investigating, things quickly began to roll.

In late April 2016, we invited our research partners to Hamburg, showed them the data and wrote down some initial areas of focus. In one of the breaks in the conference, we took a look around and couldn't believe the dimensions our project had taken on. There were around forty people from twelve different countries in the room. We were now a team. In the coming seven months, we would discover hundreds of stories in the material.

We discussed security. Football Leaks had powerful adversaries. How were we going to shield our data and research from hackers? What sort of legal protection could we hope for? We decided that every reporter team would ask their newspaper or magazine for complete confidentiality. Ideally, they would work in a space separate from the rest of the staff.

Our colleagues eventually left Hamburg, but every Friday at 9 a.m. we'd have a conference call. In the coming months, we would meet in Mechelen, Paris, Lisbon and Hamburg to discuss and plan the next steps in the project. It would be an exciting but also very taxing time.

Der Spiegel gave us a space of our own isolated from the rest of the staff. Only nine people had access to it, the computers weren't connected to the company network and you needed multiple passwords to boot up the systems. This sort of high security left us alternately amused and a bit paranoid. On the one hand, we were only working on football; on the other, we were talking about a business worth billions. Everything we published could complicate a deal or upset a club or a major functionary. We knew that we were going to make some enemies, and we didn't want them to have an easy time striking back.

That was particularly true of our partner The Black Sea, a consortium of journalists from the region around that body of water. Their research would lead them to cross paths not just with influential businessmen who had been profiting for years from crooked deals, but with mafia bosses and other outright criminals. The Black Sea reporters told us more than once about being pressured and sometimes threatened with violence.

We in the Football Leaks team increasingly began to withdraw from the rest of the *Spiegel* staff. We rarely went to departmental conferences and didn't participate much in the day-to-day life of the magazine. We were almost crushed by our work. Often, we would sit in the safe room from 8 a.m. until well after midnight, trying to get individual pieces to fit together to form an overall picture. It was a jigsaw puzzle with 18.6 million pieces – that's how many documents there were in the hard drives John had provided.

While we delved into the material, John got in touch several times, seeming increasingly agitated, exhausted and irritable. We wrote him emails explaining which stories we were working on and which directions our research was headed in. He told us that a large amount of new material had come in, including documents concerning Atlético Madrid. The whole club was externally controlled, he wrote. Atlético's glorious rise had come at a very heavy cost. He had everything in black and white, he claimed. We only needed to come and pick it up.

Flogged-Off Favourites

Saúl Ñíguez Esclápez, better known as just Saúl, is one of the most talented midfielders in the world. That became apparent to football fans at the end of April 2016, at the latest, when Bayern Munich and Atlético Madrid met in the semi-finals of the Champions League. Saúl, then aged twenty-one, decided the tie with a goal that no one who witnessed it will ever forget.

Deep in Bayern's half, the young Spaniard went on a mazy run into the penalty area, evading Bayern's Thiago, Juan Bernat, Xabi Alonso and David Alaba before putting the ball past Munich keeper Manuel Neuer. Saúl's delicate, curving shot was unstoppable. He put extreme bend on the ball with the inside of his left foot, making it cannon off the left post and cross over the goal line. The result was ecstasy in the Vicente Calderón stadium. Ever since, Saúl has been, together with forward Antoine Griezmann, the great hero of the '*Colchoneros*', or 'mattress men', as Atlético are known, thanks to their red-and-white striped kit, which resembles the colours traditionally associated with mattresses (*colchónes*) in Spain.

Saúl recently extended his contract with Atlético until the summer of 2026, despite attracting serious interest from both Barcelona and several Premier League clubs, who were said to have made him offers. Saúl had publicly pledged his loyalty, swearing not to leave as long as Diego Simeone remained Atlético's manager. The truth, however, is that Atlético will in all likelihood have to sell its massive young talent before the expiration of his contract. The reason for that is a business deal. When Saúl was sixteen, Atlético signed away 40 per cent of his transfer rights to a group of Irish investors for €1.5 million. With his signature, Atlético's managing director, Miguel Ángel Gil Marín, flogged off the future of a young talent. If Saúl stayed with the club, the investors would recoup their principal with 10 per cent interest. But of course, that wouldn't be enough. For the money men, Saúl is like a stock that keeps getting hotter and hotter.

In sporting terms, Atlético has been one of the most successful clubs of the past eight years. The club won the Europa League in 2010 and 2012, and in 2014, they landed the Spanish first-division title and made the final of the Champions League. Economically, however, things haven't been nearly as rosy. In the summer of 2015, the club was burdened by €520 million of debt, including €45 million owed to the Spanish tax authorities. Many of these debts were holdovers from the past. Atlético's former president, Jesús Gil y Gil, ruled the club like a king for sixteen years. Once, he came to the stadium leading a crocodile on a leash. On another occasion in 1996, after Atlético had surprisingly won the Spanish title, Gil rode through the streets of the Spanish capital atop an elephant. He was nothing if not decadent, even keeping a decommissioned aircraft carrier anchored off Marbella. When this eccentric patriarch died in 2004, he lay in state in his coffin on Atlético's home pitch. But the club he left behind was a financial disaster.

Gil's son Miguel Ángel came to the club in the early 1990s, when his father still ruled Atlético like a despot. Today, Gil Jr is the main shareholder, with his family owning a 55 per cent stake. The club's reputation has improved dramatically since he took over, and Atlético has successfully marketed its underdog image. Led by the rough-hewn Argentinian Diego Simeone, the club is a magnet for fans who find city rivals Real too glitzy. Atlético stands for grit, determination and a willingness to inflict pain – even on itself. One of the major reasons credited for the team's revival has been its transfer policies. Atlético is known as a club that is able to turn tidy profits by buying players low and selling them high. For example, Atlético got €36 million from Manchester City for Sergio Agüero in 2011, €43 million from Monaco for Radamel Falcao and €42 million from Chinese club Guangzhou Evergrande for Jackson Martínez. But was all truly well with Atlético?

Football Leaks has demystified the romantic story of the working-class club that dared to challenge the Establishment and that survives year after year despite losing its best players. The truth is that Atlético has depended on outside investors for its survival. Starting in 2010, the club allowed external financiers to purchase shares in the transfer rights of more than a dozen players. The investors were the ones who decreed that fan favourites would be flogged off, and it was they who profited most from the transfers. That used to be a closely guarded secret, and Atlético's CEO Gil Jr did everything in his power to keep it that way – understandably. If fans had got wind that the chief shareholder of the club was flogging off players to keep his business afloat, there would likely have been massive opposition. And no football functionary likes opposition.

Gil kept doing one backroom deal after another, keeping all contracts confidential to avoid any publicity or debate. On 29 December 2011, Atlético sold a third of Falcao's transfer rights for $10 million to a partner from Malta – none other than Doyen Sports Investments Ltd. The preamble of the contract made it clear who was making the rules. It read: 'Atlético de Madrid requires financial assistance for its ordinary activity, for which it has adressed [sic] several financial entities. At present, given the current financial crisis and market situation, the Club is finding it extremely difficult to access this bank financing, which is why it has resorted, ultimately and as a last recourse, to Doyen in order to obtain this assistance.'

Atlético concluded the majority of its rights-sharing agreements with the Irish company Quality Football. The men behind this firm were two of the most influential deal-makers in the football industry: Peter Kenyon and Jorge Mendes. We have already encountered Mendes as the agent who made Cristiano Ronaldo a global superstar. Kenyon was part of the leadership of Manchester United from 1997 to 2003, running the Premier League's biggest club for the final three years of that period. In 2004, after Roman Abramovich bought into Chelsea, he became chairman of the board at the London club. A clever businessman, Kenyon stayed there for five years before joining CAA Sports, one of world's largest sports marketing companies. Starting in 2014, he began working as an advisor for Atlético.

In June 2011, Mendes and Kenyon drew up a prospectus for investors willing to pony up at least €250,000. It portrayed the international transfer market as a humming, unshakable growth industry, in which money invested automatically grew. The brochure guaranteed a minimum return of 10 per cent annually. Where else could profits of that sort be made in the middle of a global financial crisis?

The money the two men attracted was funnelled through Jersey, the English Channel tax haven. From there it was spread among a variety of funds run by Mendes's agency Gestifute and Kenyon's then employer CAA Sports. But the third-party ownership deals were administered by a company from another low-tax country: Quality Football. Mendes and Kenyon advised this Dublin firm on which players it should invest in. Millions of euros flowed back from the Irish capital via Jersey to the clubs.

The confusing business structure Mendes and Kenyon employed raised several questions. Who were the financial backers? How much money did the funds move? To which clubs? For which players? The Football Leaks material helped us find some answers. Lawyers working for the funds maintained lists of the shares acquired in various players. In August 2011, the funds had €84 million invested in thirty-six professional footballers. In June 2015, shortly after third-party ownership was banned, they had €88 million sunk into forty players. Even in August 2016, investors still had shares in twenty-seven players' transfer rights that were worth around €45 million.

The investors were more than two dozen in number and came from around the world. One of them was a well-known actor from the *Harry Potter* films. Others – both businesses and private individuals – came from the football industry itself, opening up suspicions of conflicts of interest. One of the financiers, for example, was the wife of a Premier League manager. In December 2011, another of the investors was a company with close connections to a club in American Major League Soccer. Yet another participant in Mendes's TPO deals was a billionaire who later bought shares in a Premier League club.

Particularly questionable was the investment of Yıldırım Ali Koç, a businessman from one of the richest families in Turkey and chairman of the supervisory board and vice president of Istanbul club Fenerbahçe. In 2011, the portfolio of one of the Jersey funds, in which Koç had invested, contained a player under contract with Fenerbahçe's bitter cross-city rivals Beşiktaş. Conflicts of interest like this make football romantics' blood boil. Koç has refused to comment on the matter.

Quality Football traded in players from the Portuguese first-division clubs Sporting Lisbon, Porto, Braga and Rio Ave. But Mendes's funds did their most frequent and lucrative business with players from Atlético. When asked about his apparent close connections to the powerful Portuguese agent, Atlético's managing director Gil insisted that he maintained a healthy distance, stating to the *Financial Times* in November 2015 that he had done only a single TPO deal with Mendes.

Starting in 2010, Atlético had involved the Mendes funds in the transfer rights of at least twenty players. That brought around €58 million into the perennially cash-strapped club. But the price for those financial injections was high. Atlético gave up control over its transfer policies – and robbed fans of the chance of identifying with their favourite players. No sooner had a new star been born than he was put up for sale.

One of the players whose transfer rights were partially

owned by investors was Sergio Agüero. For a one-off payment of €2.5 million, a Mendes fund secured 12 per cent of the Argentinian striker. What happened next was predictable. Six months later, Agüero was sold to Manchester City for €36 million. Incentive clauses meant that the financiers also took in €844,000, so all told they made €2.66 million after their initial investment had been deducted.

Manager Diego Simeone has turned several of the players he's signed for Atlético into stars, but instead of securing their talents long term for the club, Gil has flogged them off. For €2 million, he gave Quality Football a 50 per cent interest in Diego Costa, for €6 million half of Arda Turan and for €5 million 50 per cent of Eduardo Salvio. Gil has refused to comment on the numerous TPO deals. Mendes and Kenyon also didn't respond to written requests for statements on this issue.

The situation with the *Colchoneros'* current idol Saúl won't be any different than with Costa, Turan or Salvio. In the files of the Mendes funds, the minimum release fee for the young star is set at €45 million. Even after the investors deduct their initial payment of €1.5 million, they're in line to make at least €16.5 million in profit – a return of more than 1,000 per cent. Aside from the cocaine trade, there aren't many businesses that offer comparable sorts of returns.

The contract signed between Atlético and the Mendes funds on 16 March 2011 provided a preview of how Saúl's sale will likely proceed. It requires the club to inform its Irish partner within five days of any offer about the size of the transfer fee, which club it came from and how the player views it. If the financiers agree to the deal, but Saúl doesn't transfer, there is a punitive clause, according to which the investors' 40 per cent stake returns to Atlético while the club has to compensate the investors for the income they would have made from the transfer.

Rebellion

John and I were by now conversing in six separate chats, all of which were encrypted and took place on different platforms. Sometimes we also used pre-agreed abbreviations and code words. John was very careful about his anonymity. His email addresses consisted of a wild mix of numbers, letters and symbols. Because of the many platforms we used, our correspondence was never constant – sometimes John would change providers in the middle of a conversation. He would give me a brief pre-agreed signal, and then I would erase the chat and switch providers as well. Sometimes we used computer programs that eliminated chats automatically.

For me, this was a completely new world, while for John it was a normal part of everyday reality. As a reporter for *Der Spiegel*, I had been trained to protect my sources as much as possible and never to betray them, even if questioned by the police or a judge. But I'd never experienced anything like the virtual game of cat and mouse John and I were playing. I often asked myself who we were hiding from. 'The police, prosecutors, Doyen and, above all, the mafia,' John once answered. He might as well have said: everybody. But given what we had found in his material, I couldn't say his caution was misplaced.

John wrote to me as many as twelve times a day. He was discovering a lot in the data and making faster progress than our team was. Often, he gave us useful tips about connections between companies, funds and accounts. He knew an enormous amount about economic and financial topics. Even Nicola Naber, the trained economist on our team and an acknowledged expert on European tax-evasion tricks, was frequently impressed at what John could tease out of the documents.

Where had he learned this? Or was he merely passing information on to us from a third party? We were still sceptical about what Football Leaks truly was and who was actually behind it. Was John really just a young man with a genius for revealing all of football's shortcomings, finding the loopholes in the system and sharing them with the world? We discussed this issue almost every day, without getting any closer to an answer.

The emails we received from John during this phase suggested that he was feeling ever more hunted and was slowly but surely losing control over himself and his life. Whenever he felt as though we weren't paying enough attention to some trail he had discovered, he always followed up, asking why we didn't find it as interesting as he did. This sort of pressure was unpleasant, and we defended ourselves. I explained that we could only work at a tempo that was right for our team and our network, and that we had to proceed strategically or we would lose our way in the mass of material. I also made it clear that even though he had shared his data with us, he wasn't our boss. We had to be able to work independently.

John reacted as a rebel does, by posting the material he thought was interesting but we initially didn't on the Football Leaks webpage. That made our work a lot more complicated. We lived in constant fear that we would lose

an exclusive on which someone from the team had worked
for days or weeks because things weren't going fast enough
for John and he simply published the documents on his own.

Colleagues repeatedly asked me why we couldn't control
John. I had tried explaining things to him, as well as begging
and pleading, but he can be pretty stubborn when an idea
gets into his head. Moreover, every time he posted something on the Football Leaks website, he would say that he
had been 'outvoted' by his team, who had decided that the
material needed to come out. What was I supposed to say,
given that I'd never met a single person from this team?

Since the two days we spent partying together, I had met
John frequently, but at irregular intervals, in various cities. We would talk about football, about our project, about
women and about everything under the sun. We grew closer
to one another, although John continued to say nothing about
the details and background of Football Leaks. I explained
the difficulties we encountered in our investigative research,
the hurdles we had to clear, how difficult it was to check
all that material and how complex the flows of money were
where many of the world's top football players were concerned. I told him that we had to obtain external advice from
tax auditors, lawyers and economic experts to untangle and
understand these structures. He would register my explanations with a nod, and then do whatever he wanted.

John often posted documents on the website very late at
night, so that I had no chance to dissuade him. When I woke
up the next morning, the social media platforms were all
full of news about the latest Football Leaks revelations, and
news outlets were quick to file reports. After such nocturnal
leaks, the documents concerned had no more value, even if

we had worked on them. They weren't exclusive any more. We could only take a deep breath, exhale and keep on working. We tried to take a somewhat relaxed attitude. What else could we do?

Nonetheless, I found myself increasingly waking up in the middle of the night to check the Football Leaks page and my Twitter account on my mobile phone. Once, my wife discovered me sitting in our kitchen at 4 a.m. She had only a vague idea of what I was working on. All I had told her was that it involved a huge cache of data and had something to do with football. Usually, she showed a lot of understanding for my work, but this research had been going on for months. I wasn't spending much time at home, and I was often quite irritable. It wasn't easy.

Now she saw me sitting red-faced at our kitchen counter angrily typing a message into my mobile because John had uploaded another contract and I knew that, in a couple of hours, our French EIC partner would be very perturbed.

'Is it worth it?' asked my wife, softly but clearly.

I thought for a while and then answered, 'I hope so.'

She gave me a long look. Neither of us spoke a word. Her eyes were saying, 'It's just football, a game with twenty-two players and a stupid ball. Now calm down and come back to bed.' But her voice was saying that she was worried and I should watch out for myself.

Trapped

It was early May when John offered me the next big cache of data. We had arranged to meet in a large European metropolis. It was warm. It felt more like summer than spring, and the entire city smelled of grilled meat. There were barbecues on almost every corner, with street pedlars selling sausages and steaks. This time, I stayed for four days. In John's last messages to me, he had seemed disturbed, as though his fear of his enemies was slowly but surely beginning to get the better of him. I wanted to have time to discuss everything we needed to discuss.

We met up in a café. John showed up nearly two hours late. I was used to that and wasn't bothered, but when he sat down at the table, I was startled. He didn't look good at all. This time it wasn't just lack of sleep after a night of boozing. A sadness that hadn't been there at the start of the year had etched its way onto his face. His skin was grey, the rings under his eyes were darker, and he sported a beard that sprouted every which way. The toes of his shoes were dirty, and the material on one side of his trousers was so thin that it looked as though it could tear at any moment. It seemed that right now other things were more important to John than his appearance.

'My friend, how are you coming along?' he said by way of greeting. He was trying to sound flippant, but his voice was a lot darker than I remembered, containing nothing of the euphoria and energy it had the first time we met. John looked like someone who was very worried.

'What's wrong?' I asked.

'Everything's shit,' he blurted out suddenly. He was staring down at the table, his shoulders hunched. Where had the bundle of energy from February gone? What had happened to him?

He ordered a cola and a brownie. There was no flirting

with the waitress, no silly jokes, not even a smile. Just an order.

'I'm sick and tired of it,' he said.

'Of football?' I asked. 'Of love? Of the project? Of what?'

'Of everything,' he answered. 'Nothing makes any sense. We've hit our limit. The other side is constantly attacking the webpage trying to shut it down. I can't sleep any more because I'm afraid someone will storm into my room and put an end to me. We're spending more time fending off hacker attacks on our system than anything else. It's no fun any more.'

'Who's attacking you?' I asked.

'Too many people, and they're professionals,' he answered. 'The people Football Leaks has published material about have all engaged specialist companies to track us down and shut down our systems. We're having huge difficulties deflecting the attacks.'

The waitress brought his brownie. John fell silent.

Was he truly so surprised? After all, he had taken on the most influential, powerful people in the world's biggest sport. What was he expecting? That they would give up without a fight? He must have known that multimillionaires would not stand being made fools of and would want to continue doing business without the intervention of any online pirates.

John poked his fork around in his brownie without eating very much of it. He had become thinner, I noticed. And his fingernails were still bitten down to the quick.

'Why don't you tell me about your research?' he said.

I started telling him about our safe room, our team and our cooperation with our international colleagues. We had succeeded in getting an initial basic, if somewhat unsorted overview of the material, I told him. But we were now able to identify certain stories and were getting a feel for the form in which we could publish them. The EIC team would meet in a few weeks' time in Paris. There, we were planning to establish small groups that would investigate individual topics in detail.

We talked about companies, bank accounts and money flows. John was like a walking Football Leaks lexicon. He could draw organigrams in the air faster than most people could talk about their last vacation. Suddenly, he seemed freer and more relaxed. The content of the project seemed to revive him. For a moment, he almost seemed satisfied with our results. He was happy that we were making progress, even though he continued to complain that we should be working faster.

'Now tell me what's getting you down,' I said.

'Not right now,' he said. 'I'm in a good mood. Let's talk about something else. We have a couple of days to discuss the rest.'

'Okay,' I said. 'What do you feel like doing?'

'I've got to pick something up not far from here,' he announced. 'Do you want to come along?'

'Of course.'

We paid the bill. After about an hour on a train, we ended up in a desert of gigantic prefab apartment buildings, uniformly grey – indeed, identical. John got his bearings, squinted and glanced right and left. 'This is it,' he said. We entered one of the buildings. The hallway smelled of mildew. John took a couple of quick steps and got in the lift. He pressed a button, but nothing happened. There was a sign in the lift, but neither one of us knew the language in which it was written. So we tried our luck. I closed the doors from the inside, while John pressed the button. The lift was not moving. We should have guessed that you had to hold the doors closed while the lift was in motion, otherwise it would grind to a halt. But we were trapped.

There was no emergency bell. The lift was, at the most, a metre and a half by a metre and a half – a shoebox that seemed to be growing more restrictive by the minute. I'm not claustrophobic, but the thought of hanging there by a cable that might well not have been serviced in living memory and having no way of sounding the alarm or otherwise attracting attention to ourselves made me feel a bit ill. John sat down on the floor of the lift, with his knees curled under him and his face in his hands. He looked tiny in that position.

'So what are we going to do now?' I asked.

'I have no idea,' said John. 'This sort of shit has been happening to me my entire life.'

I knocked cautiously on the doors. Silence. I pushed the doors. Also nothing.

'Maybe this is a sign,' John said. 'Maybe I'll end up in a tiny cell like this one.' He paused and then added: 'The football system is devouring itself. With criminals, crooks and greedy people. I can prove it, but in the end I'm the bad guy. The world is insane. We should simply turn ourselves in. Go to the police and tell them we didn't want to do anything wrong, just to clean up this whole disgusting industry. Because it's important. Then let the courts decide. At least I'd be safe from the bad guys. They couldn't hurt us in prison, could they? But you know, football is so powerful. We constantly read in the documents how investors and functionaries influenced the police. How they worked together with one another. Today everyone is a football fan.

You could make anyone happy with a couple of tickets and signed kits to impress friends with. How could we ever get a fair trial in this world?'

He was babbling. I could only understand a fraction of what he said. It was also hard to concentrate knowing that we were hanging by a fucking cable several metres in the air.

'Man, stop whining for a minute and help me,' I told him. I was having trouble breathing in this confined space, and for a change something – the solution to this very pressing problem – was more important than Football Leaks.

'Get up and press the "doors close" button,' I told him as calmly as I could, while I pushed the two doors together until I heard crackling that I hoped was an electrical contact being established. John got up in slow motion. He pressed the button, while I squeezed the doors together. One more time, in a slightly different way, and then the lift shuddered. John pressed the button for the floor we wanted. We were moving again.

He smiled. 'If journalism doesn't work out, you could always become an elevator mechanic,' he said. 'And when I get out of jail, I'll become your apprentice.'

It was good to hear him crack a joke. We both laughed hysterically.

I had no way of knowing it at that moment, but the scene in the lift would later help us continue our project in peace.

The Collector

When we got out of the lift, I felt like kissing the floor.

'We're taking the stairs on the way down,' I said.

John nodded. We had to pass through a five-metre-tall wooden door. It stuck, and we had to push together to get it to open. Why had John brought us here?

Two women no older than their mid-twenties were sitting in the room we then entered. The room felt as hot as a sauna. One reason was that one of the women was sitting at her desk wearing only a rather large bra; another was that the sun was beating down on the room through tall windows, turning it into an oven. What the hell were we doing here?

John said something in a language I didn't understand and handed a note to the half-dressed woman. She got up, arranged herself and went into a back room. John sat down on her chair and stared into a computer monitor. Only when the other woman said something to him did he smile and move his chair a bit further away. John was a curious guy. He reacted to computers like a predator does to its prey.

The half-dressed woman brought out a huge box. She was sweating. The box must have been heavy, and John moved to help her. One by one, he removed four bottles of port wine, eleven books and a large map from the box. I went to take hold of the wine, but he slapped my hand away.

'You've got grease from the lift door on your fingers,' he told me.

My mother was the last person who had spoken to me that way. I examined the wine from a distance. It was almost thirty years old and came from Portugal. I didn't know much about wine. Was the stuff even drinkable? The title of one of the books was *Dresden 1779: Concealed Empire*.

John paid, got some pieces of cloth out of his backpack and wrapped them around the items. On the way down, we took the stairs.

'What is that stuff?' I asked

'I collect antiques,' he said in a matter-of-fact tone, as if announcing that the sun would rise tomorrow.

'You're joking.'

'No, I've been collecting for many years. I earn money with it. I've got these items cheaply. They were worth considerably more than what I paid for them. I can sell them for four times the price.'

'You're talking about the port?'

'Yes, about the port,' he said.

'Where do you sell it?'

'On the Internet.'

Where else? We took the train back to the city centre, he with some antiques in his backpack and me with a couple of additional unanswered questions in my mind.

Tired Rebels

We met up again in the days that followed, taking walks, playing table football and pool and going to parties. John's nights were becoming ever wilder, longer and more boozed up. The nightlife and the alcohol were a diversion, an escape for a couple of hours at least. I tried to get him to talk about his problems, but every time he seemed about to open up, he changed the subject. I didn't understand why. I pressed him, but he wouldn't answer.

That changed on the final night of my visit. We were in a pub not far from the main street in the city centre. Lovers were making out, while bellowing tourists traversed an intersection on beer bikes. We were inside watching the

Champions League semi-final. It was a day of celebration for football fans, but John looked as though he were at a funeral. I got us some beer.

From a distance, John seemed even tenser. He glanced around compulsively, hectically wiping the sweat from his brow and eyes. The bartender gave me two large beers. I put John's down on our table. He took it in both hands, sniffed it, raised it over his head to inspect it from below and poked his finger around in the froth.

'Is something wrong with the beer?' I asked.

'Someone might have put some sort of poison in it,' John said. 'That would be the easiest way to get rid of me.'

I waited for him to laugh, but John was serious. He took a small sip.

'Yesterday you had no problems drinking beer,' I reminded him.

John took out his mobile phone and told me that a couple of hours ago he had received some new data concerning a law firm that worked for a Champions League club. He showed me a screen shot of a chat on his mobile. In it lawyers discussed whether there was any way of getting around FIFA's ban on third-party ownership. He swiped across the screen, opening another folder. It consisted of correspondence between a Kazakh and a Russian, who were discussing John and Football Leaks. The Kazakh told the Russian he should 'take care' of the situation. They listed a bunch of places where they should search for John. His enemies were getting closer.

John scrolled so quickly on his mobile that I couldn't get a good look at the names or the emails themselves. John stared at me, his eyes wide open.

'They're getting serious, man,' he told me a bit too loudly. 'They're after us.'

His hand was trembling. This was not the cool, clever John I had come to know. Sitting in front of me was someone who had come to understand that you shouldn't mess with certain sorts of people just because you wanted an adventure. That there were consequences to everything one did. Serious consequences.

'Tonight we're not going partying,' John said. 'We're going to my place. There's something I have to discuss with you in private.'

He sipped at his beer and began showing me more documents on his mobile. Something about an investor who had deposited large sums of money in Panama and Belize. A whole series of documents about a wealthy African who wanted to pump money into football. A warlord who had made a fortune with 'blood diamonds', John said.

A goal had been scored, but John seemed not to notice the jubilation of the fans. The only things that mattered to him were his data and the many dirty deals in the football industry. Suddenly, a fight broke out between two men near the entrance to the pub. A table got turned over, and a woman screamed. John didn't even look up. He just stared at his mobile phone, reading and reading. Then, shortly before the end of the first half, he quickly jumped up. I had just got two more beers for us, but John wanted to leave.

He called a taxi. Before he got in, he checked to make sure the man at the wheel was the same as the person on the driver's identification card mounted to the dashboard. John made a note of the name. He directed the driver along a park and past several cafés, back and forth. It seemed to me as though we had passed the same restaurant a number of times. Were we driving around in circles? I didn't dare ask. John, sweating profusely in his short-sleeved shirt, issued directions to the driver. He told him to stop on a side street.

John led me through a long courtyard. Adele's 'Hello' blared out of one of the windows. We stopped briefly. I had to laugh, but John didn't see the humour, even though the song could have been part of the soundtrack to his life at the moment.

John stood in front of a door that required an eleven-digit code to open. There was no light in the hallway. The walls were mouldy, and many of the windowpanes were broken. We went up a couple of flights of stairs, stopping in front of a second door that only opened after he had held a chip card in front of a small sensor. Upon entering, I almost tripped over an overflowing ashtray. There were dirty socks on the floor, and a pair of underpants hung from the doorknob.

John went into one of the back rooms and opened his laptop before he had even finished taking off his jacket. There were two crusted-over bowls of granola on his desk that would have delighted any microbiologist. John's computer was painfully slow to boot up, and he drummed his fingers on the top of the desk. Five minutes passed, then ten, fifteen. The only thing on his laptop screen was the boot-up symbol. John began to tap on the computer with his fists and shake it. It was the same sort of impatience junkies display when they need a fix.

This was their biggest problem, John told me, which is why we had to talk privately.

'Our damn computers can no longer handle the amount of data they're receiving,' he said. 'The volume of documents has nearly doubled in the past couple of months. We now have well over a terabyte, and more is coming in every day.'

This was the biggest leak in the history of sport.

Finally, the laptop was ready to go. John connected four hard drives, and another cable was inserted into a device between John's router and laptop. That was to prevent anyone from seeing where and how we logged ourselves in, John told me. The monitor came alive with links, paths and documents. He clicked on a folder entitled 'mafia'. The laptop immediately froze.

Football Leaks, John's baby, had become too big to work with. He could only upload a maximum of one or two documents per day to the Football Leaks webpage, he said. The system couldn't handle any more.

'It makes no sense like this,' he sighed.

He needed more powerful computers, bigger hard drives, more memory and better software for searching the data. A new, more user-friendly home page as well. In truth, he needed pretty much everything. He shook his head. He said that he had hoped UEFA or FIFA would get in touch with him.

'They were interested in our material,' he complained. 'So why have they never got in touch with us?'

He had dropped hints to reporters in email interviews that he could imagine working together with football's governing bodies. He took a deep breath and then a healthy swig of the schnapps he had just poured into a teacup.

'What are you going to do now?' I asked him.

'We really did consider turning ourselves in to the police,' he answered. 'Hand over everything, all the data, and put an end to it.'

'Why didn't you?'

'Because it would ruin everything. Us and the project as well.'

We talked about the possible consequences. In which country would he hand himself over? And what would he confess to?

'Nothing,' he said. 'Only that the data is here. No one could accuse me of anything more than that. Perhaps we'll leave Europe. Go somewhere in South America or Asia.'

That didn't sound very carefully considered or reasonable to me.

I suggested just shutting down the webpage for a while, as a first step. It would have the double advantage that John's enemies would think the problem had been solved and so would stop pursuing him, and it would also give the EIC the chance to keep analysing the material.

'You could relax a bit, catch your breath and decide what you really want to do in the future,' I told John.

He got up and left the room. He said that he would be right back, but it was forty-five minutes before he returned.

'That's exactly what we're going to do,' he said. 'We're going to give the project a rest.'

Neither he nor I said any more for a while.

'I think I should write an article about it,' I finally said, 'to explain to readers why you're taking this step.'

'Then please write as well that in the future we don't just want individual contracts or agents' fees to be visible, we want to tell stories about the cases in question. We want all the complex structures to be accessible to normal fans, too.'

He was building us a golden bridge across which we would travel with our EIC exposés.

We agreed that I would report that the Football Leaks page would remain on hold for at least six months. There would be no new documents, no new scandals, no new publications in the middle of the night. Only silence.

'You kept your nerve in the lift,' John told me. 'You'll be able to withstand the pressure of the football industry. I'm sure of that.'

He laughed. He seemed a bit more carefree.

We stayed for a while in that little room, saying nothing. John copied some data and transferred a couple of contracts and emails to a new hard drive.

'You'll figure your way around this new material,' he murmured.

'What are you going to do in the weeks to come?' I asked. 'Do you have plans?'

John hesitated for a moment, then took his hands from the keyboard, scratched his cheek and turned around slowly in his chair to face me.

'I think I'll spend some more time with my girlfriend and do more sports,' he said, rubbing the small mound under his T-shirt. 'I've gained a little weight in the past few weeks because of all the stress. This has to go.'

'Will you be watching any football, or have you had enough of it for the time being?' I asked.

'Enough of football?' he exclaimed. 'Are you crazy? I love this sport. No one can take that from me. No one. Now that I have more time, I'll be able to watch all the matches. Every game in the European Championship, and of course, the Champions League final. I hope Real win. I hope Cristiano Ronaldo shows everyone that he's the best football player of all time!'

The Golden Goal

By the end of May, the Champions League final was at hand. It was the biggest day in the club-football calendar. The showdown between Real Madrid and Atlético Madrid would be broadcast to an estimated 380 million people in two hundred countries around the world. There is no other sporting event like it on the planet, not even the Super Bowl.

The venue for the final was the San Siro in Milan. Tickets were going for upwards of €3,000 on the black market. Anyone who had wanted to obtain tickets legally had to have taken part in a UEFA lottery two months earlier. Those who won had no choice but to pay between €70 and €440 for tickets – without knowing whether their team was going to be in the final or not.

The Champions League final is more than just a football match; it's an event, a gigantic show, including an opening ceremony that this year would feature performances by Alicia Keys and Andrea Bocelli, one that's attended by hundreds of VIPs from the worlds of politics, business and entertainment who eat roast beef, drink champagne and network with one another in their luxury boxes. What does this have to do with football? The event in Milan took in €350 million, and the men who provide the action on the pitch want a piece of the business that's done behind the scenes.

Real and Atlético, two city rivals, were once again squaring off in a repeat of the 2014 final, which had been won by Real in extra time. The situation could hardly have been more dramatic. But there was little drama on the pitch. It was plain to see that the players weren't fresh after a long hard season. Never had the number of games been greater.

The match quickly developed into a war of attrition. After ninety minutes, things were level at 1–1, and no one was able to score in extra time, so the contest came down to penalties. This was football show business at its best. The cameras panned across the players' faces, showing their exhaustion. Some of them collapsed onto the ground while masseurs tried to rub the fatigue from their legs.

Cristiano Ronaldo, the superstar embodiment of Real Madrid, stood on the touchline with an empty gaze and an open mouth. He had been fairly invisible the entire evening – the relentless pressing Diego Simeone had instilled in his troops had taken him out of the game. Nonetheless, Ronaldo had volunteered to take the fifth – and often deciding – penalty. And of course, how could things happen any differently in a sport that lives on images and emotions? Atlético missed their second-to-last penalty, and the stage was set for CR7, the born leader.

Ronaldo once said that he loved situations of maximum pressure. He strode from the centre line to the penalty spot, his back stiff, the camera fixed upon him. Did he think in this moment how many millions were depending upon his penalty? How many people would be showered with money because of this one golden shot, amounts of money that most people won't earn in their entire lives?

The Football Leaks documents showed how tightly knit sporting and economic success are and what a difference a single penalty can make. How far removed is the world of a sports star from that of their fans? Real's Sergio Ramos earned a basic salary of €19.3 million for the 2015–16 season, Gareth Bale and Karim Benzema €10.9 million apiece, and it was rumoured in the Spanish press that every player on Real's squad would receive a €600,000 bonus for winning the Champions League. With a squad of twenty-five players, that totalled €15 million.

Ronaldo is a man not just for the big moments, but for the big contracts as well. At that point, his annual base wage was far higher than that of any other Real player – €33 million. And alone among his team, he would get a premium of €3.68 million for a Champions League victory. In his contract, this bonus was described as a 'variable payment'.

But even Ronaldo wasn't the one who stood to profit most if he converted the decisive penalty.

As the Portuguese forward stood at the spot, puffing out his cheeks and taking a deep breath, his manager watched anxiously from the touchline. Zinedine Zidane, the 1998 world champion and 2002 Champions League winner with Real, was a player for the ages. But as a manager, he was a rookie with barely three years of experience. In his first season, he had served as assistant coach to Carlo Ancelotti, and it wasn't until his third that he took over responsibility for Real – their B team, mind you.

When Rafael Benítez was fired during the 2015–16 season, Zidane's dream job suddenly became available. The contract he signed on 5 January 2016 might have given rise to the impression that Real had engaged a star manager and not a former star player – at least as far as the numbers in this seven-page document were concerned.

Zidane's contract ran for two and a half years, until the end of June 2018 – a lengthy span for a novice manager. Even more unusual was the size of his salary. Even as Ancelotti's assistant and manager of the B team, Zidane had negotiated the relatively princely sum of €600,000 a year. Now he was earning €3 million for his first six months until the end of June 2016, and €5,781,818 for each of the two following seasons. On top of that, he received the same bonuses the players got for victories and draws.

And that wasn't the end of it. Two clauses in the contract showed how important winning the Champions League was to Real. The team has defined itself for decades by how well it does in club football's premier competition. This global brand can only shine if the club regularly takes home this most coveted of trophies. Zidane profited from this like no one else. He stood to earn a €1.5 million bonus for a Champions League title, and should his team win the final in Milan, his wages for the following two seasons would be doubled. Suddenly, €5,781,818 a year could turn into €11,563,636.

So when Ronaldo approached the penalty spot, around €13 million was at stake for Zidane. The forward stood with his legs planted firmly apart, loosened his shoulders one final time, took a few short steps, shot and drilled the ball into the net. It was as though he had ice water in his veins.

Pandemonium. Zidane, too, was swept up in it. Never had a manager, to say nothing of one in his first season in charge, been able to turn the lustre of the Champions League into so much lucre with so little effort: when Zidane signed his contract, Real only had six matches to go before the final.

The icing on the evening's cake went to Zidane's predecessor, Benítez. When the Spaniard agreed in a three-page document to dissolve his contract with Real on 4 January 2016 in return for a settlement of €10.5 million, payable within a week, he knew what he was doing. In the small print, under point 3, there was a supplemental clause concerning the Champions League. It dictated that if the club were to win the title in May, Benítez would get an additional €600,000.

He, too, had reason to say a big thank-you to Ronaldo. The Portuguese superstar had caused €30 million in bonus money to be paid out with a single golden goal.

The Final Place of Refuge

I had seen John fairly frequently, sometimes for a day, sometimes for two, but rarely for longer. He was travelling a lot, sleeping and eating more, dancing and partying as if there were no tomorrow. John enjoyed life, and having put Football Leaks on temporary hold, he was able to do that again. It was the end of June, and his fears that private detectives, hitmen or other shadowy figures were trying to do him in had receded.

He talked with me a lot about what was in the Football Leaks documents, about football in general and about dealing in antiques. He kept a close eye on new auctions and was constantly mulling over what bids to make. Every once in a while, he would hand over new hard drives. I had no clue how or from where he had got hold of the material. Sometimes the hard drives were black, sometimes white. Sometimes they contained more material, sometimes less. Sometimes their content complemented the documents we already had, sometimes the material was completely new.

While my colleagues delved into the data, making one discovery after the next, I had to take a break from the safe room for a couple of weeks. Along with meeting John, I was going to France to report on the European Championship. Long before the Football Leaks project, I had agreed to cover the tournament. I had been reporting on the German national team for ten years. I couldn't very well abandon that just because I found Football Leaks more exciting.

I was tugged in two directions. On the one hand, I was writing reports on the performances of Mario Götze, Thomas Müller and Julian Draxler; on the other, I was calling my colleagues every day and hearing about the fascinating stories beginning to emerge from the data. My curiosity and willingness to dig around in the documents knew no bounds.

The most important thing in this phase was to resist the temptation to publish stories based on the material. For example, at the beginning of the Euros, Alexander Gauland of the xenophobic right-wing political party Alternative for Germany insulted Germany's half-Ghanaian defender Jérôme Boateng by saying few Germans would want him as a neighbour. Gauland's remark was unbelievably crass and ignorant, but all of Germany was talking about it nonetheless. A few weeks earlier, we had searched for Boateng in our database, and the system had coughed up an interesting match. It was hardly a newsflash, but it did illustrate that racism was not confined to right-wing political parties.

Around six months before the start of the 2014 World Cup in Brazil, a marketing agency offered a major German sponsor several German internationals for an advertising campaign promoting a product in south-east Asian countries including China, Thailand, Indonesia, Vietnam, South Korea and the Philippines. A representative of the sponsor showed interest, and the agency suggested six players. Five were white, and one was dark-skinned. 'Please take Jerome Boateng off the list, the rest reads fine,' wrote the sponsor's marketing man.

We discussed whether we should research the story further and publish it, but ultimately decided not to use it just then. For starters, we would have had to reveal that the EIC was working on the Football Leaks information, and it would also have opened the floodgates for all of our partners to use the data to write stories about players, functionaries and topics specific to their own home countries. We would lose control over the data and, ultimately, the project itself. So we let the Boateng story pass. We would later do the same with material concerning Henrikh Mkhitaryan, Paul Pogba, Mario Balotelli and, repeatedly, Cristiano Ronaldo. Our daily mantra became: Keep cool – we're going public big time in December. We accepted the risk that other outlets would beat us to the odd story, but we hoped that our big scoop would ultimately justify our approach.

But while I felt torn inside, I had to recognise that it was good to get some distance from the research. I was in a stadium in Paris watching Northern Ireland play Germany. It was the teams' final match of the group stage, and it was excruciatingly boring. The poor Northern Irish were doing what underdogs in this tournament always do: parking the bus and hoping that God, Lady Luck or a misplaced Mats Hummels foot would gift them a miracle. It was their only chance of scoring. The encounter was an exercise in tedium, not a game of football – typical of an overblown, over-marketed tournament that yielded few highlights.

After half an hour, the outcome was already decided. Mario Gómez scored what would be the sole goal of the match, and everyone knew that Germany were certs to win this game and their group. By the middle of the second half, my mind began to wander. I looked around the stadium, watching as the fans cheered and waved their scarves. In the Northern Irish section, the mood was carnival-like. Supporters were singing 'Will Grigg's on fire' over and over, with even the German fans joining in. While down on the pitch twenty-two players were running around sweating, the supporters were transforming this sporting farce into an open-air festival that was loud, colourful and heartening.

People had travelled hundreds, even thousands of kilometres to buy grotesquely overpriced tickets, kits, hot dogs, beer and caps and to sing together at a completely superfluous match. I asked myself: How would our revelations about the rapacious, greedy, often corrupt and almost always hypocritical business of football affect these fans? Would they be disappointed in their heroes? Furious? Would they turn their backs on the sport and refuse to finance it any more? Was credibility even important to them at all?

Football had been ruled for years by godfather-like figures: João Havelange, Sepp Blatter, Horst Dassler and all their spiritual brothers who followed – the Chuck Blazers, Jack Warners, Franz Beckenbauers, countless agents, investors and fools of fortune of all stripes. Anyone whose eyes weren't completely shut would have suspected how mendacious, corrupt and exploitative the industry was, how it lined its own pockets at the expense of fans and even whole countries. The system of football had been sick for quite some time, but only now could we see just *how* sick it was.

And yet, despite all of FIFA's corruption scandals, allegations that Germany paid bribes to get the 2006 World Cup, and cases of match fixing, people pack stadiums, bars and public viewing areas week after week to support their favourite players and teams – and to drink, sing and celebrate together. Every Monday, they tell their co-workers how great the weekend was. And they do this not just in Germany, England and France but in many, many other countries around the world.

Do these people even want us journalists to pester them with reality? Football may very well be the final connecting element that brings together diverse groups in our society. Football matches unite people across all professions, cultures and genders in their wishes and hopes. At a football match, an otherwise polite person can call the opponents arseholes with complete impunity. He can lose his temper and get completely emotionally carried away without anyone taking offence. Do football fans want this final place of refuge to be stripped from them? Do they even want to understand that a rapacious industry is exploiting their desire for pathos and emotion? That they're being systematically taken for a ride?

The Football Romantic

It was the semi-finals. The Euros were drawing to a close. Germany were going up against France in Marseille the day after Portugal played Wales. My mobile phone was blinking constantly. John was out of control. An online insurgent he may be, but more than anything else he's a football fan and, despite all his criticism of his native country, a patriot. He was continually sending me messages, YouTube videos of Portuguese fans and Photoshopped images of Portuguese national team players wearing crowns. In short, he was showing all the enthusiasm and creativity that all true-believing supporters pour out on the Internet.

'If Germany and Portugal make it to the final, we'll meet up in France,' John wrote.

'Is that a good idea?' I wrote back. 'It's possible the police are looking for you.' After all, investigations into Football Leaks were ongoing, and a request for legal assistance had been issued.

'I don't care,' John responded. 'You don't get to experience this sort of thing more than once in a lifetime. Portugal are going to be European champions. I told you that weeks ago!'

That was true. He had predicted Portugal versus France in the final, while I thought Poland would meet Germany. After Portugal sent Poland out of the tournament, I'd had to endure a lot of teasing.

'The tickets are very expensive,' he wrote. 'I'll have to get creative.'

John had watched almost every match of the tournament on television, as many as three games a day. Usually, he had gone out in the city with friends to watch the evening fixture. At 3 p.m., shortly before the early match began, he took a shower and then watched the game in bed with a bowl of granola.

'It's great right now,' he wrote. 'It's warm here, the sun is shining and all I'm doing is chilling out. I feel good. Life is beautiful again.'

Nonetheless, he was ready now for some adventure and wanted to come to France. I was worried that John could be arrested: at major events like the European Championship, security is at its highest level, especially for people wanting to enter the host country from abroad. If he were taken into custody, it would not only have drastic consequences for him, it would also endanger our whole project.

'The prices for hotels and flights are insanely high,' I wrote.

'That's true,' he responded. 'I'll have to see. But it would be fantastic. There's a large Portuguese community in Paris, and I'd love to celebrate this historic triumph with them.'

Portugal did indeed win their match and were now in the final. John wrote in the middle of that night that he couldn't party hard enough to express how happy he was. He was a hopeless football romantic, someone who had come to know and hate the dirty side of the industry but still loved the game itself with all his heart.

That evening, I sat in the stadium in Marseille and watched Germany get overpowered by France. They were out of the tournament. It was time to say adieu.

'Cheer up, my friend,' John wrote to me. 'After all, you Germans are still world champs. But now you must support Portugal. You owe me that much.'

It was nice to experience him being so carefree again.

The next morning, I flew to Paris for the final on Air France, a carrier I will scrupulously avoid in future. In addition to delays and cancellations, they also managed to lose my bag. I wouldn't see it again for weeks. To make matters worse, I had eaten something bad or picked up some sort of virus. My stomach was doing flip-flops. So I was doubly relieved when John wrote that he wouldn't be coming to Paris – the trip was just too expensive. At least I'd received one bit of good news that day.

We chatted a lot before the final. He explained – or so he thought anyway – Portugal's tactics and the precise weak spots in the French team. When we were engaged in conversations like this, the complicated encryption and absolute confidentiality we maintained seemed a bit absurd. Before I opened my email programme, I had to turn on an authenticator, a kind of password generator that provided random codes. It was for opening two different 'doors' I had to pass through before I could write a message. It often took several minutes just to log on. By that point, I had three separate apps that either generated passwords or saved them for me, since I was unable to remember the whole jumble of numbers, symbols and letters I was required to use. And all that effort went into shielding bits of footballing wisdom like the following:

'Renato Sanches has to exploit the space between Pogba and Matuidi. You Germans didn't see it.'

'Pepe is too slow to keep up with Griezmann. Things are going to get hot for you in the middle of the pitch.'

If an intelligence service or police force were reading our chats, I hoped that they would have a lot of fun analysing our conversations.

Portugal, the Kings of Europe

Cristiano Ronaldo was beside himself. Completely beside himself. The superstar stripped off his shirt and hopped on one leg across the pitch, unable to put any weight on the knee he had injured in the final. Ronaldo had only played for a few minutes. Afterwards he had suffered along with his teammates, experiencing the sort of passion felt only by those who share a dream – the dream of becoming European champions.

Ronaldo directed the team, yelling and arguing with his teammates as they subdued hosts France. Now, after the final whistle, this exceptional superstar was weeping with joy, embracing and shaking the shoulders of everyone who came his way. Ronaldo had achieved his lifelong goal of winning a major international title with his homeland. He was the king of Europe. It was already clear that he would go on to win all of football's big awards that year.

But to me it was also clear that our revelations about Ronaldo's secret – his diversion of many millions of euros to the British Virgin Islands – would tarnish his image as a hero. I could already see the evidence accruing on our internal platform. Every victory he achieved only increased the height of the fall to come.

I looked down at my mobile phone.

'This is one of the best days of my life! *Campeões!*'

John was going berserk. He kept messaging me the entire night. He wrote that he had cried for the first time in longer than he could remember. How could someone who loved football that much, I asked myself, have the courage to take on the industry the way he did? Maybe precisely for that reason? He remained a mystery to me.

4.32 a.m.: 'I'm out of my head! We're going to party for 24 hours!'

4.41 a.m.: 'When I'm sober again, you have to come visit me. I have to show you something.'

The next morning, I called my bosses. I was running a fever. Damn stomach. And thanks to Air France I no longer had any clean socks either.

The tournament had taken its toll on us reporters as well. I felt written out after all those weeks. All I wanted to do was sleep. My department head, Michael Wulzinger, said I should take an extra day, lie around in bed and take a walk around Paris to clear my head. But then I should think about visiting John.

Naturally.

I booked my flight the next day. I left the return leg open.

A Nice Tan and a Good Mood

Back in Eastern Europe. Another big city. It was well above 30 degrees Celsius. On the way to my rented flat, I went past a gigantic river. There were lots of people on its banks, barbecuing, playing Frisbee and splashing around with inflatable rubber lifesavers. But even these idyllic scenes couldn't stop my stomach cramps. I crawled into bed.

Hardly had I fallen asleep when a knock came at my door. The first and only time that John was on time, and it had to be today. He skipped across the doorstep, and we hugged. He was very tanned. Apparently, he had done a lot of sport in addition to partying. His shoulders were broader, and his arms looked more muscular. And his eyes were full of mischief again, gleaming with new energy.

Over breakfast – chocolate cake and lemonade for John, lemon tea without sugar for me – he told me what he had been up to over the past few weeks. And with whom. It was like listening to the Great Gatsby. John's stories were wild, adventurous and exciting. For the first time, he mentioned friends by name and told me I had to meet them.

'Do they have anything to do with our project?' I asked.

'Quit it,' he said, and laughed.

It was hopeless trying to find out exactly who or what Football Leaks was.

John said he had new material for me. Very exciting material. He had to give it to me personally, otherwise there was a chance we would miss some crucial connections. The new information was about the Premier League and players represented by Mino Raiola. Zlatan Ibrahimović's contract, for example. It was unbelievable how the English threw money around. My stomach instantly felt better.

'But before we get to that, we have to take care of something,' he said.

'Please, no more antiques,' I answered.

'Of course more antiques!' he replied. 'Come, we have to go!'

'You're going to be sorry if there's a lift,' I warned him.

We took a taxi for almost two hours, until we reached a kind of allotment-garden colony. Tiny houses with flat roofs, miniscule lawns surrounded by tall fences. A lot of children screaming. John walked along a narrow street, examining the doorbells and letterboxes. He stopped abruptly and motioned windmill-like for me to come to him. We rang the bell. A little girl, no more than four years old, approached the green fence, whose paint was peeling off in plate-sized chunks in some places.

'Is your father at home?' asked John.

The girl stared in confusion. John tried again, this time not in English. The girl shook her head. John asked again. Now the girl nodded and ran back into the house. John looked at me triumphantly, as though he had just cracked the da Vinci code. A few minutes later, a wrinkled old woman in a headscarf came out. Her words sounded as if she were berating us. I flinched, but John just nodded. We were still on the other side of the fence. The old lady went back into the house. John no longer seemed so sure of himself.

'Do we have the right address?' I asked.

'We'll see soon,' John answered, never taking his eyes from the door.

The little girl came back out dragging a bag. Suddenly, John began to fidget with his hands and shout, jumping from one foot to the other. The old lady said something to the girl, and she stopped.

'Oh man, she's going to break it,' John groaned.

He slowly opened the gate, and we headed up a path so narrow we had to go one after the other. The girl with the bag waited. John stopped in front of her, took two white gloves from his backpack and put them on, very seriously. He started to inspect the bag's contents.

'Hold it up for me,' he commanded.

I held the bag up, and he removed an old banner, two dozen books, an amulet, then another one that could be opened, and an undefinable little bottle. John wrapped each of these items in felt cloth and put them in his backpack. The old lady looked at us as though she were being visited by aliens. I must have looked at her the same way. John paid her, and we left.

'Who wants to buy junk like that?' I asked.

'You have no clue,' John told me. 'The people who sold me these items also have no clue. I've increased my money tenfold in a few minutes. Items like these are in great demand. Oligarchs, Arabs and, above all, the Chinese are mad for well-preserved historical collectibles. The market is huge.'

Well, at least John had a calling he could live from.

We drove back to the city. This time, he took me to a

kind of warehouse. The space wasn't gigantic, but there was enough room for hundreds of books, LPs, photo albums, candlesticks, amulets and swords. I seem to remember a suit of armour in one corner, but I could be mistaken. The place looked like a medieval flea market.

Along one wall, to the right of a bed and a closet, was a computer. Otherwise, it was just antiques as far as the eye could see. There was even a kitchen in this storage space, which consisted of a number of rooms. It was like a labyrinth. John crawled on all fours under a table and fumbled with a switch. When he re-emerged, he had two hard drives.

Here was all the stuff from the Premier League, he said. They were truly insane. I should just look at the contract Raiola had been able to negotiate for Ibrahimović. Unbelievable! He told me that I would also find information about a Dutch–Argentinian clique of agents who were evading taxes. It would help me better understand their system. In a few weeks, he'd give me a further cache of Premier League data, including the record-setting contract for Paul Pogba. Another Raiola client.

The Big Payday

On 1 July 2016, when Manchester United announced that they were signing Zlatan Ibrahimović, it was no longer news. Ibrahimović himself had announced his own signing the day before. 'Time to let the world know. My next destination is @manunited,' the striker had tweeted on 30 June. Ibrahimović seemed uninterested in the fact that his contract with England's most successful club would only be made official the following day. The Swedish striker isn't the type to be told when he can say something, particularly not by the suits at the PR department of a new club.

In the summer of 2016, Ibrahimović was one of the hottest properties on the international transfer market. He may have been thirty-four years old, but he seemed to have lost none of his ability. In his final season with Paris Saint-Germain, he had scored fifty goals in fifty-one matches. It was the third time in a row he had been the leading scorer in Ligue 1. More important, however, was the fact that Ibrahimović was eligible to move on a free transfer. He had run down his contract in Paris, dramatically improving his negotiating position. A player who costs nothing in transfer fees can demand bigger signing-on bonuses and a higher base salary. There are few hard and fast rules in contract negotiations in football, but this one is chiselled in stone.

One month before Ibrahimović's transfer, Raiola, who

had been his agent since the very start of his career, had remarked to Italy's *Gazzetta dello Sport* that he had been contacted by all the big clubs in Europe, with the exception of Pep Guardiola's Manchester City. This is the sort of gossip of which Raiola is a master. A little seeding of the clouds can cause a huge downpour. And if you can get in a dig at one of your enemies, so much the better. Back when he was manager of Barcelona, Guardiola had sent Ibrahimović packing to AC Milan, and ever since, the striker had considered the coach a man who thinks small. 'When you buy me, you are buying a Ferrari,' Ibrahimović once said. 'If you drive a Ferrari, you put premium petrol in the tank, you hit the motorway and you step on the gas. Guardiola filled it up with diesel and took a spin in the countryside. He should have bought a Fiat.' Ibrahimović, who has been known to refer to himself as 'God', doesn't lack self-belief.

Now the Swedish superstar had ended up with Manchester United and José Mourinho. Ibrahimović knew the manager from his stint at Milan's other club, Inter, and had nothing but praise for him. 'Mourinho is Guardiola's opposite,' he said, adding that the manager was 'basically a guy I was willing to die for'.

The question was: What was Ibrahimović's affectation worth to Manchester United and Mourinho? The rumours about his annual salary started to fly the moment he set foot in England. There was talk of the striker earning €235,000 a week, more than his then teammate Wayne Rooney, who was previously the highest-paid player in the country.

Guessing who earns what has become an integral part of the highly artificial and stylised entertainment business that is the Premier League. People are constantly drawing up lists ranking the most famous players by salary. The billions the league earns in TV revenues, together with the money provided by global investors, ensure that clubs will continue to try to attract the world's best players with record offers. As a result, salaries are going through the roof.

Ibrahimović's contract illustrated the financial excesses and absurdities of a league gone money-mad. The agreement signed by the player and the club on 1 July 2016, which ran until 30 June 2017, guaranteed Ibrahimović a basic wage of €22.62 million a year. The Football Leaks documents contained many other contracts signed by world stars – for instance, Ibrahimović's teammates Paul Pogba and Henrikh Mkhitaryan, Manchester City's Sergio Agüero and Arsenal's Mesut Özil – with Premier League clubs, but none approached the sums that Raiola negotiated for the striker.

Manchester United's agreement with Ibrahimović ran to thirty-six pages. From page 19 onwards it dealt with interesting 'additional clauses', such as goal and assist bonuses that paid the striker extra for doing his main job. A lot extra. Ibrahimović received €280,000 for his first five goals or assists, for numbers six through ten €470,000, for numbers eleven to fifteen €660,000, for numbers sixteen through twenty €850,000, for numbers twenty-one through thirty-five €1.13 million, and for numbers thirty-six through forty €2.27 million. The bonuses went all the way up to forty goals. In fact, Ibrahimović scored twenty-eight times and made ten assists in the 2016–17 season, earning himself an extra €3.39 million.

On the same page as Ibrahimović's basic wage was set, the contract contained a passage stating that at thirty-five years of age a player would 'normally' retire from football, which meant that the contract ended on 30 June 2017. However, the agreement would automatically be extended if the striker started thirty-one games in the Premier League season and Manchester United qualified for the Champions League. A knee injury prevented him from making the requisite number of appearances, but the Swede impressed the club with his speedy rehabilitation and in August 2017 was offered a new one-year contract.

Manchester United invested huge sums of money to get back into the Champions League and return to their title-winning form of the early years of the new millennium. Ibrahimović was only the beginning – if a particularly spectacular one. Other massively expensive new acquisitions included Romelu Lukaku and Pogba, who set a short-lived record for the world's most expensive transfer and whose contract was also full of secret clauses and strange details.

The Captive

In August 2016, a few days before Paul Pogba briefly became the world's most expensive football player, commanding a transfer fee of €105 million, he posted a photo on Instagram. It showed him sitting in a pool with his chest emerging from the water. He was smiling at a man with a white beer belly protruding over his red bathing trunks. Mino Raiola, Pogba's agent, was enjoying the moment. Both men were laughing.

In the photo, the two also looked relieved. Previously unknown documents, mostly from the Football Leaks cache, revealed the extent of the problems they had faced only a few weeks before.

In 2006, Pogba had met Oualid Tanazefti, a scout for the French club Le Havre. The two were very similar. Both came from poor backgrounds, and both were clever fellows who wanted to make something of themselves. Tanazefti got Pogba accepted into the Le Havre youth set-up. Two years later, he accompanied the player to England, as Pogba transferred to Manchester United's youth team.

'Sometimes it was difficult because we didn't have enough money,' Tanazefti recalled about that time in Manchester in his book *The Secrets of the Market*. On top of that, Pogba only had moderate sporting success in England, which may be why the two turned to Raiola for help. The Italian-born Dutch agent is one of the most influential movers and shakers in the industry, someone who has earned dozens of millions with his top stars. Raiola organised a transfer to Juventus for Pogba, where the nineteen-year-old midfielder blossomed, winning four Serie A titles and reaching the final of the Champions League.

Raiola has a great talent for creating sporting fairy tales, and he knows what they're worth. During Pogba's time in Italy, Juventus reported that they paid the agent €10.5 million for his services as a consultant. Meanwhile, Tanazefti was on the way out. He was allowed to accompany the burgeoning star to Italy, but he soon noticed that the young French international was growing closer and closer to Raiola.

So Tanazefti and a pal of his named Ylli Kullashi came up with an idea. Together they convinced Pogba to sell them his image rights, drawing up a contract that was pure exploitation. The agreement, dated 5 November 2014, was lifelong, could not be rescinded and was written almost entirely to Pogba's detriment. It stipulated that the two advisors were allowed to invest all income from Pogba's advertising rights. It would have taken Pogba fifteen years to see anything like a return on the marketing of his image. At that point, he would have received 70 per cent of the total revenue.

Shortly after this deal, Tanazefti and Kullashi founded a company called the Koyoz Group in the tax haven of Luxembourg. Pogba had signed up to a kind of indentured servitude. For many clubs, advertising contracts are just as important as a player's sporting abilities. They are additional sources of income. No top club would ever buy a player without a guarantee that it can use him for advertising. Pogba's deal with Tanazefti and Kullashi therefore put his own career development at risk. Once Raiola got wind of that deal, it was the start of a war between attorneys, which meant that Pogba's image rights were temporarily blocked. No one was able to earn any money with him, and the player was unable to leave Juventus in summer 2015, even though he had plenty of suitors.

Tanazefti tried to resolve the situation by offering Pogba's image rights to sports marketers. The Football Leaks cache revealed that he had contacted Doyen in late 2015. After being given the cold shoulder there, he turned to the Chinese company Fosun. They too demurred. In the end, Raiola seems to have found a solution. According to French newspaper *L'Équipe*, Tanazefti and Kullashi were paid €5 million each to release Pogba from the contract. Who paid the money? That remained unclear.

What was clear from the Football Leaks documents was that Raiola earned a fortune from Pogba's transfer to the Premier League and that the money came in from all sides. In the summer of 2016, when the midfielder returned to Manchester, Raiola and his London company Topscore Sports received €27 million of the €105 million transfer fee. That was the subject of a six-page agreement signed by Juventus director general Giuseppe Marotta and Raiola on 20 July 2016, three weeks before Pogba signed his new deal with Manchester United.

On 8 August, for his services in the Pogba transfer Raiola signed a deal with Manchester United worth €19.4 million, payable in five instalments by the end of September 2020. Pogba himself also had to pay Raiola: the club transferred €2.6 million on the player's behalf to Raiola's agency Uuniqq Sarl, which is based in the tax haven of Monaco. All told that made €49 million for a single transfer. When we asked Raiola for a statement, he forwarded our letter on to his attorney in Manchester, who replied that his client was 'fiercely protective of his reputation' and 'prepared to take whatever action is necessary to protect himself'.

The attorney's letter accused us of asking maliciously leading questions about the episode with Tanazefti and Kullashi, and of waging a smear campaign against agents and leading football personalities. Kullashi didn't respond to repeated requests for a statement. Tanazefti replied that our assertions were false or taken out of context, and he pointed out that in his thirteen years in the football business, he's never once been taken to court. He, too, threatened legal action, if his reputation were tarnished.

Such threats did nothing to dispel our many questions. Above all, why do Pogba's image rights now seem to be held in a tax haven? Several of the Football Leaks documents concerned a complex construction of companies that had an interest in those rights. Initially, they went to a company called Blue Brands Ltd in Ireland. They were then transferred to a firm named Aftermath Ltd, which was founded on 4 February 2016, about a month before Pogba inked a multimillion-euro deal with Adidas. The sportswear giant, as usual, has refused to answer any questions on this score.

Did the millions that Manchester United paid for Pogba's commercial rights also go to Aftermath? On 8 August 2016, the world's then most expensive player signed a Premier League contract with United. It was forty-one pages long, and that wasn't the only reason it deserved the appellation 'monster contract'. According to the deal, the French international tied himself to the club for five years on a basic wage starting at £8,610,616. That decreased to £7.5 million as of the 2017–18 season, but other incentives kicked in, including annual loyalty payments of €4,098,774 in 2017 rising to €4,479,200 thereafter.

Then there were the contingent bonuses. If Pogba were voted footballer of the year, he stood to earn a rise in salary of £980,393. If United qualified for the Champions League, which they did, he earned an additional £1,875,000 a season. Should the club win the Premier League title, his base salary would also be increased by £490,196. Add to that the 'commercial rights', as they are known in the contract: in the 2016–17 season, United paid £2,870,205 for their use. And because the club qualified for the Champions League, Pogba received £3,125,000 for the following campaign.

Actually, that's not entirely accurate. These payments probably didn't go to the player himself, but rather to other companies he was involved with. It was unclear from the contract whether Aftermath Ltd, which is located in Jersey, was one of those firms or not.

The Partners

It was autumn, and we were stuck. We had dug into the labyrinth of companies associated with the Dutch–Argentinian
clique of agents, but Cristiano Ronaldo's case had proven
a particularly difficult nut to crack. The networks of firms
were tightly interwoven and hard to disentangle, and we
had trouble following the flow of money. We were consulting lawyers, tax advisors and experts on international tax
law. There was a large whiteboard in our safe room covered
in the names of companies, funds, countries and people
who had cropped up in conjunction with the Ronaldo
millions. If you took a step back, it looked like a work of
abstract art.

The team had grown fatigued, exhausted even. The
research was eating away at us. We spent every day together,
sometimes making no progress at all. Often we lacked
pieces of the puzzle because certain documents weren't in
our cache of data. Or we uncovered contradictions, tempo-
ral discontinuities or dubious statements made in emails.
But we refused to get discouraged. On the contrary: our
small circle, which included deputy editor-in-chief Alfred
Weinzierl, investigative features reporter Andreas Meyhoff
and our IT expert Stephan Heffner, met every morning at
9.15 a.m. to discuss our progress and setbacks, our theses,
theories and, above all, the evidence. We collected all the

unanswered questions, made note of any problems and tried
to develop plans of action.

At this point, we were focusing on a joint trip to Lisbon
for the next EIC meeting. It was hosted by our partner in
Portugal, *Expresso*, and would be four very intense days.
It was going to be one of the most crucial meetings of the
project, and it was set to be held in the birthplace of our
whistle-blower. We needed to be particularly on our guard.
Football Leaks was the subject of an official criminal investigation in Portugal, and we had no way of determining what
the authorities there already knew.

We met early in the morning in *Expresso's* conference
room. The basics of our publishing plans – the larger topics
and the timing – had been decided upon. Now it was time
to determine precisely how to proceed and coordinate the
content. By that point, more than a hundred people were
involved in the research, including some sixty journalists.
We needed a clear strategy to keep the project from spinning out of control.

We discussed our problems and questions, considered
potential legal difficulties and examined the weak points
in our arguments. Where were we vulnerable? Were we
interpreting too much and proving too little? Where should
we back off? We argued. Our discussions were hard-fought
but always aimed at clear goals. In the end, all of the EIC
partners had to be as satisfied as possible with what we
published, and we couldn't afford to make any mistakes.
Since it dealt with issues like tax fairness, Football Leaks
was an ethically loaded project. Each and every mistake
would undermine our credibility, and our adversaries
would be quick to look for blunders. Everything we printed

had to be double- and treble-checked, including our main source.

On the final day of meetings, the discussion heated up once more. In our data, several email exchanges had emerged that suddenly cast a different light on Football Leaks, one in which it appeared less like an altruistic platform for transparency and more a means of self-enrichment. At issue was an alleged act of blackmail.

The charge that Football leaks had tried to blackmail people wasn't new. Doyen had made it almost a year previously. But the correspondence we found amidst the material made the accusations seem more concrete. Our colleagues wanted an answer to these charges. All we could say was that we had asked John numerous times about them and he had said the accusations were laughable. So how should we deal with this problem? Why would John have left these documents in the material he gave us if they could potentially discredit him and his project? Had he overlooked them? Did he want us to find them? We didn't know what to think.

Ultimately, we agreed on two points. Firstly, the material we had received was genuine and important, so we decided to publish the contents, regardless of the credibility or possible occasional unreliability of the source. Secondly, we would confront John with all the emails concerning the alleged attempt at blackmail, just as we did with Ronaldo, Mendes, Mourinho and all the other subjects of our exposés.

At the end of the meeting, we returned to a couple of stories that we'd been working on for some time and which we considered thoroughly researched and ready to be finished up. They concerned China, the new promised land for ageing football stars looking for one final big payday, and Croatia and Serbia, a true hell for young players, who were ruthlessly exploited by club bosses.

On the Silk Road

Ezequiel Iván Lavezzi's career went the same way as that of many footballers who make the move from Argentina to Europe. Successful? Yes. Stellar? No.

In 2007, the striker transferred from Buenos Aires club CA San Lorenzo to Napoli. He played for five years in Italy, scoring thirty-eight goals in 156 matches, before moving to Paris Saint-Germain. Lavezzi even made it into the Argentinian national team, but he lost his biggest match playing alongside Lionel Messi: the 2014 World Cup final against Germany. After that, things in Paris didn't go well. More and more often, Lavezzi was left out of the starting eleven, which didn't do anything for his general outlook. He was accused of having 'motivation problems'.

Then came 10 February 2016, when the thirty-year-old agreed a new contract with Chinese first-division club Hebei China Fortune. Once Lavezzi had scrawled his signature on page 21 of the document, the veteran striker was suddenly the highest-paid football player in the world. His contract with the Chinese Super League club ran until 31 December 2017. His salary for just under two years was $56.7 million. Net.

There were a couple of remarkable details to be found under paragraph 5. Lavezzi would be paid $6.7 million of his net wage as a 'signing on fee'. This one-off payment, together with a further $20 million net, was due within nine days at Lavezzi's bank Unicredit, in the tax haven of Luxembourg. The $26.7 million advance was a prerequisite for Lavezzi even making the trip to his new employer in Qinhuangdao, a port city of almost three million people around 300 kilometres east of Beijing. The Argentinian had signed the contract in Paris. He received the remaining $30 million in twenty-two monthly instalments of $1,363,636. He was earning $45,455 a day. $1,894 an hour. $32 a minute. 53 cents every second.

Lavezzi's contract is a document of insanity. Neither Lionel Messi nor Cristiano Ronaldo, the two top footballers in the world, earned the most money from their contracts in 2016. Nor did Zlatan Ibrahimović or Paul Pogba in the Premier League. No, the best-paid player in the world was a doddering striker plying his trade for a team from China that was barely known in Europe. How could that be possible?

In spring 2015, Chinese state premier and Communist Party leader Xi Jinping ordered the 'resuscitation of Chinese football'. The country's most powerful man was sending a clear message: China, which produced world champions in individual sports as though from an assembly line, was also to become a superpower in football. Xi decreed that youth academies should be built throughout the country and hundreds of thousands of kids and young people evaluated and trained. The top division of Chinese football, the Super League, which had previously only generated headlines because of its connection to the betting mafia, was to be thoroughly reformed. Xi also devoted his attention to the national team. At the time China occupied eighty-second place in FIFA's world rankings, behind Equatorial Guinea,

Haiti and Uzbekistan. In the eyes of the head of the Chinese state, that was a disgrace. He dreamed not only of China qualifying for its first World Cup since 2002, but of the country hosting the tournament. And some day winning it.

Xi's reanimation of football in China and his promotion of the sport as a national duty removed most of the constraints upon the Chinese market. The clubs are backed by the bosses of the most important Chinese real-estate, construction, consumer-goods and e-commerce companies, most of whom are billionaires. They constantly try to outdo one another, be it in marketing the sport or investing in individuals. As a result, the price for broadcast rights to the Super League increased twentyfold overnight. For the years 2016 to 2020, the TV broadcaster China Sports Media is to pay the sixteen clubs in the Super League around $1.2 billion, compared with €60 million for the same period of time prior to 2016. The transfer fees for foreign players have also risen in commensurately absurd fashion. Ahead of the 2016 season, Chinese clubs spent more on transfers than even the teams in the Premier League.

Nor has the drive for expansion among the nouveau riche Chinese economic elite been limited to the domestic football market. In 2016, the Chinese electronics company Suning, which is partially owned by Internet giant Alibaba, bought a 69 per cent share in Inter Milan for €270 million. At almost the same time, former Italian prime minister Silvio Berlusconi sold off almost his entire stake in his favourite club, AC Milan, to Chinese investors. The anti-communist Berlusconi had no qualms about the new club owners – among them the Chinese state investment company Haixia Capital – after they valued Milan at €740 million.

The Fosun investment group took over English Championship club Wolverhampton Wanderers. Previously, Birmingham City and Aston Villa had come under Chinese control, and Chinese investors also procured a stake in Sparta Prague. Wang Jianlin, the head of the Wanda Group conglomerate, acquired shares of Atlético Madrid, and Wang also took over the Swiss firm Infront, which owns television and marketing rights for the World Cup. This was a strategical masterpiece that secured the Chinese billionaire not only influence over FIFA, but the favour of Xi Jinping, who will no doubt look favourably upon Wang's entrepreneurial ambitions in his own country.

You can safely say that the Chinese aren't kidding around. They've spread out their investments strategically and have purchased positions of power in almost all of football's core areas. Such networks and enhanced influence on those pulling the strings in elite European football, together with lots and lots of money, have allowed the Chinese to persuade increasing numbers of superstars – not all of them past their prime – to join their own domestic league.

In summer 2012, Didier Drogba was an exception when he transferred from Chelsea to Shanghai Shenhua. Today, stars like Brazilian midfielder Alex Teixeira, who moved in early 2016 from Shakhtar Donetsk to Jiangsu Suning for €50 million, are becoming the rule. Quickly following in Teixeira's footsteps was Colombian striker Jackson Martínez, who in spring 2016 went from Atlético Madrid to the Chinese champions Guangzhou Evergrande for €42 million.

The Football Leaks documents contain copious material concerning these and other Chinese deals. There are transfer agreements, employment contracts, payment receipts and internal email correspondence.

Drogba, who had led Chelsea to victory in the Champions League final over Bayern Munich a few weeks before transferring to China, arrived in Shanghai on 1 July 2012. The untidy numbers in his contract, which was written in Chinese and English, set his salary at 20 million renminbi a month net. Under the exchange rate at the time, that was around €30 million a year. The transfer seems to have been a win–win for both Drogba and Chelsea: the club got the thirty-four-year-old striker off its books, and the player was able to treble his already exorbitant wages.

By contrast, Martínez only earns around €10 million annually at multiple domestic title winners Guangzhou. That's roughly what Toni Kroos got after his last pay rise at Real Madrid. But Atlético didn't resist attempts to lure the striker away from the club for a single minute. The transfer was a great deal for the team, which received €42 million for the Colombian. According to the contract, Guangzhou promised to transfer the entire transfer fee within a month to Atlético's account at Banco Santander in Madrid. That was very welcome – as a rule, clubs usually pay even transfer fees in the low millions in instalments.

Shakhtar Donetsk were likewise thrilled when Chinese first-division team Jiangsu Suning bought Alex Teixeira out of his contract for €50 million in early 2016. In an email, Shakhtar's top attorney set out the conditions of the sale: €25 million would have to be transferred to a team account with Alfa Bank in Kiev, while the remaining €25 million was payable in three instalments of €8,333,333 each by the end of the year. The Chinese quickly agreed to those terms and the deal was done. 'Dear Brooky,' the Ukrainian attorney later wrote to his Chinese counterpart at Jiangsu Suning, 'congratulations with the biggest transfer in China ever!'

European attitudes towards Chinese partners are no longer so enthusiastic. Before 2016, the Chinese had only dared approach top European clubs with inquiries about players who were approaching the end of their careers or were replaceable, players like Drogba, Martínez or Teixeira. But that changed, and the Super League began trying to lure stars in the prime of their careers who were on the shopping lists of other top European clubs. Players like Axel Witsel.

The Belgian international, who played for Zenit St Petersburg, was a player Juventus had set its sights on. But in early 2017, the twenty-eight-year-old unexpectedly went to Tianjin Quanjian. 'It was a very difficult decision because on the one hand there was a huge, top club,' he said, as though it were incumbent upon him to justify turning down Juventus. 'But on the other hand there was an irresistible offer for the future of my family.'

Even the biggest spenders in the Premier League cannot always trump the lucrative bids coming from China. In mid-December 2016, when Chelsea announced the €60 million transfer of Brazilian international Oscar to Shanghai SIPG, the Blues' manager Antonio Conte sounded the alarm. 'The Chinese market is a danger for all,' said Conte. 'Not only for Chelsea, but all the teams in the world.' Uli Hoeness, the chairman of Bayern Munich's supervisory board, fumed, 'It's sick. It's nothing but sick.'

Reading the Football Leaks documents, it was easy to agree with that assessment. Oscar, who signed a contract through to the end of 2020, is earning around €18 million net in Shanghai. The Brazilian gets €7 million in the middle of every January and a million per month for the rest of the year. All that is stipulated on page 5 of the contract he put his signature to on 16 December 2016.

The wages earned by Oscar's teammate Givanildo Vieira de Sousa, also known as Hulk, are similarly ridiculous. The Brazilian international, who transferred in June 2016 from Zenit St Petersburg to Shanghai SIPG for the ludicrously exact sum of €55,789,473.69, makes €15 million net a year in China. Most of that money flows out of the country. At the player's request, the club transfers his monthly salary of €1.25 million to an account at the Kantonalbank in St Gallen, Switzerland.

The list goes on and on. Italian international Graziano Pellè, who in the summer of 2016 moved from Southampton to Shandong Luneng in the provincial Chinese capital of Jinan, banks a cool €10 million in basic salary per season. Even a relatively mediocre striker like Nigeria's Anthony Ujah, who played for Bundesliga side Werder Bremen until leaving for Chinese first-division club FC Liaoning in an €11 million euro transfer, earned a yearly salary of €3 million net, in addition to a €4 million signing-on bonus.

The Argentinian international Carlos Tévez is at the same level as Lavezzi. On 26 December 2016, his boyhood club Boca Juniors and Shanghai Shenhua agreed a relatively moderate transfer fee of $8.75 million. But the contract the striker signed on 1 January, initialling every one of its eleven pages, brought him an astronomical salary and bonuses. Running until 31 December 2018, it gave him a basic annual salary of $22 million net. But that's not all. Tévez stood to earn an extra $1 million if he played in more than 70 per cent of the team's competitive matches, another $1 million if Shenhua won the domestic title, $500,000 if they won the cup and $500,000 if he were the league's leading scorer. If everything went his way, Tévez could earn $27 million a year. Net.

In contrast, his match bonuses were hardly worth mentioning: $2,000 per draw and $4,000 for a win. Those are the same sums that Tévez's Chinese teammates get. There are similar arrangements in the contracts of almost all the regally paid foreign players in China. No doubt, the idea is to give the impression that everyone is being treated the same.

Nonetheless, despite the possibilities for earning gigantic sums of money there, China remains a closed, alien world for many footballing mercenaries, who underestimate the cultural and linguistic barriers in Chinese society and the loneliness and boredom of living in luxury ghettos there. But Tévez took no chances. He had written into his contract an option to terminate the deal unilaterally before 30 November 2017. But there were two conditions: the only club he was allowed to transfer to was Boca Juniors; and he would have to pay $6 million to regain his freedom. Tévez exercised that option at the end of 2017.

The revelations by Football Leaks about the actual amount of money that China's clubs and companies are pumping into the sport could cause a debate in that country about the excesses associated with the sport. The leadership in Beijing wants to prevent this at all costs. After Tévez's arrival, and with the transfer market about to heat up even further, the powers that be intervened. From one day to the next, the Chinese Football Association decreed that teams were only allowed to field three foreigners. After that, the transfer insanity was noticeably dampened.

Still, it's clear that as long as the communist government maintains its fantasies of achieving total dominance in football, such restrictions won't keep the heads of Chinese clubs from flooding good old Europe with money. This creates a paradoxical situation for the English, Spanish, German and Italian leagues. For years, they have seen China as a market that had to be conquered. It was very tempting to milk a gigantic country with 1.4 billion inhabitants for money through licensed merchandise and pay TV subscriptions.

Numerous clubs from the top European leagues hurry off after the season ends to play one or two friendlies and earn a quick couple of million. But German club Wolfsburg were surprised when they did a mini-tour of China in May 2016, only to learn that the Chinese were interested solely in big-name clubs. 'Do you think it possible to have RM [Real Madrid] or MU [Manchester United] or other legendary club to join the tour?' a Chinese marketing agency charged with organising the five-day excursion inquired. 'Only teams like Wolfsburg will not succeed on box office in China.' Barcelona, Manchester City, Arsenal, Inter Milan and Bayern Munich, the agency added, had always attracted big crowds.

The Chinese may be about to turn the tables. If the state capitalism pursued by Beijing continues to free up billions to fund football, the established powers in Europe could be hoisted by their own petard. Even Russian oligarchs, Italian family dynasties and Arab royal families have a hard time competing with the sums that China has pumped into the sport.

In addition to paying Lavezzi his horrendous \$56.7 million net salary, Hebei China Fortune provided him with two rent-free houses, two limousines, a chauffeur, a chef and an interpreter. Should Lavezzi get injured, the club was required to keep paying him his full wages. Only if he were hurt for longer than two months would his salary be reduced by 30 per cent, leaving him with the still handsome sum of $900,000 net per month. Not bad for a convalescent in a country without comprehensive health insurance, where the average wage of an urban white-collar employee, the sort of person likely to be a football fan, was only around $1,000 a month.

Perhaps the most preposterous details of this monstrous contract came in connection with the unilateral option Lavezzi secured to extend the deal by a year. This passage took effect provided two conditions were met: Lavezzi had to score at least forty goals and deliver twenty assists in his first two seasons, and he had to play at least 90 per cent of all 'official matches' in terms of minutes. But here, too, there was a loophole. If Lavezzi had to travel to play for the Argentinian national team, he still received credit for having played ninety minutes, even if he had only played forty-five due to starting on the subs bench or being substituted. And what if Lavezzi were sent off for a second yellow card after committing a professional foul and was banned from the next match? No problem – as long as his manager had ordered the foul for tactical purposes.

We at *Der Spiegel* asked Lavezzi to comment on all the details of his contract but never received an answer. The club responded within a few hours to our request for precise information via a lawyer, who told us that the contents of contracts were 'confidential' and a private matter between the team and the player.

Swiss Swamps

The slightly built midfielder with flowing blond locks that Bundesliga side Hamburg had signed in summer 2016 was quick to get a nickname in the tabloids. Alen Halilović, they decided, was to be known as the 'Balkan Messi'.

This coinage was particularly unimaginative. Halilović arrived at Hamburg from Barcelona, and like Messi, early in his career things had happened very quickly for him. He had hardly turned sixteen when he signed his first professional contract with Croatia's most successful club, Dinamo Zagreb, for whom he effortlessly set a series of new records. Halilović is still the youngest player ever to play a first-division match for Dinamo, and he's also the club's youngest goal-scorer. He would go on to play sixty-one times for Dinamo before being sold to Barcelona. On 3 March 2014, the two clubs signed the transfer agreement, and some three months later, Halilović signed his first contract with the Catalan giants. His mother and father had to co-sign the deal since the talented youngster was still a minor.

The story of the wunderkind who moved to one of the world's top clubs to mature into a global superstar is one that's been told hundreds of times. But Halilović's tale also has another side, one of greed, deceit and betrayal. A circle of influential Dinamo Zagreb functionaries seem to have enriched themselves from the youngster's transfer and allowed millions of euros that should have gone to the club to seep away into a company in Switzerland.

The dark side of Halilović's story began on 3 July 2012, when Dinamo's general director signed a three-page agreement with a company called Rasport Management. It had its headquarters in the Swiss village of Alpnach, in the canton of Obwalden, which is known for its low tax rates and lax attitude towards corporate diligence. According to the contract, the Croatian club and the Swiss company agreed to divvy up income from the sixteen-year-old Halilović's transfer rights fifty–fifty. Two years later, when Halilović moved to Barcelona, this agreement came into play. The transfer fee was €2.2 million, and Dinamo retained a share of all future transfer payments as well. For example, when the player was loaned out to newly promoted Sporting Gijón in the summer of 2015, Dinamo earned an additional €1 million, and when he was sold to Hamburg a year later, the Croatians received €2.5 million – exactly half of the transfer fee paid by the northern Germans to Barcelona. All told, Halilović brought in €5.7 million in two years for Dinamo. But the club could only keep half of that sum. The other half went to Rasport Management.

Why did Dinamo chose to do business with a mysterious company in the Swiss Alps? Why had it voluntarily given up half of the transfer rights to one of its most profitable players? Why did the team unnecessarily pass on €2.85 million?

If you follow the trail of this opaque deal, three men from a family named Mamić keep cropping up. Zdravko Mamić, the clan patriarch, was the president of Dinamo Zagreb from 2003 to 2016, while his brother Zoran, a former Bundesliga player, worked for the club as sporting director and manager from 2013 to 2016. The third member of the triumvirate was Zdravko's son Mario, who's an agent representing players.

The Croatian authorities accuse Zdravko, Zoran and Mario Mamić of collaborating with five other suspects to pocket millions of euros earned from selling Dinamo's stars to clubs abroad. The transfers include Luka Modrić to Tottenham Hotspur, Eduardo to Arsenal, Dejan Lovren to Olympique Lyon and Mario Mandžukić to Wolfsburg. The alleged conspiracy included a member of the Croatian tax authorities and a high-ranking member of the Croatian national football federation, who had also worked in a leading position for Dinamo.

Does the football business in the Balkans exist in a kind of extra-legal realm? A number of former Dinamo players, including Modrić, have testified in the Mamićs' trial. The Swiss attorneys representing the Mamićs, who work for law practices in Geneva and Lausanne, didn't respond to requests for information about the accusations levelled at their clients.

In October 2016, the lead prosecutor in Sarnen, in Obwalden canton, issued a statement about the activities of her business crimes department. Croatia, she said, had made a request for legal assistance and had asked Swiss investigators for information concerning the bank activities and flows of money to and from an unlisted corporation through which Dinamo Zagreb was suspected of diverting millions of euros in conjunction with player transfers. The name of the company was Rasport Management.

The prosecutors in Sarnen uncovered numerous, possibly criminal payments made via Rasport. 'For example, there are unspecified mediation services and non-existent player transfers,' the lead prosecutor said. Rasport seems to have functioned as an intermediary holding point for money. Swiss investigators discovered large sums flowing from the firm to accounts in Belize, Hong Kong, Dubai, Panama, Gibraltar, London and Zurich. The lead prosecutor talked about 'payments in the tens of millions'. She concluded: 'What we're dealing with here is economic criminality of the crasser sort.'

Rasport's contract with Dinamo was signed by a front man in Switzerland, and it was unclear from that agreement or from the Swiss business register who really owns the company. Information from the Sarnen head prosecutor shed light on this matter. According to her, the beneficial owner of the company was Mario Mamić, the player agent. Thus, in the case of Halilović, the circle is closed.

Zdravko Mamić is no longer the president of Dinamo Zagreb, but that doesn't mean he withdrew from the club, for which he still worked as an advisor – something the team's new boss has refused to comment upon. Adversaries fear his tirades – and his connections. Mamić is said to enjoy close relations with leaders in Croatian politics, the Croatian legal system and the Croatian media. Such powerful connections are rarely made without accumulating a few enemies along the way, however. In August 2017, Mamić was shot by two masked attackers while visiting his father's grave, in an apparent assassination attempt. He was taken to a local hospital after being hit twice in the leg, but later left of his own accord.

Clubs named Dinamo have a history. In the 1970s and '80s, Dynamo Berlin – the favourite club of the head of East Germany's secret police, Erich Mielke – won the country's championship ten times on the trot, often in dubious circumstances. Dinamo Zagreb went one better, winning the Croatian first division eleven times in a row. But the attendance for home matches at Maksimir Stadium rarely exceeds a few thousand. Fans incensed at how Dinamo has been plundered have boycotted the club, and the Football Leaks information confirmed their worst fears. Documents from the cache showed how the club's leadership flogged off half of the transfer rights of a further three players.

One of them is Mateo Kovačić. In early 2013, the midfielder went from Dinamo to Inter Milan for €11 million, and in summer 2015, the Italians moved him on to Real Madrid for €31 million. Dinamo's bosses had laid the groundwork six months before Kovačić's transfer to Inter. On 17 May 2012, the club's general director signed an agreement to pay half of Kovačić's transfer fee to a company called Profoot International Ltd, headquartered in Hong Kong. The deals for the other two players followed a similar pattern. With striker Duje Čop, Zoran Mamić signed away half of the transfer rights to International Sport Company Ltd, from Malta. With defender Tin Jedvaj, who joined Bayer Leverkusen, Zdravko Mamić turned over half of the player's transfer rights to Barnes & Bell Ltd in London.

Young professional football players who promise to draw sizeable transfer fees are often like servants indentured to the bosses of their clubs. In many cases, they remain completely unaware of the wheeling and dealing surrounding their transfer rights, and if they were to resist those deals before transferring abroad, they would be putting their own careers in jeopardy. So they hold their tongues, having no option but to play along with this murky business.

That was also the case with young Serbian forward Mijat Gaćinović, who moved to Eintracht Frankfurt from Cypriot club Apollon Limassol on 11 August 2015. Gaćinović never wore the Apollon shirt. The Cypriots signed the young Serb a few days prior to his move to Frankfurt, on 31 July. The contract called for him to make €10,000 a month for four years. It was clearly an alibi agreement. Gaćinović no doubt had little choice but to sign up to the badly paid deal and agree to an intermediate posting on Cyprus so that others could profit from the Frankfurt transfer.

Gaćinović's home club was Vojvodina Novi Sad. On 17 March 2015, its president had signed a deal in the best Mamić style. It transferred 100 per cent of the rights to Gaćinović to a company named European Sports Management. Its headquarters were located in Montreal, but its house bank was in Switzerland. The goal of this deal was to sell the young player abroad as quickly as possible and cash in.

Because everyone knew there was no way a prominent German first-division club was going to pay Gaćinović's transfer fee to a Canadian consortium's account in Switzerland, another way had to be found to get the money to the Alpine country. The answer was a three-way deal, with Apollon Limassol as the third party. On 3 August 2015, Novi Sad and Apollon signed a transfer contract, according to which the Cypriots paid €1.25 million for the player. As specified by the Serbs in the contract's appendix, Apollon was to pay that sum to an account at the Swiss private bank EFG. The recipient was European Sports Management.

Eight days later, when Frankfurt paid exactly €1.25 million for Gaćinović, Apollon got their money back. At that point they were neither behind nor ahead. The Cypriots would only earn a profit later, as was specified on pages 3 and 4 of Apollon's contract with Frankfurt, which stipulated that Apollon was due half of any future transfer fee should Gaćinović be sold on. The minimum transfer fee was set at €2.5 million. If Frankfurt wanted to sell the player for less than that, they would have to ask Apollon's permission.

Neither Novi Sad nor Apollon responded to our requests for information about the murky deals concerning Gaćinović's transfer. The player himself also had no comment. Eintracht Frankfurt answered that it did not comment 'on principle on contract details or contract relationships in which we are either not involved or about which we know nothing'.

Frankfurt was taking the easy way out. It should have at least suspected that its contract partners were the profiteers from a three-way deal. What other explanation is there for a club like Apollon Limassol signing a player from Serbia in the summer transfer window and then selling him on eight days later, while retaining a 50 per cent interest in all future transfer profits involving that player?

Who was behind the company from Canada in whose account at a Swiss private bank the €1.25 million ended up? Signing the Gaćinović contract with Novi Sad for European Sports Management was a front man from the canton of Obwalden. The same front man cropped up in the Halilović deal as the director of Rasport Management.

Tax Haven Heaven

The nice thing about the data management system we used to search through John's material is that software has no emotions. While we, despite all our journalistic distance from our subject matter, were outraged by the Mamićs, the Chinese, Cristiano Ronaldo and all the tax-evasion tricks, the software just kept soberly spitting out matches. Totally coolly, with no emotional involvement. Even when it discovered the thousandth mention of the British Virgin Islands, it just provided us with the names of companies, sometimes of agents, and every now and then of economic beneficiaries, front men and administrators. Over time we identified dozens of firms that diverted salaries, marketing rights money, bonuses and supplemental payments to the British Virgin Islands. The islands are a discreet tax haven, perfect for the tight-lipped football community. This was a place we needed to visit.

Our economics expert, Nicola Naber, put together a dossier that included the most important 'subjects', as she called the front men and administrators of shell companies. She drew up lists of their Facebook, Twitter and Instagram accounts and an analysis of the financial transactions and complex labyrinths of companies.

From the aeroplane, the British Virgin Islands looked something from a fairy tale. It could have been Middle Earth from Tolkien's *Lord of the Rings*. The hills and other small rises on the many tiny islands were thickly vegetated, full of trees and greenery. The beaches were gleaming white. We couldn't see many roads. It was hard to imagine such shady deals being done via this sun-filled paradise. This was a swamp where billions of euros disappeared?

Nicola's dossier allowed us to see beyond the idyllic Caribbean surface. BVI consists of sixty small islands around a hundred kilometres from Puerto Rico. It's a major tourist attraction for sun-lovers, with 30,000 permanent residents. That's the bright side. The dark side can be summed up in a single figure: 500,000. That's the number of shell companies that are registered here. Billions' worth of dodgy deals are done here – money that is taken away from the social welfare systems of the countries where it originates. The only purpose of a great many of the offshore business constructs registered here is to get around the tax authorities elsewhere.

Life for tax evaders has become significantly more complicated over the past few years. After a number of scandals, banking secrecy has been lifted in many places, and with the global economic crisis putting pressure on government budgets, many countries have stepped up their pursuit of concealed revenue. Customs officials have intensified border controls, and European finance ministers have purchased lists of putative tax evaders from whistle-blowers and received warrants to examine hundreds of bank accounts every day. More and more nations are signing reciprocal tax enforcement agreements, and the pressure on countries that refuse to cooperate is increasing. It now takes a lot more ingenuity, and perhaps criminal energy, to hide your money from your home country's tax authorities.

The morning after we arrived, we headed down Waterfront Drive, the main thoroughfare in BVI's capital, Road Town. If you stroll along this street, it's immediately apparent that this is a place where big money feels at home. Low buildings line the road, pushed together and usually following the same pattern: on the ground floor there's usually a sporting goods, jewellery or mobile-phone shop, while the first floors are almost always occupied by banks, auditing agencies, law firms and legal administration companies. Even the island's many mosquitos have trouble getting in: as a rule, the windows remain shut, many of the law firms have CCTV cameras, and the doors can often only be opened with chipped cards. The letterbox companies rarely have any physical letterboxes outside. As we observed on numerous occasions, letters and other documents are delivered only by hand.

Our first port of call was the International Trust Building. Actually, our true goal was Paros Consulting Limited, a company numerous Dutch and Argentinian agents have used to do deals with dozens of football clubs and players from all over the world. We had the address, but the company was nowhere to be found. Instead, we ended up in front of a building with a gleaming sign reading 'Trident Chambers', which was listed often in the Football Leaks documents as Paros's mailing address – a classic shell-company trick. The building was grey, with concrete columns before the door and a symbolic sun above the entrance. CCTV cameras were mounted outside the door, so we contented ourselves with watching the comings and goings from a discreet distance.

Several times a day, messengers drove up in large SUVs with mirrored windows. They would get out of the vehicles carrying large briefcases, which they would place before the entrance. They never rang the doorbell. Someone inside the building must have been monitoring who approached, because the doors invariably opened when the messengers approached. A few minutes later, the messengers would re-emerge. Often they would head to another building in a cramped side street. Here, too, there was no sign of Paros, but there was a sign next to the narrow front door that read 'International Trust'. That was Paros's true address, as we had previously discovered on a business register.

We went up and rang the bell. Nothing happened. We waited until a messenger arrived, and asked who worked in this building. No answer. The young woman rushed past us wordlessly and disappeared behind the door.

There's a variety of reasons why BVI, with its estimated $1.5 trillion of assets under management, has become such a popular tax haven over the past few decades. Although the group of islands is a British territory, its currency is the US dollar, which is very convenient for international business. BVI's laws are mostly identical to those in Britain, and the country is stable enough politically to guarantee the security of hidden money. Moreover, and decisively, BVI maintains a strictly confidential commercial register to which the European tax authorities have practically no access. Starting a company there takes a mere three to five days and only costs around $100. In addition, letterbox companies pay no taxes on money they earn outside BVI.

There was no point in us continuing to linger here attracting attention. We weren't going to get any answers. If anything, we were going to get in trouble with the police. We continued on down Waterfront Drive and saw some small bank buildings hardly large enough for more than a handful of employees. Massive auditing companies like PricewaterhouseCoopers and KPMG also had branches, as did Mossack Fonseca, the law firm at the centre of the 'Panama Papers' revelations about the offshore dealings of politicians, actors, business leaders and criminals.

We stopped in front of a faded yellow building. On the ground floor was a chemist. We entered and saw a woman receiving a medication for lumbago. Outside, chickens were pecking at the ground. Some of them dashed out into the road, while others hopped about on the stairs leading to the first storey. Up there was where one of the biggest secrets in world football was to be found.

Nicola's dossier told us that this was the headquarters of the law firm Icaza, González-Ruiz & Alemán. The shutters were drawn. There was no seeing into the offices from the outside. No one would suspect that this was where companies owned by big-name football stars were registered. The building through which more than €100 million of Cristiano Ronaldo's wealth had been diverted was a dump.

We sat down on the other side of the street, in front of a petrol station. A couple of older men were eating sunflower seeds on a bench. They watched us watching the building. Watching grass grow would have been more exciting. Nothing stirred. There was no change of personnel or any messengers. After a couple of hours, a woman finally emerged through the door: Liz B.

We recognised the young lawyer immediately. Nicola's dossier contained dozens of pages about her. She was an offshore expert who had also worked in Panama. Now she was employed by the law firm that dealt with the flow of

Ronaldo's money. Icaza, González-Ruiz & Alemán's clients included three companies with which the Ballon d'Or winner had concluded numerous contracts. Liz B. knew the ins and outs of the business. We would have loved to speak with her, but she immediately got into a black SUV and sped off. We decided to come back tomorrow, earlier, and ask her a few questions before she arrived at work.

The following day, a little before 9 a.m., she returned with her SUV. She looked drowsy, walking slowly with hanging shoulders. We approached her, smiling, with two pictures in our hands, one of Ronaldo and the other of José Mourinho. It was a heavy-handed trick, but sometimes the simple approach works best. We asked Liz B. if she knew the two men in the photos.

Liz B. laughed and actually stopped for us. 'Cristiano,' she said, pointing to the photo on the left. 'Mourinho' – she tapped the other image.

Did she know that both of these men had businesses registered at this address? we asked, pointing to the first floor of the building.

Liz B.'s face fell. She lowered her head, raised her hands to ward us off and hurried past us up the steps.

'Are you familiar with the Tollin company?' we asked.

'Please, please,' she answered.

She held her electronic chip card up to the scanner beside the door and disappeared into the small office space, back into the world of confidentiality and non-transparency.

The Visit

After our trip to BVI, along with Ronaldo and Mourinho we focused primarily on Paros and the Dutch–Argentinian agent clique. We wanted to understand how their system worked and who was behind it. On the basis of what we'd seen in the Caribbean, we were convinced that it was aimed at making money earned in Europe disappear.

We consulted our data-management system, but for the first time it let us down. The Football Leaks cache contained encrypted documents that we could open on John's hard drives but which the system could only partially display. There were blank spots, missing pieces of the puzzle. We racked our brains but couldn't figure out how to solve the problem.

I asked John for help, but he couldn't find a solution either. Finally, he said he'd like to see the problem on the ground. In Hamburg. That made me gulp. I had no idea how he travelled. Did he use a fake passport? I couldn't rule it out. I asked whether he wasn't afraid of the authorities. After all, an official criminal investigation into Football Leaks was under way. What would happen if he was stopped at the border? Was there a Europol warrant out for his arrest? Authorities all over the continent would be on the lookout for him.

'Don't worry about it,' he wrote. 'They have nothing on me. Nothing at all.'

How could he be so sure?

I discussed his suggestion with our team. We all felt a bit nervous about it. John would have to be granted access to our safe room. Was it acceptable to let a source get so close to our research? On the other hand, no one in the world knew the data better than he did. All he was supposed to do was explain the context of the information in question. Otherwise, he would have no influence over our research.

Could we take responsibility for him flying to Hamburg? Despite the ongoing investigations? He was constantly on the go. Since I had known him, he had described taking dozens of flights, some to the most distant destinations. Surely he was able to assess the risk. We decided that he should come to Hamburg.

John welcomed the news but had a couple of conditions.

'Except for you, no one at the magazine is to see me,' he said. 'I don't want to be introduced to anyone. My anonymity is to be preserved as far as possible.'

I needed to think. If he didn't want to be introduced to anyone, we could only turn up at the *Spiegel* office late at night. At any other time, there was too much hustle and bustle. Some of my colleagues would definitely see him. He didn't have a problem with that suggestion. I told our team that our safe room would be off limits as of 10 p.m. After spending so many months there, the team wasn't unhappy about having to vacate the space a bit earlier than usual. And since he refused to tell the hotel his real name for the reservation, we just booked it under ours.

John and I arranged to meet at the main train station. When we did, he looked tired, but at least he hadn't been arrested. All he had with him was a tiny backpack slung across his shoulder. After stopping briefly at his hotel, we went for breakfast at Café Paris, in the city centre.

'What are our plans?' he asked, digging into a full English with bacon and baked beans.

'Do you want to see anything in particular?' I asked back.

He had written in advance that he wanted to go out for a night on the Reeperbahn. Now John named a few other tourist attractions: the warehouse district, the Rathaus, the port, the River Alster and Hamburg SV.

'They're playing a home match on Saturday, and I go to watch football in every city I visit,' he said.

Really? He wanted to go to a Hamburg match?

We agreed that he would do some sight-seeing alone during the day, while I continued to work on the material. Because our schedule was so tight, I couldn't afford to take a week off. We would meet at 7 p.m., get something to eat and then go either to the office or to the Reeperbahn. Sometimes both.

On the first evening, we were very disciplined. At 10 p.m. sharp, we went to the *Spiegel* offices. The building has a back entrance that very few people use, so I was able to get John to our safe room without anyone noticing. Hardly had he entered the room than he glanced at the whiteboard and said, 'There's a mistake there.' He almost tiptoed through the room, stopping before the whiteboard and tapping on a spot concerning Ronaldo's image rights.

'This here is wrong,' he said. 'Do you not have the right documents, or didn't you find them?'

I looked at him in dismay. This was one of the things we'd spent weeks working on. At issue was who actually owned Ronaldo's image rights. It was an extremely complicated question due to the construct of companies in a number of tax havens.

'There's nothing in our documents about it,' I said.

'Oh, then I'll have to send you that information,' John said.

Indeed, a few days before he left, a document arrived that fully explained the situation with Ronaldo's image rights. The guy was enough to drive you crazy.

'Let's go – boot up your system,' he said.

I showed him our software, and he listened without changing his expression. But his eyes were constantly scanning the computer screen. I showed him the emails we hadn't been able to open. John took the keyboard, typed in something, merged two documents, entered a search term, unzipped a folder, dragged it to another spot on the screen and entered a final password. Just watching made me dizzy. Then – bang! – hundreds of emails, including attachments, popped open. I still have no idea how John was able to decrypt so much information so quickly.

'Why don't you work as an IT specialist or systems engineer?' I asked him.

'I didn't study it,' he answered, as he scanned the search terms on the screen. 'Who would hire me?'

'But you can still study IT or do some training,' I objected. 'You have such an obvious talent for it. Computer freaks are in demand all over the world.'

'It's too late for that,' he said. 'At some point, every human being stands at a crossroads and has to decide. I've decided to go down a different path, and that's okay.'

John tended to be a bit dramatic.

'And where is your path going to take you?'

'That's the big question,' he said, and fell silent. We both sat there pensively for what seemed like an eternity.

'Is being a whistle-blower worth it?' I asked him finally. 'Snowden, Assange, Manning, Deltour – was it worth it? Was it worth it for them?'

John looked me straight in the eye. It was the first time that he had diverted his attention from the computer.

'It was worth it for society,' I added.

'You see?' he said. 'That's where my path should go. It should be worth it for society. Sport is such a gigantic business, and if only a bit more monitoring were to happen because of Football Leaks, if football were to once again become a bit more honest and down to earth because of the project, then it would also be worthwhile for me. I'd be satisfied.'

John clicked on a company in BVI. We sat in the safe room until four in the morning, talking about agents with all their greed, power and tricks and about why clubs went along with them. And by the end of our session, we had come much closer to putting together a comprehensive picture of the Dutch and Argentinian agents' offshore dealings.

Documents of Greed

By summer 2016, Mino Raiola was driving Borussia Dortmund round the bend. He was known for wearing down clubs to the point of exhaustion, and once again he had achieved his goal. To say that Dortmund were desperate would have been a dramatic understatement. Whatever happened, there could be only one winner: Raiola.

At the eye of the storm was Henrikh Mkhitaryan, the Armenian playmaker who wanted to leave the German side for Manchester United and the enormous riches of the Premier League. The problem was Mkhitaryan's contract. It had a year to run, and whenever there was a television studio's microphone, Dortmund CEO Hans-Joachim Watzke could be heard saying that he was not willing to sell at any price. End of story.

But Raiola wasn't going to take 'no' for an answer. He'd been peddling football players for over twenty years and had dealt with such flamboyant characters as Silvio Berlusconi, Real Madrid president Florentino Pérez and the Qatari potentate at Paris Saint-Germain, Nasser Al-Khelaifi. Someone who had done deals with people like that was hardly going to be cowed by a straight-as-an-arrow German named Watzke.

Especially not when he had an ace up his sleeve, about which the public at large had no knowledge. A three-page amendment to Raiola's agent's contract with Dortmund, dated 1 March 2014, seems to have played a decisive role in the final stages of negotiations between Dortmund and United. The supplementary agreement not only gave Raiola a stake if Mkhitaryan were sold, but also if he weren't. There was no way Raiola could lose in this deal, while Dortmund were over a barrel. If the club had refused United's offer and insisted upon Mkhitaryan seeing out his contract, it would have owed the agent millions. On 5 July 2016, Watzke sold Mkhitaryan for €38 million. Raiola seems to have been paid €2.5 million by Dortmund, on top of an additional fee of €1,185,000 from United.

Professional player agents insist upon earning quick money. In the agents' world, it's the person who's pushiest, not cleverest, who usually wins out. In this world there are lots of shadowy, behind-the-scenes figures, puppet masters and profiteers, and the most valuable character traits are ruthlessness, speed and negotiating ability. In this world, even top players who have millions of fans and earn millions in annual salaries are often nothing more than investments that are supposed to pay off.

One of the top players in this category is Julian Draxler. The German international turned in some breakthrough performances for his country at the 2016 European Championship, but even before that he was considered a hot commodity. At least that was the impression given by the contract signed between his advisor Roger Wittmann and German club Schalke in 2013. Wittmann's agency Rogon is one of the most successful in Germany. He's been in the business for decades and has built up a top international network, despite never having obtained an agent's licence. By training, he's a plumber. In recent years, he's come under criticism because multiple players of his have signed with Schalke, Hoffenheim and Wolfsburg. Critics say that gives him an improper amount of influence on the decision-making at these three clubs.

In Draxler's case, Wittmann and his people showed what hard negotiators they were. Draxler was only nineteen years old when he extended his contract with Schalke in 2013, but despite his tender age, a number of big clubs were tracking him. Although his performances vacillated from the sublime to the sloppy, Rogon was in a good negotiating position vis-à-vis Schalke. That's the only reasonable explanation for the contract signed by the club. In it, Schalke paid Rogon €1.2 million net for Draxler's extension, plus an additional €450,000 for every season he stayed at the club beyond the first one. And Rogon built into the deal a further clause that Schalke would quickly come to regret: if Draxler transferred elsewhere, no matter to which team, the club had to pay 15 per cent of the total fee to the agency. Despite these terms, the Royal Blues celebrated Draxler's extension as though it were a title, mounting a picture of the young star to a lorry and driving it around the centre of Dortmund, their arch-rivals. 'Look here,' that stunt was intended to say. 'You may have won the championship, but we have tomorrow's championship-calibre talent.'

Two and a half years later, the true winners turned out to be Wittmann's agency. Draxler's value had gone through the roof, and on the final day of the 2015 summer transfer window, Draxler moved to Wolfsburg for around €36 million. €5.4 million of that was immediately sent on its way to Rogon's bank account. In a nutshell, in twenty-eight months, the agency earned around €7 million for a nineteen-year-old's contract extension.

As professional football has grown into a business earning billions, one of the outgrowths of the industry has been the agent sector. Most players find negotiating contracts too difficult and complicated, and they usually lack the contacts to offer their services to other clubs or to attract sponsors. Agents take over these tasks. Often they also serve as pals and confidants – or what newly minted teenage millionaires mistake for pals and confidants. They buy mansions for their players, manage their assets and respond to WhatsApp messages in the middle of the night. The closer an agent is to his commodities, the less the chance that one of his competitors will poach them.

Agents' fees in Europe have doubled in the past five years or so. In 2015, agents earned more than €370 million in German and English professional football. Across the world, some 640 agents are thought to have earned €1 billion officially, plus an indeterminate amount of under-the-table money.

One of the leaders in the field is Rogon. In an interview with the *taz* newspaper in Berlin, the managing director of Rogon's Brazil subsidiary, Christian Rapp, described the trade in football talents from that country as a 'massacre of hopes'. A lot of young people competed for professional contracts, he said, 'but only very few succeed'. What Rapp failed to add, despite knowing the system as well as anyone, was that agents can earn big money even with relatively small talents.

The Football Leaks documents contained a contract, dated 28 April 2014, between Benfica and Rogon that bears

Rapp's signature. The contract is for a striker named Kevin Friesenbichler. 'Who?' you may well ask.

Back in 2014, the then nineteen-year-old Friesenbichler was playing in the Bayern Munich reserve team, facing fourth-division opponents like TSV Buchbach or Bayern Hof. So why would a Champions League club like Benfica have been interested in a player of this calibre? The answer is: they weren't. That same summer, Benfica loaned Friesenbichler out to Lechia Gdańsk. At that juncture, two close Wittmann associates were heavily involved in the deal-ings of the Polish club.

Rogon earned €1 million net from Benfica for arranging the Friesenbichler deal, and the agency also received a 50 per cent stake in all future transfer sums, minus that advance. By way of comparison, in 2013, Rogon received a fee of €1.2 mil-lion for the transfer of Brazilian international Luiz Gustavo from Bayern Munich to Wolfsburg, plus an annual bonus of €300,000–350,000 for the duration of Gustavo's five-year deal. How could a Brazilian international in the prime of his career be worth about the same as a player from the Bavarian regional league? Were Benfica being stupid? Or was there some other story behind all this money?

There is no monitoring of payments like this in the foot-ball industry. There is no limit placed upon transfer fees, and player agents aren't supervised by any anti-trust agency. Tax auditors and investigators are rarely able to follow com-plex international transactions. Even FIFA has thrown in the towel. In 2015, world football's governing body turned over the monitoring of agents to the national football associ-ations. That was tantamount to capitulation in the face of an industry in which basically anyone can take part.

As more and more money gets pumped into football – the Premier League's record-breaking £5.14 billion TV deal in 2015, for example – the more attractive the agent sector becomes to fools of fortune. With clubs willing to pay nearly any sum for quality players, agents' fees are also becoming more and more incredible.

Enter Volker Struth. The Cologne native is one of Germany's elite agents. The clients of his company SportsTotal include German internationals Marco Reus and Benedikt Höwedes, and he used to represent Mario Götze as well, until the two had a falling out and the playmaker decided to use his father as his agent. Struth was hardly mortally wounded by the end of this business relationship. A former amateur football player himself, he was an office supplies salesman before becoming an agent and made his first small fortune selling German flags ahead of the 2006 World Cup. Post-Götze, he kept putting together big deals. In October 2016, his agency received €2 million from no less a club than Real Madrid. It was part of a fee that should see Struth earn €5 million by October 2018.

The fee is an expression of gratitude for Struth's role in helping to convince German midfielder Toni Kroos to turn down bigger offers from other clubs and extend his contract with the Champions League winners until 2022. At the same time, Real gave Kroos a pay rise, from €10,909,091 to €14,545,455 a year. For an agent, a player like Kroos is like a central defender scoring a goal from 30 metres – a stroke of absolute fortune. Kroos's performances have been steadily improving for years, and the sums of money that can be earned doing business with him have increased incrementally.

Was €5 million an appropriate sum of money for an agent who helped secure a contract extension? Was this the market standard? Or an absurd exception? Both the clubs and the agents act as though such sums of money are perfectly normal. Perhaps the weirdest example of this was provided by Bayer Leverkusen. The club is known for being a stickler for everything being on the level in its dealings with agents – to the point that it requires agents to fill out special protocols to prove they have done their job. They consist of four-column tables in which agents have to enter the date, the subject, the type of agreement and the end results of the negotiations with the team or the players. Señor Eduardo Hernández Applebaum, an agent based in St Antonio, Texas, who represents Javier Hernández, was very diligent in filling out his protocol. He listed in detail everything he had done to bring the Mexican striker from Manchester United to Leverkusen: nine telephone calls, two emails and seven personal meetings with the player and representatives of the two clubs concerned. For that his agency received €1.1 million.

The Leverkusen protocols also showed how little respect agents have for any higher authorities, including national team coaches. Ahead of the 2014 World Cup, Germany's Joachim Löw forbade agents from visiting Germany's team headquarters in Campo Bahia. His players were supposed to concentrate on the tournament. Midfielder Christoph Kramer and his agent René vom Bruch found an easy way of getting round this prohibition. According to a protocol from 15 October 2014, the two met 'personally near Campo Bahia'. Vom Bruch wrote that he had discussed 'the sporting as well as the contract situation' with Kramer and informed the player that Leverkusen were interested in an extension. At that juncture, Kramer was out on loan to Borussia Mönchengladbach. As a result of the meeting, vom Bruch noted that Kramer said he'd 'think about it'. The agent didn't seem to pay any heed to that fact that the meeting with his client took place three days before Germany's knockout round match against Algeria. Business is business. And national team players bring the greatest profits.

In October 2014, Leverkusen forward Karim Bellarabi was capped for the first time, and four months later he extended his contract. Bellarabi's agent, Konstantin Liolios, listed on his protocol eleven telephone calls, two emails, a letter and nine personal meetings. Once he travelled to Leverkusen to sign his own contract with the club, and another time he signed Bellarabi's contract on behalf of the player. For those services, Leverkusen paid Liolios's agency a flat fee of €3.5 million plus VAT, €247,500 for the remainder of the 2014–15 season and €495,000 for every season Bellarabi, whose contract runs until 20 June 2020, goes on to play for the club. The agency also receives 15 per cent of the player's basic wage and bonuses.

But deals come even crazier than that. The really big money for agents comes from top transfers like Gareth Bale's move from Tottenham to Real Madrid in the late summer of 2013. Florentino Pérez, Madrid's president, had made acquiring the Welshman a top priority, so he was willing to cough up serious money. All told, Bale cost Real €101 million, which, as we have seen, had to be hushed up so as not to offend Cristiano Ronaldo. Bale's agent earned €16,373,000, which was paid in three instalments running until 15 September 2015.

Neither the clubs nor the agents reported about here have been willing to talk about these deals. Many of them didn't answer requests for statements, while others said that they were bound to maintain confidentiality concerning contract details.

The tone can get pretty coarse when there is so much money to be earned so quickly. Defaming others, talking behind their backs and spreading unfounded rumours are all part of the trade. There are running feuds between agents that are reminiscent of schoolyard fist fights. Mostly, they involve accusations that someone has been lining their pockets.

Many colleagues have pointed out that Swiss agent Giacomo Petralito does a conspicuously large number of deals with Klaus Allofs, the former sporting director of Werder Bremen and ex-chief executive of Wolfsburg. Petralito's reputation has been dented, to put it mildly, and Allofs has been accused of sending an improper amount of business the agent's way. Petralito and Allofs both deny any wrongdoing. Nonetheless, in late 2016, Wolfsburg's supervisory board prohibited Allofs from doing any further deals with Petralito.

The Football Leaks documents included a contract that seemed to support the scepticism surrounding Allofs' business practices. It was dated 27 October 2009, back when Allofs was still sporting director at Bremen. In this two-page, English-language agreement, which bears Allofs' signature, a maximum of €600,000 is set for the agents representing Brazilian defender Naldo. Agents? Why plural?

When Naldo arrived at Bremen in the summer of 2005, his agent was his fellow Brazilian Paulo Fernando Tonietto, and in July 2012, when Naldo left Bremen for Wolfsburg, Tonietto was again the only agent involved. The 'agreement of fees' in Naldo's 2009 contract extension included the names of two other agents who apparently played a role: a Serbian and a Montenegrin, who, according to the document, were licensed agents. Even more strange is the fact that these two men's company, Tumod Ventures Ltd, has its headquarters in Road Town, the main city of Tortola, one of the British Virgin Islands. Its only address is given as 'Trident Chambers, PO Box 146'.

Why would Allofs have signed such a document? And who pocketed the €450,000 that Bremen paid for Naldo's extension?

Allofs himself has refused to comment on these questions. When confronted with the document, Werder Bremen first said they were having difficulty reconstructing what had happened and, after two days, asked for our 'understanding that researching the matter in-house will take some time'. One day later, the club answered: no comment. Tonietto told us that he had wanted to involve the other two agents because he valued their 'expertise'. He said that he personally had made sure he paid all the applicable taxes. He could not, of course, vouch for his two colleagues from the Balkans and their company on BVI.

Hundreds of documents from the Football Leaks cache showed that anyone doing deals with agents whose address was Trident Chambers – PO Box 146 in Road Town, Tortola – was getting close to the less-than-transparent side of football. That same address is also home to Paros Consulting's letterbox. It's a dark spot in the global football world.

Paros Consulting has specialised in South American football stars like James Rodríguez of Bayern Munich and Real Madrid, Gonzalo Higuaín of Juventus and Ángel Di María of PSG. But the company's name never appeared in any of the contracts agents signed with clubs. Those documents were signed by European agents to whom Paros had granted negotiation rights in other secret agreements.

Paros's front men, most of whom are from the Netherlands, work and bill for their services under their own names. The huge agent fees clubs pay upon signing big stars usually goes to one of these front men. Then the booty is divided. Depending on their agreements with Paros, the Dutch front men usually get to keep only between 5 and 7.5 per cent of this income. They transfer the remainder of the money to a Paros Consulting account in Europe. One of Paros's house banks is in London, another in Lisbon, a third in Lichtenstein – a savings and loan institution in the village of Schaan.

It is unclear what happens next to the millions that are siphoned off year in, year out from the international football business and paid into the Paros coffers. What is clear is that this is a perfect way to extract the maximum net from the gross. Paros's associates in the Netherlands declare their single-digit-percentage fees as income, but 90 per cent-plus of the agents' fees they pass on apparently end up untaxed in Paros's European accounts.

The Football Leaks documents suggested that the key figures behind Paros were several South American entrepreneurs. One of them was agent Marcelo Simonian. The Argentinian, whose agency Dodici is based in Buenos Aires, is a major player in his country's football scene. Another main Paros figure was his fellow Argentinian, former football player Omar Walter Crocitta. He had power of attorney and was entitled to sign documents on Paros's behalf. He

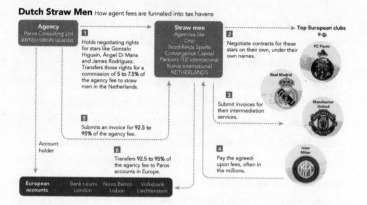

Dutch Straw Men How agent fees are funneled into tax havens

is the sole owner of the agency Merham Ltd in Panama, a company that works together with the same front men that Paros does.

When doing deals, the Paros connection insists on strict secrecy and internal emails are almost always encrypted. But the network was now exposed. The Football Leaks documents allowed us to trace in detail who helped the company earn its millions.

A good example of how the system worked was the case of Colombian international James Rodríguez, who was the leading goal-scorer at the 2014 World Cup and subsequently moved to Real Madrid. The previous year, Rodríguez had moved from Porto to Monaco for €45 million. At that point, the Dutch agents Orel BV officially owned 10 per cent of his transfer rights. But Orel provided just a facade. The real owners of the 10 per cent were located on BVI, as became apparent a few months after Rodríguez's transfer, when Paros Consulting demanded its share. The offshore company sent Orel a bill for €4,121,185.13, payable to a Volksbank account in Liechtenstein. The purpose of the payment was given as:

'Transaction Porto Futebol Club – Orel B.V. connected to the football player J. Rodríguez.'

One of Orel's bosses is Martijn Odems, an agent licensed by the Royal Netherlands Football Association. Orel has often offered its services when Paros needed help doing its deals in Europe: for example, with the 2011 transfer of Argentinian midfielder Ricardo Álvarez to Inter Milan; the 2014 transfer of Argentinian midfielder Fabián Rinaudo to Calcio Catania; or the 2015 transfer of Argentinian striker Ezequiel Ponce to Roma. As a result of these deals, almost €2 million went to Paros via Orel.

Odems has also served as the chief executive of a company called Kunse International N.V., which is located on the same floor in the same building as Orel. Kunse provided a facade for another large deal, one concerning Ángel Di María, the biggest star in the Argentinian national team other than Lionel Messi.

On 18 August 2014, Kunse signed a contract with Paros for the rights to send Di María from Real Madrid to Manchester United and collect 7.5 per cent of the accompanying agent's fee. Several days later, the transfer was completed. On 31 October 2014, United sent €2 million to Kunse in Holland. The front men kept €150,000 and transferred the rest to the Paros account at Bank Leumi in London.

This Argentinian–Dutch connection has functioned for years as a well-oiled money-making machine. The Football Leaks documents showed that the men pulling the strings in South America maintained half a dozen football-player agencies in and around Amsterdam as fronts. One of them was owned by writer Marco Termes, who lives near the Dutch capital. He is the author of eight novels as well as short stories, three volumes of poetry and thousands of aphorisms. In late 2008, when his writing was no longer going so well and after consulting with a friend, Termes changed career. He was suddenly the director of two football-player agencies, one of which was registered at his home address, a social welfare-subsidised flat. These were mere shell companies. In reality, Termes was acting on instructions from a trust. He would fly to southern Europe carrying the contracts of South American players, get the documents signed by club bosses and then head back to Holland.

Termes barely ever saw some of the well-known players he supposedly represented. In late 2013, the man of letters took his leave from this bizarre parallel world. 'I was a goldfish in a piranha tank,' Termes told the *NRC Handelsblad* newspaper, which is part of the EIC research network and which succeeded in locating him. But he didn't provide any specific names or sums of money. They were 'confidential', he explained, adding that he'd already 'said much too much'.

None of the Dutch companies that the Football Leaks documents suggested were doing deals with Paros away from the eyes of the European authorities wanted to comment on the suspicions of possible tax evasion. Odems, who according to the Football Leaks information was one of the most active front men, also refused to give a statement. Nor did we get an answer from Crocitta, even though *Der Spiegel* personally presented him with a list of questions in front of his house in the province of Buenos Aires.

Simonian, the man who in dozens of encrypted emails from the Football Leaks cache appears to be pulling the strings in deals with Paros, was the only one to respond. Paros? he said. Never heard of it. In a telephone interview he said that it was a 'scandal' to connect him with suspicions of tax evasion and a company in BVI. Orel? Never heard of it either, he claimed. 'I am the biggest tax payer in the world of Argentinian football,' Simonian claimed. 'I pay all of my taxes. Are you paying for this call? I am very poor because of all the taxes I have to pay!'

Paros's system of having millions in untaxed agent's fees paid into European bank accounts has worked so well because the clubs have played along. It's possible that the teams in question aren't guilty of breaking any laws. They paid their fees to the Dutch agents with whom they sat down together, and there's nothing illicit about Dutch bank accounts. But many of these clubs must have suspected that the money would be transferred to offshore financial institutions. That much was clear from an email sent by the general director of Sevilla football club to the team's head lawyer in October 2014.

The Dutch front men of an offshore company had offered Sevilla a player. The club boss wrote: 'I have a bad feeling about this.' The company behind the Dutchmen, he added, resided 'in a tax haven'. The general director was afraid of being asked difficult questions about money laundering by the Spanish tax authorities, if they were able to trace the path the transfer fees took.

Sevilla's lawyer wrote back to the attorneys representing the front men that the club 'didn't feel comfortable and couldn't countenance payments by a Dutch company to a consortium in countries with no tax transparency'. It was one of the few documents of honesty amongst thousands of documents of greed.

Hero or Blackmailer?

There he was, the guy everyone – including the police and private detectives – was after. The man who was being hunted by the biggest clubs and the most powerful agents. The man who was always on the run because so many people were afraid of him, afraid of losing money and having their secrets revealed. There he was sitting in the stands of the Volksparkstadion, home of Hamburg SV football club.

In his right hand was John's fifth plastic cup of beer. Down on the pitch, Hamburg were being slaughtered again. The visiting supporters were singing, 'Welcome to division two!' John laughed. The tickets cost €75 a piece. They were located in the middle of the stand, very close to the pitch. Insanely expensive. Here, John seemed like just another fan. He had swayed to Hamburg's theme song 'Hamburg, meine Perle' and been dismayed at every goal the visiting side had scored. When you go to the stadium as a neutral, he told me, you have to support the home team. After all, you're a guest. I took that on board.

After the game, Hamburg supporters showered their team with whistles and catcalls. John got up and took a sip of beer. We had had our fun, and it was time to get to work. We went back to the office. John sat down at one of the work stations in the safe room, a computer with two monitors and a laptop in front of him. He wanted to show me something in the documents about a Maltese company, and he had remembered a point about an agent and his tax-evasion tricks. Documents cascaded over the computer screen. John's legs fidgeted and his pupils jumped up and down, up and down, seeing nothing other than names, figures and addresses in a jungle of data.

It was our final evening together in Hamburg. Up until then, I had avoided the subject, but I no longer had a choice. I had to confront him with the allegations of blackmail we had found in the data, and which we'd discussed with the EIC team in Lisbon. In the meantime, I had taken a closer look at the emails in question and had to admit that they didn't show him in a good light. It was an unpleasant subject.

A number of companies had been charged with tracking down Football Leaks, including IT specialists, highly regarded law firms and private detective agencies. These were real pros, tough and ruthless when it came to achieving their ends. One of the crisis response managers was the head of a company belonging to a shady Russian oligarch. One of the private detectives was a graduate of a military academy in the UK. They had applied pressure to the people behind the Football Leaks page for weeks and months. The whistle-blowers had their website rendered inoperable several times.

John had told me about this over the course of the past few weeks. It was a time of panic, he had said, during which he had almost lost his mind. I was never sure whether he was exaggerating a little, but his worries were well founded. What he hadn't told me about was the other side of Football Leaks, the dark side. But there were emails that allowed us to reconstruct it.

The story began on 3 October 2015, only five days after the project went online. Nélio Lucas, Doyen's head of football marketing, received an email from a certain Artem Lobuzov. That could well have been a pseudonym. The email was sent from an account with the Russian provider Yandex, which was also used by Football Leaks. In it, Lobuzov described the sorts of documents he had in his possession: unsavoury material, photos, text messages and emails. 'All this and much more may come online, and afterwards in all European press,' Lobuzov wrote. 'You certainly don't wish that to happen, do you? But we can talk.'

Lucas seems to have suspected what he and Doyen were in for, but those accustomed to asserting their power over others aren't used to being put under pressure themselves. They need to stay in control. Their secrets are simultaneously the secrets of their success. So Lucas did what he could and tried to cut a deal with this unknown entity. Lobuzov agreed and responded on 5 October that he could imagine doing business with Lucas. For a sum of between €500,000 and €1 million, he wrote, 'the info I have will be eliminated'. He added: 'We can solve this easily in the biggest possible secrecy, preferably between lawyers.'

Lobuzov's attorney was named Aníbal Pinto, a small-time lawyer from Porto, by no means a legal star. He would be charged with handling the rest of the negotiations with the giants of the football industry. In late October, there was allegedly a meeting between Lucas, his lawyer and Pinto at a petrol station in Lisbon. Lucas, wrote a Doyen manager in an email, suggested that Lobuzov receive €300,000 in return for an end to the leaks. Other emails allowed us to reconstruct what happened next: the three men went their separate ways, and it would be two weeks until Lucas got a response from Lobuzov.

Who was Lobuzov? One of John's associates? Did John know him personally? Or maybe Lobuzov was John himself. Was the real point of the project not to inform the public about corruption, but rather to fill his own bank account?

John snorted. He had been sitting in the safe room with me for almost five hours. His cheeks were flushed, and he repeatedly rubbed his eyes. He had taken off his shoes. One of his socks had a large hole in the heel. The otherwise ever so cool online whistle-blower was visibly irritated by this subject. Before he replied, he sat staring at the computer screen and scratching his chin for several minutes.

'We never hacked anyone, and like we have always stated, we are not hackers,' he finally said. 'All we have is a good network of sources. All those ridiculous allegations are coming only from a criminal organisation. That is what Doyen is for us, a mafia organisation.'

There was nothing left to say. Period.

One thing needs stressing at this point: John never received any money from EIC for his information.

Later, we confronted Doyen with the blackmail story. A company spokesman reacted as though he were insulted, telling us that our information was 'completely false and manipulated' and that Doyen would defend itself in the courts. We followed up with the question: Which of the questions we asked had made Doyen think our information had been manipulated? The spokesman declined to specify what he meant. And months later, we still hadn't heard anything from Doyen's lawyers regarding this matter.

We also asked the other people involved about what they

recalled about the alleged extortion attempt. Aníbal Pinto declared that he hadn't helped Lobuzov blackmail Lucas; he had merely been hired as a middleman to conclude a deal with another attorney. When he realised over the course of the meeting that the deal could be an attempt to extort money, he had ended the negotiations, informed his client as to the possible legal repercussions and advised him to end the blackmail attempt. A request for a statement that we sent to the Lobuzov email address went unanswered.

What were we to make of all this? For journalists, working with whistle-blowers like John almost invariably makes you question yourself. Is your material really relevant enough to outweigh the personal motivations, biography and possible criminal past of a source? Do the documents uncover a problem that would otherwise remain concealed? People become whistle-blowers because they are prepared to cross boundaries. Those boundaries can be of proper conduct, morality and even the law. Often they are heroes with character flaws, but they are very rarely saints.

We would later decide to publish stories drawing upon our cache of data, even though we could never fully determine what had happened in the incident of alleged extortion. The material was genuine and it had a high degree of relevance. These stories deserved to be told. They revealed the true face of a football industry that had got out of control. The public had a right to know about this, and it was our duty to inform them.

Another reason to go ahead with publication was that Artem Lobuzov, this unknown key figure with his unpleasant documents, never actually did a deal with Doyen. Nothing came of the whole affair. No money changed hands, and

Lobuzov rejected Doyen's offer. The reasons why remain unclear. Perhaps Lobuzov got cold feet, or maybe he had a falling out with his attorney, Pinto. That's conceivable. But even more likely was another explanation, for which we also found email evidence among the Football Leaks documents: the police had the meeting between Lucas, his attorney and Pinto under surveillance and made a secret recording of it.

It's possible that Lobuzov got wind of this later on. In any case, he extracted himself from the deal. 'Keep your money,' he wrote to Lucas. 'You are going to need it.' Lucas reacted in a manner familiar from mafia films, writing back saying: 'I'm not threatening you with a beating, which is what you deserve, but we are not bandits. We are people of character and principles. Your lesson will be another one that will hurt more!!!!'

Staying Cool

The final phase. We reporters had drawn up lists of hundreds of questions we wanted to be checked. Our lawyers then weighed up every word and advised us on how to pose those questions so that they were clearer and more binding. Now it was up to us. Everything we wrote had to be spot on. Anyone whose research wasn't up to scratch or who had missed a crucial detail could endanger the whole project. Every question that was badly put or incomplete could open the door to lawsuits and damage our credibility. The lawyers and PR people who worked for our adversaries were just waiting for us to slip up.

We sent our questions back and forth within the EIC, checked them over one last time and shared the addresses of people we wanted to contact. We had worked hard, and we hoped we had been careful enough.

All the EIC partners sent their emails, letters and faxes with questions and requests for statements at the same time on the same day. Then we called the recipients to ask whether they had received them. By that point, at the latest, the footballing world would find out what we had been working on the past few months. Now all we could do was wait and hope that no outside authority would intervene, that there would be no restraining orders and that we could publish our articles as planned.

One of our partners got in touch that evening, saying that their publisher had received a text message from one of the lawyers we had confronted. At issue was the Ronaldo story. The content of the text message was simply: 'Give me a call!' That was the tone we would be confronted with. We were in for nine long days.

The following morning, a PR guy representing an agent got in touch, saying that people at Real Madrid were nervous. What did we intend to do with the information we had? He had heard about something to do with Ronaldo. In the football world, rumours spread like wildfire.

In the evening, John wrote that the football world was panicking. Lawyers and PR companies had been hired as troubleshooters, and they would try to entrap us – he had heard that from his sources. The situation was very serious.

Eight days to go.

John vacillated between anticipation and anxiety. He wrote that he hoped the world would learn about all the dirty deals, the insane sums of money and the moral turpitude of the football industry. But he was beginning to have his doubts. In one of his emails, he wrote: 'What's going to happen to all of us afterward? They'll try to find and destroy us.'

Destroy us. To judge from how various Football Leaks adversaries expressed themselves in their emails, John could well have been right. The pressure on John and his associates was about to become enormous. Once we had published our reports, private detectives, underworld musclemen and the police wouldn't be the only ones trying to track down the people behind Football Leaks. Tabloid journalists from all over the world would also be on their trail.

'We are going to have to go completely underground for a few days,' John wrote.

Five days to go.

One of the attorneys who had worked on the offshore business construct for Ronaldo's image rights companies denied all allegations of wrongdoing. We knew from the emails in the Football Leaks cache that he was aware of Ronaldo's tricks to minimise his taxes and had even been asked for his advice on the matter, but he still denied everything. By the end of his email, we wouldn't have been surprised if he had denied ever meeting Cristiano Ronaldo. The lawyer's denials weren't going to do him much good. We had too much concrete evidence to the contrary.

Four days to go.

John wrote that he wished it was already 2 December, when his information would be presented to the world. He said that there was no going back. The waiting was driving him crazy. He knew, he wrote, that he was a wanted man and that the Portuguese police were being pressured to find him. An IT specialist had been hired to determine his whereabouts using special software designed to draw

conclusions about who was behind Football Leaks by analysing the website.

The game of cat and mouse continued. John believed
that he had an advantage, but he still hoped that the world
would soon be talking about corruption in football and not
about him.

Three days to go.

We could tell that our lists of questions were being passed
around among players, clubs, functionaries and their lawyers
and PR teams. They were exchanging views, coordinating
their activities and working on strategies for how to defuse
the stories we were planning to write. The answers we
received came from different people, but they were often
identical, right down to the punctuation.

As a rule, we received answers directly from the other
side's attorneys, and they contained four central points:
firstly, the information we were using had been stolen; secondly, the material had been falsified; thirdly, it violated
individuals' right to privacy, and thus no comment could be
given; and fourthly, should we publish the material, we were
risking legal action. This was what we had expected. Most of
our questions were left unanswered.

Some of our partners were contacted by functionaries and
sports marketers requesting an off-the-record chat before
they answered our questions. Such requests were problem-
atic. We were entering a phase in which we would be held
legally liable for what we did. Off-the-record conversations
didn't do us any good. On the contrary, the other side would
have an opportunity to tell us stories that would win them
time and be difficult for us to check out. We wrote back, trying to be diplomatic, requesting that the people and entities

concerned first answer our catalogue of written questions, then we could see how to put their replies in the proper context. The requests for off-the-record meetings immediately ceased.

Two days to go.

An extraordinary situation arose. Shortly before 9 p.m., one of our EIC partners from Portugal got in touch with the news that our questions had been passed on to another newspaper and that a Ronaldo story would be published tomorrow. They had no idea where the story would be appearing and knew only that it had something to do with the Real Madrid forward.

It all sounded rather vague, but even this information was enough to further tax our already jangling nerves. We gathered in the safe room to decide how to react to this tip-off. The phone rang. It was our Spanish colleagues. They had been alerted that a large-scale Ronaldo story was set to run tomorrow on the online platform *El Confidencial*. The report was about offshore companies. It was our story.

The room was silent. We stared at one another in dismay. Could this be true? Forty-eight hours before our major exposé was published, the same story would be appearing elsewhere. We were almost paralysed. Someone suggested calling a conference of all the EIC partners. Stefan Candea, our coordinator, set up the meeting on our internal platform.

A call came in from Portugal. Our partner said that an informant had told him that *El Confidencial* was planning to publish exactly our story. They had been briefed by the Ronaldo side. The article was intended to 'shoot us down'.

Everyone in the safe room began talking at once, only to fall silent again. The worst-case scenario had come true. We had been working on our exposés for months, and now it felt as though someone was trying to rob us of the rewards for all our hard work. But maybe it was all a ruse, an intentionally baseless rumour.

Our colleagues from *El Mundo* in Spain and *Expresso* in Portugal repeated what they had heard. The information was still sketchy, but both of our partners had concluded, independently of one another, that *El Confidencial* would be publishing an article tomorrow about the construct of companies owned by Cristiano Ronaldo.

What should we do? Voices got raised during the conference, with some of our partners demanding that we publish all our stories tomorrow. Put everything online, they said. Another countered that we should merely announce that EIC was planning a major Football Leaks story for the coming weekend.

Our network was made up of websites, newspapers and magazines. We had tinkered around for weeks trying to orchestrate a publication schedule that reflected how hard the various partners had worked on the story. It had taken what felt like for ever to talk over all the eventualities and agree which stories should appear when. If we all had to go online with our stories in the next twelve hours, it would be chaotic. We might make mistakes, and our collective power would be lost. We took a deep breath and tried to stay calm. It was important to keep a clear head and not panic.

What would an intentionally placed Ronaldo story that depicted him in a good light actually look like? we asked ourselves. We ran through the possible PR strategies. Ronaldo had diverted well in excess of €100 million to the British Virgin Islands in a plan designed to save on taxes. How could this secret be revealed in a story that was positive for him? None of us had any idea.

Our discussions were going around in circles. Everyone's fear of standing there empty-handed the following morning, of seeing all our work over the previous months go down the drain, was palpable. Stefan said that he wanted *Der Spiegel* to decide how to proceed, since that was the publication that had originally received the cache of data. We decided that we would stick to our publication schedule. This was a big risk. We were betting everything on a single card.

We wrote to John, telling him that there had been problems and that *El Confidencial* might be pre-empting our Ronaldo story tomorrow. We would have to examine the story and perhaps react. His response was curt, merely wishing us the best of luck. Even whistle-blowers were apparently at a loss for words sometimes.

We left the office shortly before midnight. As a rule, *El Confidencial* put articles online between 3 and 5 a.m. We wanted to grab a shower and catch at least a few minutes of sleep beforehand.

One day left.

El Confidencial appeared a little before 3 a.m. The headline was about Ronaldo, and the teaser used the phrase 'tax haven'. Nicola Naber, who speaks very good Spanish, translated the article that night and sent it to us by email. But before we got her translation, John had written to us that we shouldn't panic. The article was very thin, he wrote. There was nothing in it.

Nicola's translation confirmed that assessment. *El Confidencial*'s story was very primitive. It was exclusively about Ronaldo's endorsement business and two companies that worked for him in Ireland. It didn't mention BVI. That was less than half the story, but it gave Ronaldo's team of advisors the chance to declare that he didn't have any problems whatsoever with the tax authorities.

When those in the football industry want to pull the wool over the public's eyes, they almost always find a way. They can lull the media to sleep, do deals with them, release quotes and place stories. But those techniques weren't going to be of much use in this case. The story about Ronaldo that Football Leaks told could no longer be pre-empted.

Friday, 2 December 2016.

We had been working towards this day for months and spent weeks coming up with a structure. During the 10 p.m. news, we would present the results of our research on ZDF, one of Germany's two main national public TV stations. Over the past few weeks, we had taken colleagues into our confidence about our research. They had helped us come up with ways of publicising Football Leaks on a variety of platforms so as to reach the largest possible audience. It had become a mammoth project, in terms of both the scope of its content and its organisation.

At 9 p.m., we all gathered on the thirteenth floor of the *Spiegel* building. We had agreed that all the EIC partners would publish their stories at the top of that hour.

We hit the button. And Football Leaks was released into the world.

John wrote only a few seconds after the Ronaldo story had gone online.

'This is the most important day of my life,' he told us. 'I am convinced that there will be a better football after these publications.'

Burning Issues

It was bitterly cold, minus 15 degrees Celsius, with a biting wind and snow. Winter in Eastern Europe is hard, but John still wore the same thin denim jacket he had worn a year ago when we first met him. Now, in February 2017, we were meeting again. More than two months after our first publications, we wanted to take preliminary stock and discuss the reception Football Leaks had received. And the consequences.

The mission and goal of all of our major investigative reports is to shed light on things. We want to get as close as possible to the truth. That may sound simple, but it's not. The massive collection of data from Football Leaks had given us a unique opportunity to illuminate a parallel universe that previously believed it could escape detection behind a shiny facade. That's what we could do. We could describe the excesses of the football industry, the criminal energy contained within and awakened by it, and its susceptibility to tax evasion, embezzlement and corruption. We could tell the public about a rotten system and bad practices, such as the global deals done with teenage talents. We could also dissect the megalomania of the whole scene, the brazenness of corrupt club patrons and politically connected football association functionaries.

But what would follow exposés like ours was another question. Would they help bring to justice those who paid and accepted bribes? Would they put a stop to the trade in players who are still children? Would they force football associations to institute tighter controls on the flows of money for transfer and agents' fees and far stiffer penalties for violations of the rules? Would it make the profiteers from all these dirty deals fear that they could be the next ones to be uncovered? And would it open the eyes, at least a little, of all the people that loved the game?

Or was it naïve to think that increased transparency could impress a football business that is corrupt in so many ways? Or change the minds of football fans, especially as almost everyone assumes and accepts that in huge industries such as football the rich are permitted to help themselves and get even richer?

'Should I tell the truth?' John said. 'I'm frustrated. I'm asking myself whether it was all worth it. The stress, the risk, the hard work and the fear. The football world was startled for a moment, that's true, but now it's back to business as usual. Nothing has changed.'

He took a couple of documents from inside his jacket and spread them out on the table. They were contracts, with the name Nélio Lucas printed in bold. The manager – whose company Doyen Sports had nearly driven the Dutch club Twente Enschede into the second division, who had worked together with shady Kazakh business moguls and whose business practices allegedly included the use of prostitutes – was still sitting at the negotiating table with the powers that be in world football, sewing up the next contract deals worth millions. The proof was right there in these documents.

Lucas was now operating with a different company. At least, the papers John smoothed out with his hand made no mention of Doyen Sports. Instead, in late November 2016, Inter Milan concluded a contract with Vela Management Ltd. The company was based in Malta and was represented by Lucas. This time the Portuguese entrepreneur functioned not as an investor, but as a regular agent. It was his task to ensure that Croatian midfielder Marcelo Brozović extended his contract with the club.

'How can this be?' John asked. 'We've been describing Nélio Lucas's business practices for almost a year and a half now. Anyone can read about how little he's interested in the welfare of his players. Or whether his players have successful careers, make good decisions and are happy. Nélio and his kind don't care about any of that at all as long as they are earning profits for themselves. And the money they get for their deals disappears in tax havens. Why are players, agents, clubs and football associations still working with him? Why aren't people like that taken out of circulation? What are the police doing?'

He laid out another document on the table. On 14 December 2016, in the midst of the Football Leaks publications, Vela Management received €1 million from Inter Milan. The money was paid to the VP Bank (Verwaltungs- und Privat-Bank Aktiengesellschaft) in Liechtenstein. The contract stipulated that Lucas was owed a further €1 million, payable by 31 May 2017. Brozović extended his contract until 2021.

'He doesn't care at all whether a couple of journalists write about him and his deals,' John complained. 'He just keeps on going as usual, and the football industry allows him to.'

John was talking a bit too loudly. A guy looked over the top of his newspaper at us, interested.

'I'm so angry,' John murmured, much more quietly.

There were several ways of looking at the Football Leaks revelations. On the one hand, they made waves, kicked off a lot of discussions and were passed on and commented upon by other media outlets. For example, Germany's respected *Süddeutsche Zeitung* newspaper wrote: 'Those who celebrate their heroes are celebrating an elite. In terms of what they earn and how they behave that's what pro footballers are. And the current Football Leaks research shows just how elitist they are. A rapacious clique has formed and is increasing its wealth with dirty tricks.' Another source reported: 'In the professional realm, the top echelons of football are rotten. Calculated trafficking in human beings, ostentatiously displayed wealth – and the business eats up funds from social welfare programmes.'

If the football industry had been a business that had promised to abide by a code of conduct for good management, such bleak judgements would have shaken it to the core. But hardly any of the decision-makers in the industry pay much heed to moral or ethical limits. The main goal is to beat the competition and gain an advantage, even if it means exploiting human beings, bending the sense of what's right and wrong, or skirting laws.

The football industry's response to the Football Leaks revelations was stony silence. Club bosses, players, agents and football association functionaries rarely commented on our exposés. But internally, the industry was panicking. For the heads of the European leagues and clubs, the most important question was not which dirty deals Football Leaks would make public, it was how all of this could have become public in the first place. For the bosses, the priority was to stop the leaks and identify their source.

On 19 December 2016, a good two weeks after the start of the Football Leaks publications, the heads of the Premier League, the Bundesliga and the Primera División wrote a joint letter to FIFA, in which they voiced their suspicion to the association's head lawyer, Marco Villiger, that the leak might be located in FIFA's Transfer Matching System (TMS). For roughly ten years, in an attempt to fight corruption, kickbacks and illegal agreements, FIFA had been collecting in a strictly confidential file all the information that it required clubs to provide about their business dealings, including transfer and labour contracts and the fees agreed with agents.

The European Club Association (ECA), which represents the common interests of the continent's leading teams, had sent a similar letter on 13 December. The lobbyists for the individual clubs also suspected that the TMS system had been hacked. They demanded that Villiger provide them with a clear plan for how FIFA planned to ward off possible attacks.

The FIFA lawyer rejected the charge that the sensitive information had been leaked from within world football's governing body. He drew attention to numerous security measures FIFA employed for confidential TMS information: no direct connection to the Internet, regular mandatory password updates for all users and, since 2016, the obligatory use of watermarks on every FIFA document. None of the contracts published by *Der Spiegel* or any of its partners bore any such watermark, Villiger stressed. He added that Football Leaks had emphasized on its own website that no one had been hacked.

The last things the football industry wanted were a loss of control, unwelcome internal supervision, persistent external questioning and the publication of stories about ethically dubious deals. That became clear at a meeting of the most important European club bosses at Munich's Hilton Airport hotel on 30 January 2017. The exclusive circle included the heads of Bayern Munich, Juventus, Barcelona, Manchester United and Paris Saint-Germain.

On the agenda was Football Leaks. Then-ECA chairman Karl-Heinz Rummenigge opened the session. The protocol reads: 'KHR emphasised the damage of these leaks to the atmosphere in the dressing room in many clubs and that it is still not clear where these leaks originate. He called for action. Jean-Michel Aulas [the owner and chairman of Olympique Lyonnais] stated that certain information did not come directly from the TMS system, like information on third-party ownership. He suggested checking the system, but mentioned that the source of the leaks is more important.' Killing the messenger to get rid of the message is a classic response of systems of power when their strategies for maintaining dominance are made public and questioned by anonymous third parties.

It's surprising that the football associations and clubs that saw their interests threatened by Football Leaks should have singled out FIFA as the source of the leaks. Via *Der Spiegel*, John had offered to give the governing body documents illustrating the dirty deals connected with transfers and TPO agreements. But FIFA hadn't reacted to this offer. It seemed as though world football's governing body wasn't interested in clearing up these issues in the slightest.

At least FIFA president Gianni Infantino had agreed in mid-December to talk to representatives of the EIC. The interview was supposed to cover the big questions raised by the Football Leaks exposés: credibility, transparency and the monitoring of agents and flows of money.

The value of such group interviews is directly proportionate to the clarity with which the conversational partners express their positions. Infantino had no such positions. But the interview was interesting insofar as Infantino's empty phrases, evasions and hemming and hawing showed that FIFA can't be expected to do anything to drain the swamp of modern-day football. In almost all of his answers to our questions Infantino lost himself in generalities. Again and again he told us he would have to think things over, take another look or discuss the matter with others. 'We reach some limits here,' he said. 'FIFA is not the world police.' It sounded as though he were capitulating.

'If Football Leaks has shown anything, it's that football is in dire need of help,' John said. 'The sport isn't able to help itself. It needs assistance from the police, tax authorities and, above all, the politicians.'

John had registered with great interest how leading politicians across Europe had taken notice of Football Leaks, in particular criticising the tricks used to evade taxes. German finance minister Wolfgang Schäuble had vowed to take on tax havens more directly, British Labour MP Meg Hillier had called for an investigation into the revelations, and the Socialist Party in Spain had demanded a comprehensive inquiry into the director of the Spanish tax authority and the country's finance minister, Cristóbal Montoro. German politician Sven Giegold, the financial and economic spokesman for the Green Party in the European Parliament, put it best: 'The leak is a red card for football millionaires. Income resulting from sporting performances must be taxed in the country where the player is active. Football players' evasion of taxes is a serious foul against the common welfare. With their tax evasion tricks, football millionaires are hurting the people that cheer them on in stadiums. With their socially damaging behaviour, football players aren't living up by any means to their function as role models for young people.' The Football Leaks revelations were the subject of an EU investigative committee hearing in September 2017.

'As upset as I am about how the football industry has dealt with the publications, I'm quite happy that politicians have recognised the problems and want to do something about them,' John said. His documents had illustrated how tax havens, letterbox companies, the lack of transparency in the global flow of money and the holes in EU law had given the super-rich the chance to increase their wealth to the detriment of the general public, whether their money was invested in football or in another sector. The explosive nature of our exposés went far beyond football itself. The revelations were about issues that concerned everybody.

'Precisely these sorts of discussions were what we wanted,' John said. 'But the best thing about the journalistic articles was that eight European tax authorities have contacted us. They read the articles and want help pursuing tax evaders. We will support these efforts.'

The judicial authorities seem to have found John's material very useful. The French and English tax authorities opened investigations into a number of players and their agents. The German and Dutch authorities also found evidence for further investigations, while the Spanish tax authorities are currently investigating numerous professional football players, and even Cristiano Ronaldo's books have been examined. But such investigations can take years.

'It's a little bit crazy,' John said. 'On the one hand, half of Europe is going after criminals in the football industry on the basis of our data, and on the other, at least three national police forces are searching for us because they think we're hackers.

'What I told you at the start of our meeting was wrong,' he went on. 'Of course, it was all worth it.' It was the best, most exciting time of his life, and all in all we had set a lot of things in motion. 'But the pressure has to be kept on football so that the sport understands that it will commit suicide someday if the lack of transparency and all the swindles go on.'

Did that mean he was going to continue? we wanted to know. And what about his associates?

'Football Leaks isn't over,' he answered. 'On the contrary, while you were working with our material, we've been collecting new data. Several terabytes' worth, an even bigger pile than what we previously gave you. This material is explosive, and it concerns other professional players than in the other documents. We want this material to be published too, so that the football industry finally realises that it isn't exempt from laws and ethics.'

He had prepared a new hard drive, he told us. We could take it with us that very day.

The Earthquake

With John firing on all cylinders it was increasingly impossible to take any sort of a break from journalistic scoops and research. Since our meeting in February, he was sending us new messages almost every day. He seemed increasingly to be drawing his information from official investigative circles. .

'Something big is going to happen soon – the Spaniards are taking Ronaldo and Mourinho seriously,' he wrote.

The Spaniards?

'Prosecutors intend to file charges quite soon.'

Where did he get that from?

'Just believe me.'

A few weeks later, in May 2017, the Spanish media began reporting that Ronaldo's financial practices might be about to get him into hot water. The state authorities were taking a closer look at his tax returns, particularly the large sums of money passing through a company in the Caribbean. Cristiano Ronaldo barely commented on the matter in public. He only touched on the issue in an interview with the magazine *France Football*, saying: 'I've done everything correctly. There are lots of innocent people in prison – that's a bit how I feel at the moment. You know that you've done nothing wrong, but you're accused of acting immorally.' Ronaldo is nothing if not dramatic.

By this point, however, investigators throughout Europe weren't allowing themselves to be fobbed off with protestations of innocence and were following up on the Football Leaks revelations. For example, in France, the Central Investigative Office for Fighting Corruption and Financial and Tax Crimes carried out raids on Paris Saint-Germain and the homes of several top players in late May. They were looking for material connected with deals done by agent Marcelo Simonian, who was alleged to have funnelled millions of euros in fees into a construct of offshore companies, with the help of Argentinian player advisors and Dutch middlemen. In the early hours of 23 May, this special French police unit spent hours searching the PSG headquarters at the Parc des Princes stadium and club offices in the Paris suburb of Boulogne-Billancourt. At roughly 6 a.m., other officers paid visits to the homes of PSG stars Ángel Di María and Javier Pastore, as well as Nantes player Emiliano Sala.

'Slowly but surely, our work is paying off,' John wrote.

There was something surreal about the whistle-blower commenting on the latest developments in this manner. John was sitting in front of his computer somewhere in the world, watching as investigators carried out raids and interrogations based on his revelations. And he made no bones about how pleased he was.

'It took a while but now they're doing something,' he wrote. 'Good!'

The investigations concerning Simonian and his business partners will take months, and they have also led to raids on English clubs. The inquiry has become international, so the national authorities are currently cooperating via Europol. It is unclear how long the investigations will take and whether they will result in any indictments, but the case of Ronaldo suggests that they could cause a sensation.

In mid-June 2017, prosecutors in Madrid issued a brief but explosive press release. It accused Cristiano Ronaldo, European champion and multiple Ballon d'Or winner, of having evaded, 'wilfully' and 'knowingly', some €14.8 million in taxes between 2011 and 2014. Prosecutors found that the construct of companies in Ireland and the British Virgin Islands that managed Ronaldo's money served to conceal his advertising revenues from the tax authorities, and they announced that they would ask a court to consider criminal charges. Ronaldo could be put on trial.

The Madrid prosecutors were acting on advice from the Spanish tax authorities and following up on Football Leaks revelations from the previous December. A spokesman for Ronaldo claimed that even though the player hadn't paid all his taxes, he had never intended to break the law. 'I am not a saint, but I am also not a devil,' added Ronaldo himself. Amidst the breaking scandal, it was rumoured that Real Madrid had called up the Spanish newspapers and asked them not to use any pictures of their star forward wearing the club's kit.

At the time of writing, a Spanish judge is examining Ronaldo's case. She will decide if and when the forward will have to appear in court. At the same time, investigators are honing in other superstars, with Real Madrid a particular focus. As of March 2018, Luka Modrić, Pepe, Marcelo and Fábio Coentrão have all received correspondence from or been interviewed by investigators. And other players, such as former Barcelona star Alexis Sánchez, have cut deals with the Spanish authorities, obliging them to pay millions in back taxes.

Videos have been posted of Monaco striker Radamel Falcao being interrogated. The financial authorities think that between 2012 and 2013, while at Atlético Madrid, he evaded €5.6 million in taxes, and the Football Leaks material shows that he used a number of letterbox companies and middlemen. Spanish prosecutors have accused Falcao of using a system of concealment 'with the sole purpose of hiding money from the Spanish tax authorities'. After being summoned for an interview, the Colombian striker paid €8.2 million to those authorities. In the video, the striker takes a seat in the first row of a small courtroom, with space for fewer than two dozen people. He's all alone. At the beginning of the interview, he seems very confident. Outwardly, there's no difference to the cool, calm and collected forward, lurking with intent in the box, unimpressed by the steely central defenders trying to keep him away from goal. But sometimes judges can be tougher opponents than fullbacks.

The initial questions generally concern where and when Falcao was liable to pay taxes. Soon, the striker begins to fidget in his seat, searching for words and often ending up saying nothing more than that his advisors took care of everything. When the questioning turns to letterbox companies and the millions of euros transferred around the globe, Falcao's shoulders droop. The fidgeting continues – it's hard not to be reminded of a schoolboy who needs to go to the toilet. He seems unable or unwilling to answer questions, as though he is only now, in the courtroom, learning that he is responsible for his own financial affairs and that earning millions also entails certain social obligations. Falcao keeps repeating that he only came to Europe to play football and that his financial advisors took care of everything else. One of those advisors was Jorge Mendes, who also represents Ronaldo and José Mourinho.

It was at this point that the court began to scrutinise the 'Big Three' in world football – and our attention was directed to the Madrid community of Pozuelo de Alarcón, where Falcao was made to testify. The court is presided over by Judge Monica Gómez Ferrer, who would also go on to question Ronaldo, Mourinho and Mendes. Why is it that three of the world's biggest tax investigations come under the jurisdiction of this one court?

Real Madrid's biggest stars barely think twice about where to live. La Finca is a luxury neighbourhood full of mansions with swimming pools in the north-west of the Spanish capital, only half an hour from Real's training ground. Entry into this exclusive community is carefully restricted. There are parks and ponds. It's surrounded by trails for jogging, which is as close as the residents of La Finca usually get to the outside world. Real's Gareth Bale and Toni Kroos live there, as has Ronaldo for the past nine years. Mendes, too, owns a house in La Finca. Since the community is part of the district of Pozuelo de Alarcón, tax cases concerning La Finca residents usually end up on Judge Ferrer's desk. And she has a reputation for being strict, persistent and utterly uncowed by the glamour of football.

In June 2017, she summoned Mendes to appear before her. The court building is the polar opposite of La Finca – a concrete eyesore on a busy road. Mendes had been driven to the court in a limousine like a statesman. He got out wearing his usual trim dark suit and brushed aside questions from journalists with a dismissive wave of his hand. The agent was brought for questioning to a small room of barely thirty square metres, where he was given a hard wooden chair to sit on. Mendes is known as an antsy guy, but when the judge began to question him, he was even more restless than usual. When asked who thought up all the constructs of offshore companies for his many superstar clients, he answered decisively. It wasn't him. Definitely not. It must have been others. Who, he didn't know. Financial advisors, certainly. He was only responsible for contracts, he swore. The judge, who was well versed in the facts, background and context of such deals, didn't bat an eye.

Mendes's agency Gestifute has its headquarters in Ulysses House, the most expensive office building in Dublin. The companies Polaris and MIM, both of which played central roles in the offshore company constructs of Mendes's players, are also registered on the same floor of that building. One of the top managers for both Polaris and Gestifute is Mendes's nephew Luis Correia. Another manager, Irishman Andy Quinn, works for all three firms. Mendes has earned some €6 million in dividends as an investor in Polaris. That's quite a sum, considering that Mendes testified that he had no idea what Polaris and MIM do.

A number of Mendes's clients have had to make costly appearances in Pozuelo de Alarcón in the wake of Football Leaks revelations. Aside from Falcao, Portuguese defender Pepe paid back €1.8 million, Ángel Di María and Fabio Coentrão, €1.3 million apiece, and Ricardo Carvalho a mere €500,000. Tax investigations against other players are ongoing, with further fines possibly forthcoming.

The tax authorities are also examining the case of James Rodríguez, who moved from Real to Bayern Munich in 2017. Like other Mendes clients, Rodriguez's advertising revenues were paid to Polaris and MIM, and his case also involves a company in the British Virgin Islands: Kenalton Assets. In late 2014, €12 million were paid into James's account at the St Galler Kantonalbank in Switzerland. It's entirely possible that Bayern will have to give the midfielder a few days off from work in order to answer a few questions from Judge Ferrer about these flows of money.

Portuguese international Carvalho told a court that when it came to his image rights deals, he always listened to Mendes and his lawyer, Carlos Osório de Castro. It is conspicuous how many Mendes clients work with the same people and companies: Castro, for instance, or Miguel Marques, a banker at the Portuguese branch of the St Galler Kantonalbank, or Polaris and MIM. These football stars often put their trust in the same attorneys to deal with their tax problems.

While Judge Ferrer was conducting her interviews, we kept exploring the Football Leaks database, where we found a document entitled 'Meeting Gestifute'. There was a note reading: 'Tax authorities' campaign against Jorge. Risk of being classed as *cooperador necesario*. Criminal offense.' Under Spanish law, anyone aiding and abetting a crime can be charged as a '*cooperador necesario*', or accessory. Thus, if the court in Pozuelo de Alarcón finds that there was a 'Mendes system' behind the tax-saving tricks of players, the agent could face criminal charges as an accessory to tax evasion.

Judge Ferrer may be weighing that option. In the months to come, she intends to summon Mendes confidants such as Castro and Correia to testify. First, though, she wanted to talk to Ronaldo and confront him in court about his tax arrangements. Unfortunately for her, Judge Ferrer also learned that world superstars like Ronaldo live in a parallel world of appointments that simply cannot be cancelled. The court and the player's attorneys fought a veritable tug-of-war over the proper time for his questioning. In summer 2017, after a long season, Ronaldo played for Portugal in the Confederations Cup in Russia, then used the only time available to take a vacation with his family, and after that it was back to training for his next season at Real.

After the Ronaldo tax story broke, he published a video on Instagram that showed him running around his estate in La Finca and blabbing this or that into the camera. Suddenly, Ronaldo said he had a message for all his haters: they should continue – it only spurred him on. Then he jumps into his pool.

A short time later, headlines began to pop up in newspapers all over Europe: Ronaldo, who had just won an unprecedented second straight Champions League title with Real, wanted to leave Spain. Sources 'close to him' were cited as saying that he was dissatisfied with how he was being publicly treated and felt hard done by. He wanted to leave it all behind: his tax problems, the investigation and his club Real, which the source said was not doing enough to defend its star players against the accusations. Perhaps, a number of tabloids speculated, Ronaldo would return to England, maybe to his former club, Manchester United. Or he might head to PSG, where Qatari oil money has wiped away all the limits on transfer fees.

Judge Ferrer remained unperturbed by the entire circus. She ignored all the headlines and summoned Ronaldo to testify. The superstar ended his holiday on a gigantic yacht in the Mediterranean and returned to Madrid.

According to the prosecutors' report, Ronaldo sold his image rights to Tollin on BVI, only for that company to pass them on ten days later to MIM in Ireland. Investigators found that the sale to Tollin was completely superfluous. The only possible point, they argued, was to hide the suspect's image rights revenues from the financial authorities. It was a serious accusation – and one that supported a central element of our reporting based on the Football Leaks data.

On a Monday morning in late July 2017, more than two hundred journalists from all over the world, including reporters from the globe's biggest TV stations, gathered in front of the court in Pozuelo de Alarcón. That morning, Ronaldo had a date, not with his teammates on the training pitch, but with Judge Ferrer. At 10.58 a.m., a black saloon with tinted windows entered the parking garage underneath the building. None of the journalists waiting in front of the main entrance got a glimpse of Ronaldo.

In court, the player told Judge Ferrer that his only talent was for playing football, and that was why he hired advisors and 'paid them so well'. He said he had instructed the experts in his employ that he didn't want any 'nonsense' and that they should calculate his taxes honestly. Judge Ferrer kept pressing: so who had taken care of Ronaldo's taxes for him?

The striker's answer was something like a process of elimination. The first thing he did was to exonerate Mendes, whom he claimed was 'even dumber than I' on tax matters. Mendes, Ronaldo said, was only in charge of transfers and employment contracts. Meanwhile, Mendes's nephew Correia, the striker asserted, was charged exclusively with acquiring sponsors. Ronaldo added that he had instructed Castro to find him the 'best tax accountancy in Spain' to handle his affairs.

Judge Ferrer continued to press him. Ronaldo's construct of Caribbean companies had existed even before he joined Real Madrid, she pointed out. 'Look me in the eye,' the striker told her. He assured her that he had never intended to deceive anyone. She simply had to believe him. Tollin, his letterbox company, had been the idea of a lawyer at Manchester United. 'He said all football players did that,' he told Ferrer. 'I didn't want to be the exception. I may be exceptional on the pitch, but off the field I just want to be like everyone else.'

A few weeks before Ronaldo's testimony, we had stumbled across some strange documents in the Football Leaks database. They centred on a contract Ronaldo personally signed with Tollin, according to which, between 2009 and 2014, the company would receive and store the player's money from his advertising contracts. Ronaldo apparently provided the authorities with these documents during the course of their investigations. In the database, we found a draft of the agreement, with a note from one of Ronaldo's advisors, who wrote that 'a bank account that had existed in 2008' should be added. That was the year the contract was allegedly signed. But was it in fact backdated?

An internal email from June 2009 indicated that Ronaldo's British advertising rights 'currently' resided with his British image rights company – despite the fact that the contract Ronaldo had personally signed gave them to Tollin in January 2009. 'Backdating documents for the tax authorities would constitute forgery,' says Carlos Cruzado, the president of the tax experts' association in the Spanish Finance Ministry.

German-Spanish business attorney Rafael Villena adds, 'According to Spanish law, that could be considered fraud.'

This contract has rocked Ronaldo's defence strategy. His lawyers have always argued that nothing changed about the role played by Tollin since 2004. Ronaldo played for Manchester United until 2009 and, his solicitors claim, even the Inland Revenue service checked his Caribbean business dealings and found nothing untoward about them. Ronaldo's conscience was clean. He never intended to evade any taxes. At least that's what he repeatedly told Judge Ferrer.

What Ronaldo never mentioned was that his image rights initially belonged to the Brockton Foundation, which his mother founded in Panama. As of 2004, his worldwide advertising revenues went to Tollin, but England was excepted from that deal. At that point, Ronaldo played in the English Premier League and was liable for taxes in Britain. He set up a separate company for his English advertising revenues. According to the contract in Football Leaks, it wasn't until January 2009 that all of his advertising millions went to Tollin. Thus, in contrast to what his attorneys were saying, he had changed his constellation of companies. Both Ronaldo's lawyer and his advisors declined to comment upon the suspicions surrounding Tollin and the possible backdating of contracts.

Judge Ferrer and her colleagues didn't get any answers on this score either. In her questioning, Ronaldo was confronted directly with our revelations, but the superstar only asked the judge to speak more slowly, saying that he had no idea about tax matters.

Ronaldo – the man who has many millions invested in companies, who maintains an impressive collection of luxury cars and has a private jet at his disposal, and who presents himself on all his social media platforms as an extremely successful entrepreneur – seemed completely at a loss in front of Señora Ferrer. It was as though a judge in Pozuelo de Alarcón had blown down a house of cards.

As Ronaldo was being questioned, his fans assembled in front of the court building. Some chanted, 'Free Ronaldo!' Others carried placards – one fan had written on his that rich people, too, should have to pay taxes.

Ronaldo had originally intended to make a statement about the accusations after his hearing, and Real Madrid employees had set up a microphone on the front steps of the court building. But following several sound checks, a lawyer for Gestifute appeared in Ronaldo's stead and informed the crowd that the questions had ended. Ronaldo had testified for ninety minutes before Judge Ferrer and would not be appearing personally in front of the press. Everything was 'fine', the solicitor declared. Ronaldo was already heading home. The player only commented on his court date later in a prepared statement, repeating that he had never intended to evade any taxes and had nothing to hide.

As we write, the ball, so to speak, is in Judge Ferrer's court. She will decide whether and when to put Ronaldo on trial. If charged, the football superstar could face a prison sentence of up to seven years and hefty fines. Ronaldo seems to have realised how serious the situation is: in late 2017, he began to hire more top-flight attorneys to defend him and prepare for a possible trial.

For the football world, Ronaldo's interrogation was definitive proof that the Football Leaks documents are genuine.

*

In his office in Nyon, on Lake Geneva, UEFA president Aleksander Čeferin doesn't officially name either Ronaldo or Mendes, but he's clearly pissed off. 'It is completely unnecessary to evade taxes if you earn that much money,' Čeferin says. The Slovenian, who has held the job since September 2016, has been following the reports based on Football Leaks data closely. 'The scale of the revelations surprised me,' he says. 'It's not good at all for the reputation of our sport, but it is good that these things come to light. That way they won't happen any more – or at least only rarely.'

Čeferin, a lawyer, eagerly awaits all court dates in Pozuelo de Alarcón and believes that in general football players don't know very much about their own finances. 'Of course, legally, they're responsible for their tax returns,' he says. 'But I don't think they know much about what is going on there. They have people around them who take care of their books and say, "Don't worry! We'll sort everything out!" We're talking here about men who think about nothing but football all day. I know these players. They may want this or that, but they don't want to bother themselves with taxes.' Čeferin suggests that in future football players only use state-registered accountants to deal with their tax returns and financial affairs. 'A system needs to be built up to help the players,' he says.

But to take the conclusions drawn from the Football Leaks revelations to their logical extreme, Čeferin's idea needs to go further. Players aren't the only ones who have encountered problems with the law because of Football Leaks; coaches and advisors have, too. Spanish prosecutors have accused José Mourinho, during his stint at Real, of failing to pay €3.3 million in taxes in 2011 and 2012. Football Leaks documents showed how the superstar coach, a Mendes client, diverted assets to letterbox companies and trusts in the Caribbean and New Zealand. In the wake of our reports, Castro wrote to Mourinho's London PR agency, saying, 'The house is on fire.'

Mourinho was another resident of La Finca, where from 2010 to 2013 he rented a €20,000 a month mansion. Like other Mendes clients, his money – around €6 million in 2011 and 2012 alone – was chanelled via MIM and Polaris to a Caribbean letterbox company to which he had signed over his marketing rights.

In July 2014, Mourinho was put under audit by the Spanish tax authorities, who noticed this construct of companies. A year later, he was forced to pay €3.25 million in back taxes plus a €1.15 million fine. The case seemed to be closed. But then we published details about a trust in New Zealand that was behind the Caribbean company. A mere ten days later, New Zealand's Inland Revenue department contacted the trust in Auckland, demanding to see its records.

That set off feverish activity in the Mourinho camp. One of the lawyers wrote that he was sure the British Inland Revenue service would also want to check the manager's tax returns. Mourinho was advised not to take his records to England. The coach, who had managed Manchester United since the summer of 2016, had had enough. His banker told his lawyer that their mutual client had decided to sell off all his interests in such offshore companies to avoid any, presumably unpleasant, surprises and media attention in the future.

Such rectitude came too late to ward off investigations by the Spanish tax authorities. They re-examined Mourinho's

Irish–Caribbean–New Zealand business connections and are now accusing him of failing to pay taxes on €7 million in advertising revenue. The judge in charge of the case is Señora Ferrer.

Meanwhile, in Croatia, the Mamić brothers were put on trial in connection with payments to letterbox companies, the many millions of Dinamo Zagreb money that seem to have gone missing, and the questionable contracts and exorbitant fees charged in conjunction with talented Dinamo players. One of the witnesses in the trial was Real midfielder Luka Modrić, who tied himself up in convoluted explanations and partly contradicted what he had previously told police. At one point, the defendant Zdravko Mamić jumped up from his seat to praise the 'lad' for his testimony. In early March 2018, Croatian prosecutors charged Modrić with perjury.

The investigations concerning Mendes's companies and clients could also be somewhat protracted. Judge Ferrer isn't the only one interested in the super-agent's dealings. Portuguese investigators have their eyes trained on him as well, examining dozens of transfers, worth hundreds of millions, in which Gestifute played a role.

The Football Leaks revelations led authorities in a number of European countries to scrutinise documents and transactions connected with players, functionaries and advisors. The investigators formed networks and they now try to solve cases jointly. John continued to comment almost every day on the latest developments, testimonies and legal cases.

For example, in late September 2017, he followed the live stream of a European Parliament investigative committee discussing fraud in football. The Football Leaks revelations had also made waves in the highest echelons of politics, and parliamentarians wanted to know whether EU regulations could bring the runaway market back into line.

'I don't put much hope in this committee, but we'll see,' John wrote.

The politicians were particularly interested in tax equity and reining in letterbox companies, and their tone of voice was correspondingly pointed, with parliamentarians explicitly accusing FIFA functionaries of wrongdoing. FIFA's compliance representative Kimberly Morris was asked whether she was in favour of tax equity and fair play. Morris answered all the questions during the session with the argument that the problem was a matter of national regulation. FIFA's authority was limited, she said, but officials at football's governing body were doing what they could to investigate the sporting aspects. Gregor Reiter, a representative of the European Football Agents Association, also said that differences in national laws made it difficult to impose sanctions on advisors who misbehaved.

The football functionaries presented themselves as helpless representatives of a billion-euro business that had been forced to recognise that the whole system was beyond its control. Committee chairman Werner Langen described the answers given by those questioned as 'not entirely satisfactory', and one of the MEPs said that the testimony of the FIFA representatives was 'a magnificent example of double talk'.

'Today, even the stupidest person must realise that politicians have looked the other way for too long with this industry,' John wrote. 'The football business needs rules that can be enforced internationally.'

Football Leaks has achieved a lot. The revelations have shaken up the industry politically and legally. But it will take years until the sport gets the sort of binding rules that will save it from itself.

Days before the EU committee hearing, we found a number of promising items in the material that John had given us on his last visit and which he had irregularly updated ever since. This time the documents concerned the mega-transfers of the summer of 2017: Neymar, Ousmane Dembélé and Kylian Mbappé. We also found thousands of contracts and emails connected with the Premier League that illustrated how the billions earned from English football's last TV contract encouraged rampant spending by the league's clubs.

'We've been warning for two years that the market was going to explode,' John wrote. 'This summer it's happened, and the effects on football will be deadly.'

Hostile Takeover

The entire lunacy of unrestrained commercialism in football is summarised by a document no bigger than a single sheet of toilet paper. It's a cheque from the Société Générale bank containing a sum in large red numbers:

€222,000,000.00.

The cheque was issued on behalf of Paris Saint-Germain, and it was signed in August 2017. A short time later, an employee of FC Barcelona's house bank sent an email to Qatar National Bank: 'We're pleased to inform and confirm that the account has been credited and the funds are at the clients [*sic*] complete disposal. We would like to take advantage and thank your Paris branch as well as yourself for the great support and professionalism with which this matter was handled.'

The biggest deal in football history had been done. PSG had bought Brazilian striker Neymar da Silva Santos Júnior from Barcelona for €222 million. The news hit the footballing world like a hurricane. A ranking member of UEFA would write in a desperate-sounding email to a colleague: 'The transfer system is out of control.'

UEFA president Aleksander Čeferin asked the EU Commission for help, and Bayern Munich president Uli Hoeness said that things couldn't keep going the way they were – otherwise everything would be *'kaputt'*. Even German chancellor Angela Merkel would call upon football associations to 'ensure greater competitive balance'.

Who really pulls the strings in football? This question has become even more urgent since the Neymar deal was announced.

Clubs and associations organise the game. Fans, managers and players fill it with life. But since the summer of 2017, another entity has made its influence felt. An entity capable of buying the sport.

The story of the Neymar transfer is the story of a hostile takeover. The Football Leaks documents John provided illustrated how brutally PSG pursued its own interest in acquiring Neymar and how little billionaire investors care about football association rules when they want to take their clubs to the summit of world football.

In 2011, the emir of Qatar ordered the company Qatar Sports Investments to take over PSG, a club previously drowning in debt. The firm is a subsidiary of the state-owned Qatar Investment Authority (QIA), the eleventh-largest governmental investment fund in the world. QIA invests the profits from Qatari sales of oil and gas, and in the autumn of 2017, it had interests in companies that were worth $338.4 billion. By comparison, the German Bundesliga's richest club has an annual turnover of €640 million (approximately $780 million). By PSG's standards, Bayern Munich are pygmies.

In the few years preceding last summer, PSG's owners had pumped €700 million into the club so that it could buy new players. In 2017, they added €400 million to that total. Along with Neymar's record-setting transfer, the club committed itself to buying Mbappé for €145 million, plus €35 million in bonuses, from AS Monaco in the summer of 2018. Within a matter of days, PSG had negotiated the two most expensive transfers in football history.

Club boss Nasser Al-Khelaifi has a clearly defined task. Qatari emir Tamim bin Hamad Al Thani, a boyhood friend of Al-Khelaifi, has his sights set on international football as a way of increasing the significance of his tiny country. Qatar has already secured the rights to host the 2022 World Cup; next up, the emir wants to win the Champions League. And Al-Khelaifi's job is to deliver.

In March 2017, a few months before PSG's two spectacular transfers, Al-Khelaifi, a former professional tennis player turned football potentate, experienced a nightmare. PSG was matched up with Barcelona in the first stage of the Champions League knockout phase, and the French team won their home leg 4–0. Then came the away leg. The Spaniards had already erased that deficit after ninety minutes, when in the fifth minute of added time Neymar, who had already scored a brace for Barça, made the decisive pass for Sergi Roberto to complete the 6–1 final score. PSG, Al-Khelaifi and the emir were humiliated.

One day after that Champions League return leg, a PSG employee wrote to Barcelona's headquarters, saying: 'I was very sad yesterday evening. The match is an evidence that PSG has a lot to learn, still.' That sounded like a gesture of subordination, but in reality it was the start of a plan to attack the Catalonian giants.

In Brazil, Neymar is regarded as the heir to the great Pelé. The circumstances surrounding his transfer from FC Santos to Barcelona in 2013 – which brought his father riches and Barcelona president Sandro Rosell a brief stretch behind bars in investigative custody – continues to interest the legal authorities, but everyone at Barça was happy to have the forward, who was seen as an eventual replacement for Lionel Messi.

For his part, Neymar also seemed happy to be at Barça. He was the club's top earner: in the 2016–17 season, he made €54 million – almost €8.5 million more than Messi. By comparison, Uruguayan striker Luis Suárez, the third member of Barca's 'Big Three', was earning a paltry €28 million a year.

At the beginning of July 2016, Neymar had signed an early three-year contract extension with the Catalonians that would have kept him at the club until 2021, but by the summer of 2017, relations had soured between the forward and his employers. Barcelona's new main sponsor, the Japanese company Rakuten, had agreed with the club that five 'top players' would travel to Tokyo for a marketing date.

One of the players was, obviously, Messi. Another star the Japanese didn't want to do without was Neymar. The plan was for him to join his Barcelona teammates on the flight to the Far East, but there was a problem: while on vacation in Brazil, Neymar had neglected to get a visa for Japan, causing panic and diplomatic tension between the Japanese and FC Barcelona.

'I have the impression that he intentionally missed his plane to drag everything out and ensure he wouldn't be granted a visa,' a Barcelona employee surmised in an email. Rakuten demanded an explanation for why Neymar hadn't completed the necessary paperwork. Oscar Grau, Barcelona's chairman of the board, forwarded an email describing the whole disaster. According to it, Neymar's personal assistant had flown from São Paulo to Rio de Janeiro to pick up the player's passport and bring it back to São Paulo the following morning, where the Japanese consulate issued Brazilian citizens visas to visit that country. Neymar himself had a private advertising engagement somewhere else in Brazil, but his passport was kept in a movable safe that could only be unlocked by the player's own fingerprint. The assistant did as any loyal servant would and picked up the safe and headed to the airport, where Neymar was arriving by private jet.

Neymar's plane landed late. When the assistant finally got hold of the player's passport, he rushed off to catch a flight himself back to São Paulo before the Japanese consulate closed, but he got stuck in Rio's infamous traffic. As if that weren't enough, his mobile-phone battery ran out of power because he was constantly making calls: with Neymar's father, with FC Barcelona and with the people from Rakuten. By the time the assistant made it back to São Paulo, the consulate was closed for the weekend. 'He was crushed,' Barcelona's sporting director wrote to the chairman of the board. 'Everyone blamed him, and he was very frustrated because he felt there was nothing that he could do.'

The episode neatly illustrates the challenges of working with superstar athletes and the hoops that clubs and sponsors jump through just to bask for a moment in reflected glory. Not surprisingly, Rakuten, which had influential diplomatic contacts, ended up solving Neymar's visa problem. Thanks to the sponsor's intervention, Neymar was given an early Monday morning appointment at the Japanese consulate in Rio. The Japanese also arranged for the Brazilian star to make it on time for the photo shoot in Tokyo. Instead of flying to Japan via Europe, Neymar took the Pacific route and appeared punctually at the promotional event.

Nevertheless, the episode left Barcelona bosses feeling uneasy. Rumours were flying that PSG was interested in signing Neymar and that the forward had intended to skip the appointment in Tokyo. Ironically, in the summer of 2017, the Brazilian had every reason to be happy about his Barcelona deal: in July, he was set to receive the second instalment of his 'signing bonus' – a cool €64.4 million that the club had agreed in exchange for Neymar's signature in July 2016. He had received €20.75 million that year and now, in 2017, stood to pocket the remaining €43.65 million.

On 31 July, Grau wrote the player a letter complaining that for weeks there had been a 'cloud of rumours and comments' that Neymar wasn't going to honour his contract and that neither the player nor his advisors had denied them. For this reason, Barcelona were going to withhold the second instalment of the signing bonus. Grau also said that Barça was examining whether it could demand the first instalment be paid back in case Neymar transferred to another club.

On 1 August, Neymar sent a letter to Barça's president giving the club twenty-four hours to pay up the €43.65 million. But Barça was having none of that. The team transferred the money to a notary public and informed Neymar that he would only receive it under two conditions: that he would not negotiate a transfer with another team and that he guaranteed he would stay at Barça until 2022. Neymar was unable – and unwilling – to do either of these things.

Neymar's contract with Barcelona contained a release clause allowing him to leave the club for a set fee of €222 million. On 2 August, the player appeared before a notary public in Barcelona and gave two Brazilian lawyers power of attorney to activate that clause. That same day, PSG's chief executive authorised two lawyers and the team's head of finance to write a €222 million cheque made out to FC Barcelona.

On 3 August, Neymar signed a contract running until the end of the 2021–22 season with the French giants. His monthly base salary was €3,069,520. The Football Leaks documents contain no information about the premiums and special payments that might be due, but we can probably conclude that they were in excess of €20 million a year. It's highly unlikely that Neymar would accept being paid less than at Barcelona, where he earned €4.5 million a month in 2016–17.

Barça fans don't have many kind words for Neymar, and after the transfer, the club sued him to recoup some €8.5 million plus interest. In Paris, by contrast, he was given a hero's welcome: his kit was a big seller from the first day he joined the team, and when he was officially introduced to supporters and the media in early August 2017, the Parc des Princes stadium was full almost to capacity. At that event, Neymar grabbed the microphone and bellowed the PSG battle cry: '*Paris est magique, ici c'est* . . . [Paris is magical, and this here is . . .]' The stadium bellowed back: 'Paris!'

PSG's owners, for whom the club, Neymar and the youngster Mbappé are all part of a geopolitical strategy, were happy about the hype. Qatar's fossil fuel resources are not infinite, and the country is seeking to prepare itself for a future without oil and natural gas revenues. Sport is a major part of this endeavour. Even though PSG still operates very much in the red, by investing money in professional clubs and the marketing of sporting events and TV rights, Qatar hopes to bolster its long-term earnings.

The hundreds of millions PSG forked out in the summer of 2017 overwhelmed the football market, unleashing an absurd chain reaction. The aftermath of the spectacular Neymar transfer fulfilled many of the dark prophesies made by Football Leaks, which had been warning for two years about the dangers associated with such investment models. Now it was clear that the massive sums being pumped into professional football were influencing how the game was played, how squads were put together and how competitive various clubs could even be.

With Neymar's departure, Barcelona felt an urgent need to replace him and began to court twenty-year-old Borussia Dortmund forward Ousmane Dembélé and twenty-five-year-old Liverpool playmaker Philippe Coutinho. Both players had contracts without release clauses, but that didn't deter Barcelona.

On 20 July 2017, Barça had already tendered a formal offer for Coutinho, but Liverpool's sporting director, Michael Edwards, brushed it off, saying that the midfielder had just extended his contract and was not for sale at any price. That was a clear no, but the Catalonians had already designed their new squad with Coutinho in mind, according him a status in their internal payroll between Suárez and 'elite' players like Gerard Piqué, Sergio Busquets and Andrés Iniesta.

'No question, this is an expensive operation, but the market this summer is insane,' Barcelona's sporting director Raúl Sanllehi wrote.

Barcelona, of course, was itself partly responsible for the insanity. In August, Grau once again contacted Liverpool, citing the good relations the two clubs had maintained since Suárez transferred from Merseyside to Barça three years previously. Grau increased his initial offer to €90 million as a set transfer fee, plus an additional €40 million in add-ons.

'I kindly ask you to stop your pursuit of Philippe both publicly and privately,' Edwards wrote in an email. 'No amount of money will make us change our decision.' In another message Edwards wrote to 'dear Oscar', he said: 'Recent media reports and interviews given to the press combined with your recent email would suggest that FC Barcelona employees or individuals acting on behalf of FC Barcelona have entered into formal talks with the player and the agent without permission.' Grau acted affronted, replying that the charge that Barcelona were negotiating with the player was 'pure invention'. FIFA rules prohibit a suitor club from talking to a coveted player without his current club's permission, as long as the player isn't into the final six months of his contract. After that, players can talk to whomever they want.

In Coutinho's case, in January 2017, the player had signed a five-year contract extension that would have kept him at Liverpool until 2022. After inking that deal, in front of the team's cameras, the beaming midfielder told fans how happy he was and how much the club had given him. He said he had signed a new contract because he wanted to stay for several years. Six months later, it seemed that he had changed his mind completely. As the first rumours emerged about him and Barcelona, he reported himself injured – his back hurt. Throughout that summer, he trained only sporadically.

How could Barcelona present a fully formulated twenty-page draft contract with the player without ever having spoken to him or his agent, as Liverpool had forbidden them from doing? This document, dated 31 August, the last day of the transfer window, was among the Football Leaks data. In it, Barcelona offered Coutinho a guaranteed salary of €115 million over five years. A separate email suggests that the player's agent would receive €10 million for a transfer not exceeding the fixed sum of €100 million.

Coutinho's transfer didn't come off in the summer of 2017. Liverpool stuck to their guns initially, but their resistance was only temporary. In January 2018, during the next transfer window, the midfielder left for Barcelona. The Brazilian deserted the Reds in mid-season, even though they had reached the knockout phase of the Champions League. The bitter aftertaste left behind by this deal was all the more acrid when it emerged that a few days before the official announcement of Coutinho's move, Barcelona's equipment sponsor was advertising a personalised kit on its website, with the words: 'Philippe Coutinho is ready to light up Camp Nou. Get your 2017/18 FC Barcelona kit with the Magician's name on it.'

After losing Neymar, Barcelona were determined to restock on talent, whatever the cost, and as a result the 2017 summer transfer window became an object lesson in how easily people can be seduced with lots of money. This was a new development. Suddenly, violating contracts became perfectly acceptable. The case of Ousmane Dembélé was a paradigm.

The young French winger also received an offer from Barcelona in the summer of 2017, and despite being under contract with Dortmund, he jumped at the chance. Dembélé simply went on strike, refusing to attend training sessions. The club's management suspended him. The squad was unsettled, and fans were outraged. On 21 August, Dortmund sent a six-page letter to Barcelona containing a kind of ultimatum and putting a price tag on Dembélé. The Spanish giants were to tender an offer of at least €115 million, with an additional €30 million in add-ons, or else there would be no deal.

On 27 August, the player officially dissolved his contract with his club, and the following day, Dortmund and Barça signed a nine-page transfer agreement. The Germans received a set fee of €105 million, payable in two instalments, with the prospect of variable additional premiums of up to €40 million more, including one-off payments of €5 million after Dembélé's twenty-fifth, fiftieth, seventy-fifth and hundredth matches for the Catalonians. For every time Barça won the Champions League over the course of the winger's contract, Dortmund would get €5 million – with a cap of €10 million in total. The same conditions applied to Barcelona winning La Liga.

Dembélé had been a professional for only two years. He was just starting out, but he was already set for life, thanks to the dream contract his people had negotiated with his new employer. The winger earned €12 million euros in annual base salary at Barcelona, with all manner of special premiums, including a €1.25 million bonus for playing in 60 per cent of all competitive matches in a season.

Unfortunately, the youngster seriously injured himself in only his fourth game for Barça, tearing a thigh tendon, and was out of action for months. As he was starting his comeback, he suffered another injury setback. Nonetheless, he didn't have to worry about any financial losses because of all the time he missed. The 60 per cent clause only applied to matches in which Dembélé was physically able to play.

The winger is also protected against the eventuality of a long title-less stretch at Barcelona. If he doesn't earn at least €48 million within his first three years, including bonuses, the club will make up the difference. It's almost as if the team has agreed to pay the player damages, if they let him down. That was the sort of absurd deal clubs like FC Barcelona were concluding in the summer of 2017. No desires on the part of players were considered too costly or ridiculous. (Barcelona refused to comment on either the contracts or the emails.)

A few weeks after Dembélé had been presented to Barcelona's fans, the winger went under the knife in a special clinic in Finland, and the football world was debating whether the transfer tug-of-war and the sums involved had put the young man under undue psychological strain. Perhaps he had injured himself because he was simply overwhelmed.

Whatever the case may be, Neymar, it seems, has no problems with his role as the world's most expensive player. In his first season with PSG, he scored for fun in Ligue 1. In one of his first matches for the French side, against Toulouse, he dribbled his way past five helpless opponents in the box before slotting home. PSG toyed with opponents like a cat with a mouse, but that seemed to bore the Brazilian superstar. No sooner had the second half of the season started than speculation began about whether and when Neymar could leave the club. In January, Real Madrid's president Florentino Pérez publicly mulled over signing the Brazilian. Things were spiralling skywards, with no end in sight.

There has been an intense debate in the world of football about the Neymar transfer and its effects on the game. In September 2017, club presidents, marketing experts and former professional players convened for a 'football summit' in Frankfurt to talk about the insane transfer sums of the previous summer. Among the hot topics were the Neymar deal and Qatar's ambitions with its investments in the sport. Javier Tebas, the president of La Liga, sat low in his chair, his arms crossed, and criticised the competitive advantage enjoyed by clubs like PSG. If the team needed new players, the bosses in Qatar simply 'opened the gas pumps' and the emir's administrator Al-Khelaifi could go back into the market. This, Tebas complained, amounted to 'financial doping', to the detriment of football. Neymar's transfer fee had nothing to do with the normal laws of the market, which had been destabilised by all the money pouring into it. The pumps needed to be turned off, Tebas pleaded. The domino effect had to stop.

But who would be able to make that happen? Who had the power in football? The national associations? The clubs? Or the emir of Qatar himself? In 2011, UEFA had instituted Financial Fair Play (FFP) rules to limit the amounts clubs could spend on players. The governing body has repeatedly punished clubs that have spent too freely, but the overarching impression is that the world's top teams don't care about the FFP regulations.

When UEFA got wind that PSG intended to buy Mbappé after splashing out so big on Neymar, in what would have seemed to be a clear FFP violation, the governing body threatened sanctions. In the final week of the transfer window, a UEFA delegation even travelled to Paris to make the potential consequences clear to Al-Khelaifi. Yet hardly had the delegates left the club's headquarters than PSG announced that they had signed Mbappé. The Qataris had negotiated a contract with the youngster some time ago, availing themselves of a transparent trick.

On 31 August, PSG and Mbappé's previous club, Monaco, signed a deal sending the forward to Paris on a free loan and giving PSG an option to buy him. To trigger it, the Paris club needed to inform Monaco's general director, Vadim Vasilyev, and his deputy, Nicolas Holveck, in writing between 30 May and 30 June 2018, at which point they would owe a fixed sum of €145 million euros. A first instalment of €90 million euros would be due on 15 July 2018, and a second one of €55 million on 15 July 2019. Moreover, PSG would owe a further €35 million if Mbappé extends his contract, which runs until 30 June 2022, or if PSG sells him on.

As a result of the deal, Mbappé has become a very rich young man. The eighteen-year-old earned €7 million net in 2017–18, and in the following years, his base salary was set to increase to €9.33 million, then €10.33 million, then €11.33 million, and finally €12 million. As the cherry on top of it all, Mbappé also pocketed a signing-on fee. Qatar has won the day. Half the clubs in Europe tried to sign up the young forward, and he is now scoring goals for PSG.

The football industry is still waiting to see whether UEFA will hand down any sanction to PSG. Others mock football's governing body. Liverpool manager Jürgen Klopp, for instance, was quoted as saying: 'I thought FFP was made so situations like that could not happen. But it seems it is more of a suggestion than a rule.'

UEFA president Aleksander Čeferin keeps a steady face in his Nyon office when asked about the PSG case. He has decided to stay calm. Circles within the governing body say that the French club won't face any punishments. The team has been given until June 2018 to prove that its books are balanced. Only after that will a decision be made about possible sanctions.

And what if PSG refuses to provide that proof? Internally, UEFA has discussed a variety of scenarios, including docking the club six points for the next Champions League season or forcing it to reduce its squad for international competitions. Banning the team from competing internationally at all, which was mooted in the past, is off the table. FFP is a sword with a dull blade. UEFA seems unwilling to exclude one of the most glamorous sides from its premier competition – the financial losses from marketing and TV revenues would be too great.

On 8 August 2017, after the Neymar deal was done, a senior UEFA lawyer wrote an email to a colleague, complaining that the transfer system was out of control, that it didn't encourage a level playing field, a fair distribution of money or stable contracts between players and teams. The system, the lawyer went on, favoured the interests of agents and the clubs with the deepest pockets. He also compared today's football market with the robber baron capitalism of the late-nineteenth-century US.

These sentiments were never meant for general consumption, but thanks to Football Leaks they are now part of the public record. The lawyer's email reads like a capitulation, but perhaps it's just the most realistic assessment ever to emerge from inside the football business.

Paris Saint-Germain and the emir of Qatar are not going to rest until the club wins the Champions League. Thus far, they have been allowed to stockpile talent year after year, transfer window after transfer window, in their effort to reach the next level. They have no need to worry about money since they've potentially got €300 billion at their disposal. The consequences of this arms race for the rest of football are obvious. Other investors and financiers will follow suit. Predatory capitalism will spread. How far? The Football Leaks documents concerning the Premier League give a taste of the dimensions the market could take on in the years to come. And they are overwhelming.

A Team Bus Worth a Billion

Ever since 52 per cent of the UK voted to leave the European Union in June 2016, the country's economy has been in turmoil. The one business sector that has been utterly immune to the effects of the downcast mood surrounding Brexit is the Premier League. England's top-flight domestic football competition is a leader in the global entertainment industry, and it's positively booming. Since its founding in 1992, professional football's flashiest national stage has never experienced a single period of economic decline. The numbers have gone up and up and up.

Indeed, the Premier League has become something of a special economic area, and English clubs seem to not know what to do with all the money pouring in, particularly from the sale of global television rights. In the 2016–17 season alone, the twenty Premier League clubs earned some €2.75 billion – half a billion more than in the previous season. League champions Chelsea took in £153 million, while even last-placed Sunderland got nearly £100 million – more than what Germany's top club Bayern Munich received for winning the Bundesliga for the fifth time on the trot.

As a rule, the big English clubs are owned by billionaires from the US, Russia or Abu Dhabi, men used to luxury and for whom living within one's means is not a priority. All of this together has caused transfer fees and salary for players to skyrocket around the world, potentially overheating the market.

The top superstars aren't the only ones who are courted and coddled. Suddenly, even comparatively average performers are worth huge sums. Consider Everton's £40 million fee to bring in midfielder Gylfi Sigurdsson from Swansea – with an additional £2.5 million bonus to be paid should the Toffees qualify for the Champions League. By way of comparison, in summer 2017 Bayern Munich, the undisputed financial and sporting powerhouse in German football, paid €41.5 million, plus variable bonuses of up to €6 million, for French international Corentin Tolisso. That was the largest transfer fee ever shelled out in the Bundesliga.

The Football Leaks material contains dozens of transfer agreements and employment contracts, documenting in great detail the inflationary leap in fees in the summer 2017 and winter 2018 transfer windows. The motor is constantly revving higher and higher, and the transfer sums, basic salaries, premiums and agents' fees are truly dizzying. Even the Brexit-related devaluation of the British pound isn't a problem. If a player insists, as some big-name ones indeed have, his Premier League contract will stipulate that he gets paid in euros.

Some deals contain twenty-three pages of financial clauses. Such is the case with Belgian international striker Romelu Lukaku, who transferred from Everton to Manchester United on 7 July 2017. The transfer fee was a cool £75 million, plus a premium of a further £10 million should Lukaku score at least twenty-three goals in each of the next four seasons; another £5 million was due if the player extended his contract beyond June 2022 or transferred to another club. The total cost of the deal, excluding Lukaku's salary and agents' fees and the like, was £90 million.

The contracts for players who moved to Manchester City, Chelsea, Liverpool and Arsenal in the summer of 2017 all guaranteed them staggering wages. But the craziest provisions were contained in the agreements signed by Manchester United. There, players can earn eight-figure annual salaries. A case in point is the deal Mino Raiola got for the twenty-four-year-old Lukaku. In 2017–18, the striker was guaranteed a basic wage of £7,824,658, payable in monthly instalments. He also stood to earn £4.5 million if he contributed at least fifty goals and assists, as well as a £2.4 million loyalty payment and £1,956,164 for his marketing rights. If all went well, Lukaku had the chance to earn £16.68 million in his first season at Old Trafford.

Lukaku was brought in as a replacement for Zlatan Ibrahimović, who had earned a basic wage of €22.62 million a year, plus a premium of €3.39 million for scoring and assisting thirty-eight goals. Then, in April 2017, he tore a cruciate ligament in his knee. On 23 August, Ibrahimović signed a new one-year extension that was oriented far more around incentives. The Swedish striker's weekly wage was reduced to €50,000, but he had the chance to earn astronomical premiums. For every competitive match he started, he stood to earn €200,000, rising to €250,000 after fifteen starts. He would also get an additional €5.2 million for contributing twenty goals or assists. Not bad for a thirty-five-year-old trying to come back from a serious injury.

Ibrahimović underwent surgery in the US, and afterwards the striker posted a photo of his knee, with the caption: 'Fixed, done and stronger. Once again thank you for the support. We will enjoy my game togheter [*sic*] soon.' And in November 2017, Ibrahimović did indeed return to the pitch. 'Lions, they don't recover like humans,' the ever-modest striker told the press after the match. 'Different day, same quality.'

Still, the bosses at Manchester United apparently lacked faith in Ibrahimović staying healthy and, on 22 January 2018, two months before the Swede's transfer to LA Galaxy, brought in twenty-nine-year-old Alexis Sánchez from Arsenal. Sánchez didn't cost a transfer fee; he was acquired in a straight swap for playmaker Henrikh Mkhitaryan. But the wage package the Chilean forward agreed with the Red Devils was enough to cause a serious case of vertigo.

The contracts between Sánchez and Manchester United, which run until the end of June 2023, encompass forty-three pages. In basic wage and for his marketing rights, the Chilean stood to earn £391,346 a week – or £20.35 million annually – provided the Red Devils qualified for the Champions League. He also got a loyalty bonus of £1.12 million a year and a premium of £75,000 for each match started. His bonus for forty goals or assists: another £2 million. Additionally, Sánchez stood to earn £1 million for winning the Champions League and £500,000 for triumphing in the Premier League. If the Chilean managed to avoid injury and established himself as a regular starter, it was possible for him to make £25 million a year.

In one of the great ironies of football, even the bosses at Chelsea – the club that initially spent their way to the top after Roman Abramovich bought the team in the summer of 2003 – threw up their hands in the face of such inflated figures. When the Sánchez signing was announced, Chelsea's manager Antonio Conte complained: 'Only one or two clubs can pay this type of salary . . . We never were in this race. Ever.'

But before we feel too sorry for poor Signor Conte, we should recall the enormous sums of money Chelsea themselves splashed out in the summer of 2017. French international Tiémoué Bakayoko, for instance, was worth a transfer fee of €42.5 million, payable in two instalments by 30 June 2018. And Chelsea broke the club record to bring in Spanish striker Álvaro Morata. In public, Conte talked about a transfer fee of €55 million, but that was an understatement.

In the transfer agreement between the Blues and Morata's old club, Real Madrid, the sum was €65 million, due in three instalments, with the final one coming on 31 July 2019. That truly was an inflated sum for a striker who had started only fourteen of his twenty-six league matches in his final season with Real. And his salary, paid in euros, matched his transfer fee. Morata was on €11,257,176, including his marketing rights, and stood to earn €943,397 for starting at least half of all competitive matches and €1 million for scoring twenty-five goals in a season. Morata's agent also had reason to smile: Chelsea paid him €6 million as part of the deal.

The hypocrisy of big clubs complaining about being outspent by even bigger clubs isn't restricted to Conte and Chelsea. In late January 2018, Manchester City manager Pep Guardiola said with a straight face: 'City are not so different from other clubs. There are salaries we cannot pay. There are transfers we cannot afford. That's why academies are so important, because you must find players of your own.'

Guardiola is a clever man, but occasionally he talks rubbish. Despite the wild spending spree by the sheikhs behind PSG in the summer of 2017, the most aggressive actors during that transfer period were the sheikhs backing Manchester City, who between May and August 2017 spent around €250 million in bringing players to the club. And the sum City paid for just four of them was higher than the entire annual budgets of thirteen of the eighteen firstdivision clubs in Germany in 2016–17.

City forked out over €55 million to Monaco for French defender Benjamin Mendy, payable in three instalments to an account at the Compagnie Monégasque de Banque in the principality. Guardiola's team also tapped Monaco for

Portuguese midfielder Bernardo Silva, transferring €50 million to that same account. £45 million, plus £5 million in variable premiums, went to Tottenham for defender Kyle Walker. And for goalkeeper Ederson, City was willing to pay €40 million into Benfica's account at the Banco Comercial Português. €55-million-man Mendy played exactly 389 minutes before blowing out his knee, while by early March 2018, €50-million-man Silva had started only nine matches out of twenty-seven in the Premier League. But Walker and Ederson did establish themselves as first-team regulars. That's what City got for an expenditure of just below €200 million.

City's strategy is to create a squad with two top-quality players for every position, allowing Guardiola, if necessary, to replace a €50 million player with another €50 million player. The sheikhs in Abu Dhabi have pushed the envelope further than ever before. If they continue down this road, it's conceivable that the players inside the team bus as it rolls along to an away match will be worth €1 billion.

Liverpool, too, have spent astronomical sums on transfers, if not across the board as City have done. On 1 January 2018, Klopp was allowed to shell out £70 million for former Southampton defender Virgil van Dijk, with a further £4 million due should the Dutchman play 150 matches for the Reds and Liverpool regularly finish in the top four in the Premier League. Van Dijk's contract, which runs until 30 June 2023, guaranteed him a weekly wage of £124,658, which is more than goal-machine Mohamed Salah, the club's new hero, who arrived in the summer of 2017 from Roma – the Egyptian forward's basic wage is a mere £123,030 a week. Still, Africa's 2017 Footballer of the Year was clever enough to negotiate some lucrative premiums, including a goal and assist bonus that earned him an additional £2.5 million for scoring or setting up thirty-five goals. Salah had already reached that mark by February 2018.

Van Dijk, for his part, also stood to receive a £5 million loyalty bonus, a £6 million signing-on bonus and £20,000 per goal scored in the Premier League or in European competition; assists were also worth £20,000. But as a defender, Van Dijk was probably more interested in the generous premiums his contract guaranteed for him for every clean sheet Liverpool recorded. The agreement was complicated. If van Dijk started and played at least an hour in fifteen competitive matches in which the Reds didn't concede a goal, the Dutchman would get an additional £250,000 at the season's end. For eighteen such matches, the reward was £375,000, for twenty, £500,000, and for twenty-two, £750,000.

The contracts of the Premier League's biggest stars give us a glimpse into a world in which absurd is the new normal. In their efforts to retain players or bring in new ones, clubs draw up deals containing all manner of nonsensical conditions. On 22 January 2018, Henrikh Mkhitaryan transferred to Arsenal, receiving a loyalty bonus of £8.65 million, plus an annual basic wage of £7.5 million until the end of the agreement on 30 June 2021. Arsenal have an option, to be triggered by 5 January 2021, to extend the contract for a further year, but it's an expensive one: Mkhitaryan's annual basic wage would jump from £7.5 million to £12.5 million. There's no rhyme or reason to this. Why should a player who will by then be thirty-two earn two-thirds more in his fifth season than in his previous ones?

Nine days after Mkhitaryan arrived, Pierre-Emerick Aubameyang also joined the Gunners. Arsenal agreed to pay

Dortmund €63.75 million in three instalments by 15 March 2020. With this deal, the club broke its previous transfer record, which had only just been set on 6 July 2017, with the €53 million deal, plus €7 million in add-ons, the club had agreed with Olympique Lyon for Alexandre Lacazette.

Aubameyang's move was finalised on the final day of the winter 2018 transfer window. The Gunners urgently needed a replacement for Alexis Sánchez, and their weak bargaining position was reflected in the sums Aubameyang would earn under his new deal. His average annual basic wage was £10.3 million, and if Arsenal qualified for the Champions League and Aubameyang started games in which 60 per cent of the points needed for that qualification were collected, the striker would bank an additional £2.26 million. For every Premier League match started and won, Aubameyang got £50,000, and he stood to earn £300,000 for twenty-five or more assists and goals.

As if that weren't enough, the Gunners agreed to pay a loyalty bonus of £15.15 million, split into four instalments to be paid before the expiry of the contract at the end of June 2021. Can there be anything more cynical than a loyalty bonus for a player like Aubameyang, who skipped training sessions and played listlessly in matches towards the end of his final half-season at Dortmund, seemingly in an attempt to force the Arsenal transfer? And the Gunners rewarded him for that behaviour.

It's mind-blowing how willing Premier League clubs are to prostrate themselves in front of the players they want and their agents and to sign on to the most absurd of clauses. Are there any boundaries left? Well, one, perhaps. Alexis Sánchez's contract with Manchester United contains a passage in which the club actually explicitly distances itself from its new employee. The clause concerns a tax controversy dating back to Sánchez's time with Udinese Calcio in Italy, where he was fined €30,000 for filing an incorrect tax return in 2011. Paragraph 16.2 of his United contract 'acknowledges' that Sánchez was under investigation by the tax authorities in Spain, where he played for Barcelona until 2014. A few days after joining the Red Devils, his agent, Fernando Felicevich, confirmed that after a plea bargain, a Spanish court had sentenced him to sixteen months in prison, suspended, and a hefty fine for tax evasion. Sánchez remained a free man because the sentence was for fewer than two years and because he had no prior record. Manchester United's contract with Sánchez acknowledged the player's legal difficulties and required him to indemnify the club for any third-party claims. Teams apparently still draw the line when players breaking the law is a potential concern.

Euphoria

From afar, I was able to keep abreast of how John was doing, and in mid-December 2017, we met up in a large European city. John strode across a bustling square, his back straight and his eyes fixed ahead of him with determination, almost like a cowboy. He was the picture of self-confidence.

There was little to recall the John of a few months ago, full of paranoia about poisoned beer and private detectives. We embraced, and he said, while grabbing my stomach, that he could tell I was enjoying my food. Very funny. A grin split his face. There was something different about him. He seemed more lively and euphoric than he had recently.

'Why are you in such a good mood?' I asked.

'Because things are getting under way,' he answered, not specifying what he meant. He loved keeping me in suspense – something that drove me crazy.

'How about some pasta?' he suggested. 'I fancy something with lots of melted cheese on top.'

We strolled through some side streets past parks and cafés, getting further and further away from the city centre. It was the first time we had met in this city, but John moved through it as if he had grown up there, without using a map or asking for directions. I trailed a step behind him. The pavements were too narrow to walk side by side. Only then did I notice that John's hands were balled into fists. Was he stressed about something after all? Was his coolness just a facade?

'We're getting more encouragement for our work than ever before,' John said.

'From whom?' I asked.

'From the public, from fans, but the main thing is that we can see that things are moving.'

'Money is moving, in any case,' I replied. 'Neymar gets sold for €222 million, and Dembélé, Coutinho and even Lukaku make €100 million transfers seem normal. Things may be moving, but you can't like the direction they're going in.'

John stopped in front of a small, very dimly lit Italian restaurant. He peered through the window, rapped on the glass and waved. The door opened. John and the owner greeted one another in a language I couldn't identify and kissed each other on the cheek three times. The owner – a grey-haired fellow with a loud voice who talked with his hands and wore an apron over his suit – hugged and kissed me, too, as he steered us through the restaurant's narrow entrance. Then he locked the door from the inside.

John and the man laughed. They seemed to know one another quite well. Filipo, as he called himself, seated us at a table towards the rear. There were no windows in the back room, which had a high ceiling with wooden beams. It smelled a bit damp.

'This place has the best pasta in the world,' John announced.

'Where do you know this guy from?'

'I know lots of people.'

'I know that. But where did you meet him?'

'We've known each other for a long time.'

'Sure. But where from?'

Talking to John was often reminiscent of a Monty Python sketch. We would go round and round in circles, and somehow, using the simplest of means, he would always manage to say nothing.

'I'd recommend the pasta à la chef,' he said. 'You might think it's nothing special, but I tell you, you have to try it. It's made with truffles.'

I gave up. He wasn't going to tell me where he met Filipo. But I still wanted to wind him up a bit.

'How often have you been in this city?' I asked. 'You seem to know your way around.'

'I know my way around lots of cities.'

I stood up and asked Filipo where the toilets were.

When I returned to the table, a well-chilled bottle of white wine, bread, bruschetta and carpaccio had arrived. John may have guarded his secrets closely, but where restaurants were concerned, he rarely left any wishes unfulfilled. Filipo brought another plate of antipasti. Obviously, John intended for us to be here for a while.

'You don't think Aubameyang, Coutinho and Dembélé are bad for our work?' he asked, as he shovelled a forkful of carpaccio into his mouth.

'That's not what I meant. I said I thought that you wouldn't approve of such excesses.'

'That's not true,' John said, with his mouth full. 'They're super for us.' He took a big drink of wine. 'For more than two years, we've been writing that the transfer market and the whole business of football are on a path towards getting completely overheated, right?'

I nodded.

'We've always said that investors are exerting massive influence on the game and that the sport is getting more and more dependent on them with every infusion of money. Our warnings often went unheard. Many football fans only live in the present and don't stop to consider what might happen to their favourite sport tomorrow. Functionaries are even worse in this regard. All they want are quick returns, and they think the only way to get them is with new money, no matter what the source. But when things get so far that every six months there are absurd transfers with insane sums of money and players moving this way and that, even the dumbest fan will see that sporting competition has been destroyed. In the worst case, every team can be plucked apart in a couple of months, and only a couple of clubs will be able to afford such gigantic deals. Then those teams will decide all the titles amongst themselves, year after year. Not very exciting.'

He added that clubs with tradition would be among those crushed – a point that seemed to be important to him since he raised his voice.

'They won't be able to keep up financially with the new clubs. The result will be that a lot of traditional fans will disappear with their clubs from the top leagues. The new clubs, which are really more like businesses, don't bring a comparably stable fan base with them. You can already see that for many European matches the stadiums aren't full and that the TV viewership for matches between clubs with big investors is often laughably small.'

His hands were in a whirl as he spoke, putting olives, capers, cheese, grilled vegetables and carpaccio onto his plate. As euphoric as he was, he still had an enormous appetite.

We talked for around three hours about the transfers in a market solely concerned with success and profit. The rhythm of the Premier League was become increasing frenetic, we agreed. Buoyed by horrendous amounts of money from TV and investors, it was seeking to become something of a global league. There was no escaping it. The rapacious sponsors of this gigantic show constantly demanded new superstars, new sensations and new records. That was the only way to make the Premier League even more attractive to the investors upon whom it had come to depend. The trade in TV rights was as radical a business as the football industry itself. If English clubs didn't deliver sufficient fireworks, if the Premier League got boring, it would soon experience how radical the external money providers could be. They would simply turn off the pump, move on and develop new strategies. The same was true for agents.

All of this led the many nouveau riche English clubs to try to outbid one another with practically every transfer. It was a vicious battle, without limits, for putative sporting saviours. Many of the top clubs in Spain, France and Italy felt compelled to try to keep pace with this spending game and to find new financiers. In Germany, too, the voices calling for the Bundesliga to lower the hurdles for investors were growing louder and louder.

The prices may have spiralled out of control, but the clubs' spending frenzy continues unchecked. That is why more and more players behave the way Aubameyang, Coutinho, Dembélé and Riyad Mahrez have recently. Players who essentially go on strike are a product of an unfettered market. They act completely selfishly because there's always some club that will fulfil their every wish. Together with their agents, players like this will hound clubs, playing them off against one another to drive up prices.

'It's one thing that the flurry of transfers runs the risk of cooling off the love of fans for their favourite teams and leagues,' John said. 'It's another that we're increasingly talking about money that's illegal, or at least very unethical. Agents' fees are becoming a kind of bribe clubs pay to gain influence over the agents' players. The billions moving around this market must be subjected to more intense external scrutiny.'

He had polished off a huge plate of pasta and was now enjoying a glass of grappa that Filipo had brought to our table, unasked. In the background, music began playing, instrumental sounds like those I had once heard in Russia. Was Filipo Russian? There was nothing stereotypically Italian about his appearance or behaviour, but then again, such clichés meant less and less in the globalised world. And in any case, Filipo didn't remind me of a Russian either.

John interrupted these thoughts.

'In the months to come we will be providing lots of insights into the football industry that will convince even the most ardent fan how far removed the sport has become from the common man. We'll be presenting football's investment models in much greater detail. We'll show how oligarchs and their football clubs avoid international sanctions, how financiers simultaneously invest in multiple clubs, how money gets transferred from tax haven to tax haven, and how helplessly the football world just sits back and watches all this happening. We're going to focus more sharply on the money flows of players and agents, on their supposed charitable activities, their letterbox companies and middlemen. We're going to increase the pressure so that the politicians stop talking and start drawing up new laws – internationally valid laws. We're going to hold Čeferin to his word and chronicle how many changes UEFA actually institutes. And we'll be keeping a close eye on Qatar and Paris.'

Once John gets going like this, he's hard to stop. In the past few years, I've accompanied him through his highs and lows, his combative and exhausted phases. You can't put full stock in everything he says in his higher moments, but I was slightly relieved to find him in a mood in which the sunshine outweighed the clouds. He was more fun to be around, and usually John doesn't get in a good mood without reason. I couldn't wait to see what he got up to next.

John stood up and said it was time to go. He was travelling that day to 'meet a few people'. He donned his thin denim jacket, hugged Filipo, whose accent I still couldn't place, and skipped to the door. Filipo locked it behind us.

'We have a massive amount of new data,' John whispered to me in the taxi to my hotel. 'And there's constantly more and more coming in. People out there seem to have realised that the football industry needs greater transparency and are starting to take matters into their own hands. We've become one of the most important contact points for everyone who wants to publicise the bad things about football.'

During our journey, he removed a hard drive from his rucksack and put it in mine.

'This is really exciting stuff!' he told me.

The taxi stopped, and John got out. He stretched his back and then strolled down a side street.

There would be a lot of work awaiting us in the months to come.

Acknowledgements

This book would not have been possible without the assistance, knowledge and support of many colleagues. They threw themselves into the work, guiding us through the ocean of data, digging and searching until they found answers. Sometimes the search was tough going; mostly it was electrifying. The most important thing we learned from it was that such a project depends on teamwork.

We spent hundreds of hours with our wonderful *Spiegel* team in the safe room, in the corridors of our offices, on research trips and on the phone. With their effort, determination and curiosity, Jürgen Dahlkamp, Christoph Henrichs, Udo Ludwig and Jörg Schmitt allowed us to put together the numerous pieces of the puzzle to create the bigger picture.

Without our head of IT, Stephan Haffner, we would have drowned in the sheer volume of data. His hard work, technical know-how and patience, especially in view of our ignorance, remain invaluable.

Fact-checkers Nicola Naber and Andreas Meyhoff not only prevented us from making mistakes, they invested countless hours of research, sometimes overnight, in the project and repeatedly impressed us with what they found. Their love of facts, devotion to detail and constant critical questions were what allowed us to see the connections between many of the firms and flows of money. Kurt Jansson supported us on the technical front in particular. Thanks to him, we arrived at a structure to search through our data. A big thanks also goes to the head of the fact-checking department, Hauke Janssen, who allowed us to work with such fantastic colleagues.

We're very grateful to Gerhard Pfeil, who as head of the sports department supported our research from the very beginning.

From Roman Lehberger, Thomas Heise, Hendrik Vöhringer, David Walden and Jochen Blum we learned a lot about just how difficult, complicated and exhausting film-makers' work really is. The *Spiegel* TV team flew halfway around the world with us, supporting our efforts with more than just their cameras. Their clever ideas and encouragement to constantly rethink our assessments always ensured our results were a little bit better.

The *Spiegel Online* and *Spiegel* digital teams around Peter Ahrens, Jule Lutteroth, Frauke Böger, Mike Glindmeier, Christian Gödecke, Jörn Sucher, Ayla Mayer, Torsten Beeck, Heike Janssen, Jens Radü, Olaf Heuser and Roman Höfner spent weeks on research and developed new formats, forms of visualisation and background explainers. Without their efforts, we would never have been able to reach so many readers with a topic as complicated as this one.

We're grateful to our lawyers Jan Siegel, Uwe Jürgens, Sascha Sajuntz and Oliver Srocke for their faith in our research and their fortitude. Although we encountered fierce legal resistance, we never felt alone with this project.

Our thanks go to Heike Drinkuth, who never lost sight of the bigger picture, no matter how stressful things got, and who always had a smile for us.

Without the wonderful, tireless and always friendly support from Martina Hasch, Kirsten Beitz, Gordon Bersch, Frauke Ernesti and Agnes Ruckdäschel from the *Spiegel* travel department, we would never have been able to undertake our research trips to far-flung corners of the globe.

We'd like to thank Angelika Mette, Antje Wallasch and Karen Guddas at Spiegel Publishing and DVA for their ideas about this book, their professional editing and their many encouraging words.

We're very grateful to *Der Spiegel*'s management, in particular Klaus Brinkbäumer and Alfred Weinzierl, for freeing us up for months to pursue this mammoth project and for believing right until the end that all the effort would be worth it. In the name of our entire staff, we are also grateful to chief executive Thomas Hass and publishing director Jesper Doub, who together with our editorial bosses invested tens of thousands of euros during difficult economic times in the data management system Intella. This decision will prove a blessing for many future research projects.

Our partners from the research network European Investigative Collaborations helped us get across the finish line with their research, sources and ideas. They examined every document, every email and every contract from all possible perspectives in an effort to get closer and closer to the truth. Our EIC colleagues and their employers are:

El Mundo (Spain): Paula Guisado, Javier Sánchez, Quico Alsedo, Pablo Herraiz, Pablo Medina, Alberto Hernández

Expresso (Portugal): Pedro Candeias, Miguel Prado, Raquel Albuquerque

Falter (Austria): Lukas Matzinger

L'Espresso (Italy): Vittorio Malagutti, Stefano Vergine

Le Soir (Belgium): Alain Lallemand, Joel Matriche, Stéphane Vande Velde, Xavier De Cock

Mediapart (France): Michaël Hajdenberg, Michel Henry, Donatien Huet, Martine Orange, Yann Philippin, Nicolas Barthe-Dejean

Newsweek (Serbia): Milorad Ivanovic, Blaž Zgaga

NRC Handelsblad (the Netherlands): Hanneke Chin, Hugo Logtenberg, Merijn Rengers, Esther Rosenberg

Politiken (Denmark): Jakob Sorgenfri Kjar, Jeppe Laursen Brock, Frederik Storm

Romanian Centre for Investigative Journalism/The Black Sea (Romania): Michael Bird, Zeynep Sentek, Craig Shaw, Vlad Odobescu, Costin Stucan, Alex Morega, Gabriel Vijiala, Dan Achim, Raluca Ciubotaru, Dragoş Catarahia, Victor Avasiloaei

Sunday Times (UK): Jonathan Calvert, George Arbuthnott, David Collins.

Special thanks goes to the EIC coordinator Stefan Candea, who kept this flea circus under control with great charm and unshakable diplomacy.

We thank our wives Sonja Buschmann and Brigitte Wulzinger for their love, strength and patience in putting up with this craziness.

But the biggest thanks of all goes to our whistle-blower John, the man without whom none of this would have been possible. Take care.

Index

Football clubs denoted by **bold**

AC Milan, 84, 126, 179, 193
Adidas, 111, 120–9; sponsorship deal
  with Manchester United, 121–2;
  sponsorship deal with Real Madrid,
  120–4
Aftermath Ltd, 185–6
agents, 1–10, 20, 24, 32, 40, 44,
  49–50, 60, 62, 65–6, 71–3, 77–81,
  102, 105, 107–11, 128, 140, 158,
  177–87, 219–34, 235, 240, 248, 251,
  254–62, 270–1, 287–9, 295, 301;
  Dutch–Argentinian clique, 177–87,
  210, 214, 218, 219–34
Agüero, Sergio, 137, 141, 180
Al-Khelaifi, Nasser, 274–5
Allofs, Klaus, 227
Alonso, Xabi, 63, 135
Apollon Limassol: and Gaćinović
  transfer, 206–7
Arif, Arif, 17, 20–6, 33
Arif, Refik, 21, 22–3, 26, 28, 33
Arif, Tevfik, 20–4, 26, 28, 30–1, 33
Arsenal, 47, 48, 71, 180, 199, 203,
  289, 290, 294–5
Assange, Julian, 70, 92, 109, 218
Atlético Madrid, 29, 71, 105, 134,
  160–1, 135–42, 194–5, 259
Aubameyang, Pierre-Emerick, 294–5,
  299, 301
Aznar, José María (Spanish PM), 51

Bale, Gareth, 58–60, 98, 162, 226, 260
Ballon d'Or: linked to footballers'
  contracts, 56, 63
Balotelli, Mario, 83–4, 167
Barcelona, 26, 47, 121, 126–7, 135,
  179, 199, 201–2, 252, 258, 272–83,
  296

Barnett, Jonathan, 60
Barrada, Abdelaziz, 27
Bayer Leverkusen, 78, 81, 105, 118,
  205, 225
Bayern Munich, 8, 20, 26, 34, 63,
  65, 75, 83, 105, 121, 124, 135,
  195, 196, 199, 223, 228, 252, 261,
  273–4, 288
Bayrock, 23
Beckenbauer, Franz, 124, 168
Becker, Boris, 19, 25
Beckham, David, 19, 25, 51, 58; 'Lex
  Beckham', 51
Beiersdorfer, Dietmar, 34
Beister, Maximilian, 34
Belize, 126, 155, 204; *see also* tax
  havens
Benfica, 6, 29, 50, 56, 222–3, 293
Benítez, Rafael: contract with Real
  Madrid, 164
Benzema, Karim, 162
Bergkamp, Dennis, 48
Berlusconi, Silvio, 193
Bermuda: *see* tax havens
Birkenfeld, Bradley, 37
The Black Sea (RCIJ), 3, 134
Blatter, Sepp, 124, 168
Boateng, Jérôme: victim of racism, 166
Bolt, Usain, 19
Borussia Dortmund, 20, 74, 99,
  122, 219–21, 279, 282, 295
British Virgin Islands, 1, 10, 30, 45,
  53, 54, 128, 173, 208–13, 228, 244,
  258, 262; *see also* tax havens
Brockton Foundation, 53, 266

Cádiz, 34
Can, Emre, 82
Candea, Stefan, 243, 245
Carrizo, Juan Pablo, 65

Carvalho, Ricardo, 49, 51, 261, 262; back taxes/fine, 261
Castaignos, Luc, 13
Castrillón, Jan Piers Advíncula: transfer saga, 115–16
Čeferin, Aleksander, 268, 273, 286, 303
Champions League: *see* UEFA
Chelsea, 16, 47, 71, 121, 138, 194–6, 288, 289, 291–2
China: Chinese investors and FIFA, 194; Chinese investors in English football, 194; Chinese investors in Italian football, 193
Chinese Super League, 192–200; TV deal, 193
Chodiev, Patokh, 22
Cléber, 34
Coentrão, Fabio, 258, 261; back taxes/fine, 261
Comaro Management GmbH, 117–18
El Confidencial: Ronaldo scoop, 243–5
contracts, 11–15, 26–29, 34, 37, 58–60, 63–5, 75–84, 89–90, 96, 98, 114–18, 135–6, 162–4, 175, 177–81, 183–6, 191–2, 197–8, 223, 227, 231, 248; German Football League (DFL), 80–1, 118–19; *individual player deals:* Aubameyang, 295; Bale, 58–60; Balotelli, 83–4; Can, 82; Coutinho, 281; Dembélé (Ousmane), 282–3; Draxler, 220–1; Drogba, 195; Firmino, 116–18; Halilović, 201–2; Hernández (Chicharito), 78, 81; Hulk, 197; Ibrahimović, 178–81, 290; John, 29; Kiessling, 78–9; Lavezzi, 191–2, 199–200; Lukaku, 289–90; Martínez, 195; Mbappé, 285–6; Mkhitaryan, 219–20, 294; Morata, 291; Nastasić, 79; Neymar, 278; Oscar, 196–7; Pogba, 182–6; Ronaldo (Cristiano), 162; Salah, 293–4; Sánchez (Alexis), 290–1, 295–6; Schweinsteiger, 75–6; Teixeira (Alex), 195; Tévez, 197–8; Van Dijk, 293–4
Correia, Luis, 261, 262, 264
corruption, 11, 40–1, 57, 8, 108, 124, 168, 237, 242, 247, 251; World Cup 2006, 11, 40, 87, 124, 168
Coutinho, Philippe: transfer saga, 279–82

Croatia: corruption trial, 203; *see also* football

Dahlkamp, Jürgen, 132, 305
Dassler, Horst, 124–5, 168
De Gea, David, 89–90; transfer blunder with Real Madrid, 89–90
Deltour, Antoine, 70, 218
Dembélé, Ousmane: Barcelona transfer, 279, 282–3
Denos, 31–2; *see also* Doyen Sport
DH-Holding Verwaltungs GmbH, 114, 117–18
Di María, Ángel, 73, 228, 230, 231, 257, 261; back taxes/fine, 261
Dinamo Zagreb, 201–5
Doyen Group, 25, 32, 34
Doyen Sports Investments Ltd, 12–15, 16–19, 24–6, 30–3, 37, 38, 40, 61, 71, 138, 248–9; blackmail allegations, 236–9
Draxler, Julian, 166, 220–1
Drogba, Didier, 194–5, 196

Eintracht Frankfurt: and Gaćinović transfer, 206–7
English Premier League, 10, 47, 53, 57, 58, 75–6, 80, 135, 139–40, 175, 177, 179–80, 184, 186, 193, 196, 219, 224, 251, 266, 272, 287–96; as global league, 301; leader in global entertainment industry, 179–80, 287; overheating transfer market, 288; TV rights, 80, 180, 224, 301; vs Bundesliga, 287–8
Etihad, 43, 52
European Club Association (ECA), 251–2
European Investigative Collaborations (EIC), 2, 45, 132–4, 146, 149, 158, 187–90, 235, 237, 239–46; publication of Football Leaks data, 239–46
European Sports Management, 206–7
Expresso, 3, 188

Falcao, Radamel, 19, 71, 137–8, 259–60; tax fraud investigation, 259–60
Falciani, Hervé, 37
Falter, 3
Ferrer, Judge Monica Gómez, 260–2, 263, 264–7
FIFA, 7, 8, 11, 12, 28, 33, 34–5, 40,

60, 61, 117, 154, 168, 194, 223, 251, 252, 253; and EU committee, 270–1; and football agents, 223; response to Football Leaks, 251–3; study of transfer market, 60; third-party ownership (TPO), 12, 28, 34–5, 117, 154; Transfer Matching System (TMS), 61, 251

Financial Times, 140

Firmino, Roberto, 80, 81, 116–18

football: corruption, 11, 40–1, 57, 68, 108, 124, 168, 237, 242, 247, 251; criminal underworld (mafia), 107, 134, 143, 157, 192, 237; embezzlement, 2, 57, 247; entertainment industry (show business), 2, 7, 44, 160–1, 179; hooligans, 9; image vs reality, 8–9; in China, 72, 106, 137, 190, 191–200; in Croatia, 190, 201–7, 270; in Serbia, 190, 206–7; industry response to Football Leaks, 250; kickbacks, 6, 57, 108, 251; match fixing, 40, 87, 168; money laundering, 68, 233; parallel universe, 10, 247; predatory capitalism, 272–87; secrecy, 2, 6, 14, 19, 31, 39, 42, 57, 58, 65, 68, 74, 100, 173, 181, 212, 229, 234, 236; shell firms, 19, 30, 31, 49, 93, 106, 208–11, 232; sponsorship deals, 41–2, 43–54, 120–9; substitute religion, 87; the super-rich, 17, 45, 254; tax evasion/fraud, 2, 38, 44–5, 51, 53, 68, 98, 208–13, 253–4

football fans: attitudes of, 4, 58, 63, 71, 87, 108, 113, 119, 165–9, 205, 248; treatment of by clubs/industry, 9, 14, 66, 137, 140, 169

Football Leaks (FL), 6–7, 36–42, 61, 67–71, 86, 98–9, 102, 108–9, 139, 148, 158–9, 188–9, 234–46, 251–3, 256–96; aftermath, 256–96; attacks on, 39, 70, 108, 148, 150, 235; blackmail allegations, 61, 189, 234–46; *El Confidencial* scoop, 243–5; email communication with *Spiegel Online*, 67–71; enemies, 40, 67, 108–9, 158; fending off hackers, 139, 148; hacking allegations, 37–9, 60, 69, 97, 237, 251, 255; international watchdogs, 39; motivation, 39, 67–8, 70, 86, 98–9, 109; offers to buy FL data, 102; put on hold,

158–9; responses by FIFA, 251–3; responses by football clubs, 251–2; responses by politicians, 253–4, 270–1; responses by tax authorities, 254–5; tax investigations as a result of leaks, 256–96; under criminal investigation in Portugal, 188

footballers: as indentured servants, 75–84, 183, 205–6; as large international corporations, 44–5, 52–3; greed, 46, 219–33; image rights, 41, 53, 46–9, 54, 183–4, 185, 208, 216–17, 241, 262, 264, 266, 269, 290, 291, 292; megalomania, 7, 46, 247; third-party ownership (TPO) transfer rights, 12–13, 16–18, 25–6, 27, 28–9, 33, 34, 35, 39, 114–15, 117, 154

Gaćinović, Mijat: transfer, 206–7

German Football League (DFL) (also Bundesliga), 1, 29, 78–82, 87, 105, 117, 118–19, 251, 274, 288–9, 301

Gestifute, 45, 52, 54, 71, 139, 261–2, 267, 270

Gil, Jesús, 136–7

Gil Marín, Miguel Ángel, 136–7

Goddard, Mark, 61

Gomes, André, 49

Grindel, Reinhard, 8

Guardiola, Pep: on transfer fees, 292

Halilović, Alen ('Balkan Messi'), 201–2

Hamburg SV, 34, 83, 201–2, 234

Hart, Joe, 48

Havelange, João, 168

Hebei China Fortune, 191

Heffner, Stephan, 187

Hernández, Javier (Chicharito), 74, 78, 81, 225

Higuaín, Gonzalo, 73, 127, 128–9, 228, 230; sponsorship deal with Adidas, 127; sponsorship deal with Nike, 128–9

Hoeness, Uli, 124, 196, 273

Hoffenheim, 111, 112–19

Hong Kong: *see* tax havens

Hopp, Dietmar, 111, 112–19

Hulk, 57, 197

Ibragimov, Alijan (Alik), 20

Ibrahimović, Zlatan: contract and

transfer to Manchester United, 178–81, 290

Icaza, González-Ruiz & Alemán, 212–13

image/marketing rights, 41, 53, 46–9, 54, 183–4, 185, 208, 216–17, 241, 262, 264, 266, 269, 290, 291, 292

Infantino, Gianni: response to Football Leaks, 252–3

Inter Milan, 19, 65, 193, 199, 205, 231, 249

Ireland, 41, 47, 52–3, 185, 246, 258, 264; *see also* tax havens

Januzaj, Adnan, 32, 33

JCLC Promotions, 48

Jersey, 139–40, 186; *see also* tax havens

John, Ola, 29

Júnior Ponce Pardo, Alexander: transfer saga, 115–16

Junuzović, Zlatko, 79

Juventus, 1, 129, 183–4, 196, 228, 252

Kaká, 126

Kazakhstan, 20–3, 30, 107–8, 154, 248; 'aluminium war', 21–2

Kenyon, Peter, 138–9, 141

Kiessling, Stefan, 78–9

Klopp, Jürgen, 76, 110, 286, 293; on UEFA Financial Fair Play (FFP), 286

KNVB (Dutch Football Federation), 14–15

Kondogbia, Geoffrey, 16–18

Kroos, Toni, 63–4, 77, 195, 224, 260

Kullashi, Ylli, 183–4, 185

La Finca, 260, 263, 269

Lasogga, Pierre-Michel, 34

Lavezzi, Ezequiel Iván: contract with Hebei China Fortune, 191–2, 199–200

Lazio, 65

L'Équipe, 184

L'Espresso, 2

Le Soir, 2

Levy, Daniel, 58–9

Liverpool, 48, 80–2, 83–4, 117, 279–82, 286, 289, 293–4

Lobuzov, Artem (possible pseudonym): blackmail allegations, 236–9

López, Mariano Maroto, 117–18

Löw, Joachim, 8, 225

Lucas, Nélio, 248–9; blackmail allegations, 236–9; Doyen Sports Investments Ltd, 12–15, 16–19, 24–6, 30–3, 37, 38, 40, 61, 71, 138, 248–9; Vela Management, 249

Lukaku, Romelu, 289–90

Luxembourg: *see* tax havens

Malta: Doyen Sports Investments Ltd, 12, 30, 138; International Sport Company Ltd, 205; Vela Management Ltd, 249

Mamić, Mario, 203, 204; trial, 203, 270

Mamić, Zdravko, 202–3, 204; assassination attempt, 204; trial, 203, 270

Mamić, Zoran, 202–3, 204; trial, 203, 270

Manchester City, 19, 57, 137, 141, 179–80, 199, 289, 292–3

Manchester United, 1, 32, 47, 56–8, 60, 74, 75, 78, 81, 89, 121, 126, 138, 178–85, 219, 225, 230, 231, 252, 265–6, 269, 289–91, 295–6

Mangala, Eliaquim, 9, 57

Manning, Bradley (Chelsea), 37, 92, 109, 218

Martial, Anthony, 56

Martínez, Jackson, 195

Mashkevich, Alexander (Sasha), 20–2, 31

Mata, Juan, 126

Mbappé, Kylian, 272, 274, 279, 285–6; PSG transfer, 274, 285–6

Mediapart, 2

Mendes, Jorge, 49–52, 71, 109, 138, 260–1, 262; tax fraud investigation, 260–1

Merkel, Angela (German chancellor), 8, 273

Messi, Lionel, 40, 126–7, 275

Meyhoff, Andreas, 187

Mkhitaryan, Henrikh, 167, 180, 219–20, 290, 294

Modrić, Luka, 97, 203, 258, 270; perjury charge, 270

Monaco, 18, 19, 27, 56, 137, 184, 230, 259, 274, 285, 292

Morata, Álvaro, 291–2

Morris, Kimberly, 271

Mourinho, José, 49, 51, 179, 189, 213,

214, 256, 260, 268–9; back taxes,
269; marketing rights, 269; tax
affairs, 268–70
Multisports & Image Management
(MIM), 41, 43, 52, 53
El Mundo, 3, 244
Munsterman, Joop, 12

Naber, Nicola, 144, 208, 212, 245
Nastasić, Matija, 79
Nazarbayev, Nursultan (president of
Kazakhstan), 21
New York Times, 6, 38, 71
Newsweek, 3
Neymar, 19, 25, 58, 97, 272–3, 275–9;
PSG transfer, 272–3, 275–9; effects
on football, 279–83, 284; Rakuten
saga, 275–7
Nice, 84
Ñíguez Esclápez, Saúl, 135
Nike, 52, 121, 128–9; contract with
Higuaín, 128–9; contract with
Manchester United, 121
NRC Handelblad, 2, 232

Odems, Martijn, 65, 73, 231–2
Orel B.V., 65, 230–3
Oscar, 196–7
Özil, Mesut, 1, 68, 71, 105, 180

Panama, 45, 53, 65, 73–4, 155, 204,
230, 266; *see also* tax havens
Paris Saint-Germain (PSG), 26, 50,
178, 191, 219, 229, 252, 257, 272–9,
285–6; and Financial Fair Play
(FFP), 285–6; and Mbappé transfer,
272, 285–6; and Neymar transfer,
272, 275–9; and Qatar, 272–9
Paros Consulting Limited, 128, 210,
211, 214, 228–33
Pepe, 49, 97, 258, 261; back taxes/
fine, 261
Pérez, Florentino, 16–19, 59, 219,
226, 284
Petralito, Giacomo, 227
Pinto, Aníbal: blackmail allegations,
236–9
Pogba, Paul, 105, 167, 177, 180, 181,
182–6; contract with Manchester
United, 182–6; image rights, 183–4,
185
Polaris Sports, 41, 261–2, 262
Politiken, 2

Porto, 6, 50, 57, 140, 230
Pozuelo de Alarcón, 260–2, 264, 267,
268
Puma: sponsorship deal with Borussia
Dortmund, 122

Qatar: Al-Khelaifi, Nasser, 274–5;
football as part of geopolitical strategy, 272–9, 284; Qatar Investment
Authority (QIA), 274; Qatar Sports
Investments, 273; Sheikh Tamim
bin Hamad Al Thani, 274
Quality Football: image rights,
138–41

Raiola, Mino, 175, 177, 178–81, 182–
6, 219–20, 289; and Ibrahimović
transfer to Manchester United,
178–81; and Pogba transfer to
Manchester United, 182–6
Rakuten, 275–7
Ramos, Sergio, 162
Ras al-Khaimah, 31
Rasport Management, 202–4, 207
Rauball, Reinhard, 8
RCIJ/The Black Sea, 3, 134
Real Madrid, 1, 16–18, 26, 43–4,
58–60, 63, 71, 74, 86, 89, 120–4,
127, 160–4, 226, 230–1, 240, 258,
260, 267, 284, 292; 2016 Champions
League Final, 160–4; sponsorship
deal with Adidas, 120–4
Reuben, David, 21
Reuben, Jamie, 25
Reuben, Simon, 21
Rixos hotels, 22
Rodríguez, James, 49, 73, 228, 230–1,
261
Rodríguez, Ricardo, 79
Rogon Sportmanagement, 117,
220–3; and transfer of Kevin
Friesenbichler to Benfica, 223
Ronaldo, Cristiano, 1, 41, 43–5,
49–50, 51–2, 53–4, 160–4, 241,
243–5, 244–6, 258, 264–7; 2016
Champions League Final, 160–4;
companies, 244, 245–6; contract
with Real Madrid, 162; court hearing, 264–7; criminal investigation,
258, 264–5; *El Confidencial* scoop,
243–5; image rights, 41, 53, 241,
264, 266; tax affairs, 244–6, 258,
264–7

Rooney, Wayne, 48
Rummenigge, Karl-Heinz: response
    to Football Leaks, 252

Şahin, Nuri, 74
St Galler Kantonalbank, 197, 262
Salah, Mohamed, 293–4
Sánchez, Alexis: back taxes, 258; con-
    tract and transfer to Manchester
    United, 290–1, 295–6; guilty of tax
    evasion, 296
Schalke, 79–81, 220–1
Schmitt, Jörg, 132
Schweinsteiger, Bastian, 75–6
Semzov, Vladimir, 25
Serbia: *see* football
Sevilla, 16–17, 233
Shakhtar Donetsk, 195–6
Simonian, Marcelo, 229, 232–3, 257
Snowden, Edward, 37, 70, 109, 218
Southampton, 59, 197, 293
Der Spiegel/Spiegel Online, 1–4, 41,
    67, 73, 132–4, 232, 245, 252; first
    email communication with Football
    Leaks, 67–71; *see also* European
    Investigative Collaborations
Sporting Lisbon, 6, 140
SportsTotal, 64, 224
Stoneygate Ltd, 48
Struth, Volker, 64, 224
Süddeutsche Zeitung, 114, 117, 250
Sunday Times, 3, 47
Switzerland, 45, 125, 201–7; St Galler
    Kantonalbank, 197, 262; *see also*
    tax havens

Tah, Jonathan, 34
Tanazefti, Oualid, 182–4, 185
tax: evasion/fraud, 2, 38, 44–5, 51, 53,
    68, 98, 208–13, 253–4; footballers'
    image rights, 41, 53, 46–9, 54, 183–
    4, 185, 208, 216–17, 241, 262, 264,
    266, 269, 290, 291, 292; havens,
    45, 53, 65, 73–4, 139–40, 126, 155,
    183, 186, 192, 201–7, 204, 208–13,
    230, 262, 266; letterbox companies,
    31, 32, 33, 45, 49, 108, 210, 211,
    254, 259, 265, 269, 270, 271, 302;
    'Lex Beckham', 51–2; shell firms,
    19, 30, 31, 49, 93, 106, 208–11,
    232; tourists, 43–54
tax authorities, 30, 45–9, 51–2, 54, 58,
    126, 127, 136, 203, 209–11, 233,

    246, 253, 254, 258, 259, 261–2, 269,
    296; raids on players, 257–8
Teixeira, Alex, 97, 194, 195
Termes, Marco, 231–2
Tévez, Carlos, 71, 197–8
third-party ownership (TPO) transfer
    rights, 12–13, 16–18, 25–6, 27,
    28–29, 33, 34, 35, 39, 114–15, 117,
    154
Tollin Associates, 53, 213
Topscore Sports, 184
Tottenham Hotspur, 58, 60, 71,
    203, 226, 293
Transfer Matching System (TMS),
    61, 251
Transfer Rights Monetisation Society
    (Transfair), 113–19
Twente Enschede, 11–15, 25, 28–9,
    38, 56, 61, 248

UEFA: censor images of hooligans,
    9; Champions League, 78, 81, 99,
    120–2, 135, 154, 159, 160–4, 181,
    186, 195, 274–5, 281, 282, 286–7,
    288, 291, 295; Financial Fair Play
    (FFP), 285–6; views on tax evasion,
    268; views on transfer system, 273,
    286–7
Uuniq Sarl, 184

Van Djjk, Virgil, 293–4
Vela Management, 249
Vojvodina Novi Sad: and Gaćinović
    transfer, 206–7
Von Heesen, Thomas, 34

Weinzierl, Alfred, 132, 187
Werder Bremen, 79, 197, 227–8
WikiLeaks, 37, 61, 70, 98
Witsel, Axel, 196
Wittmann, Roger, 116–17, 210–11,
    227
Wolfsburg, 29, 79, 82, 105, 199, 221,
    223, 227
World Cup 2006, 11, 40, 87, 124, 168
Wulzinger, Michael, 88, 173

Yandex: Football Leaks host, 39, 236

Zahavi, Pini, 24
Zenit St Petersburg, 57–8, 196–7
Zidane, Zinedine, 58, 162–4; contract
    with Real Madrid, 162–4